묘신계록 제1권

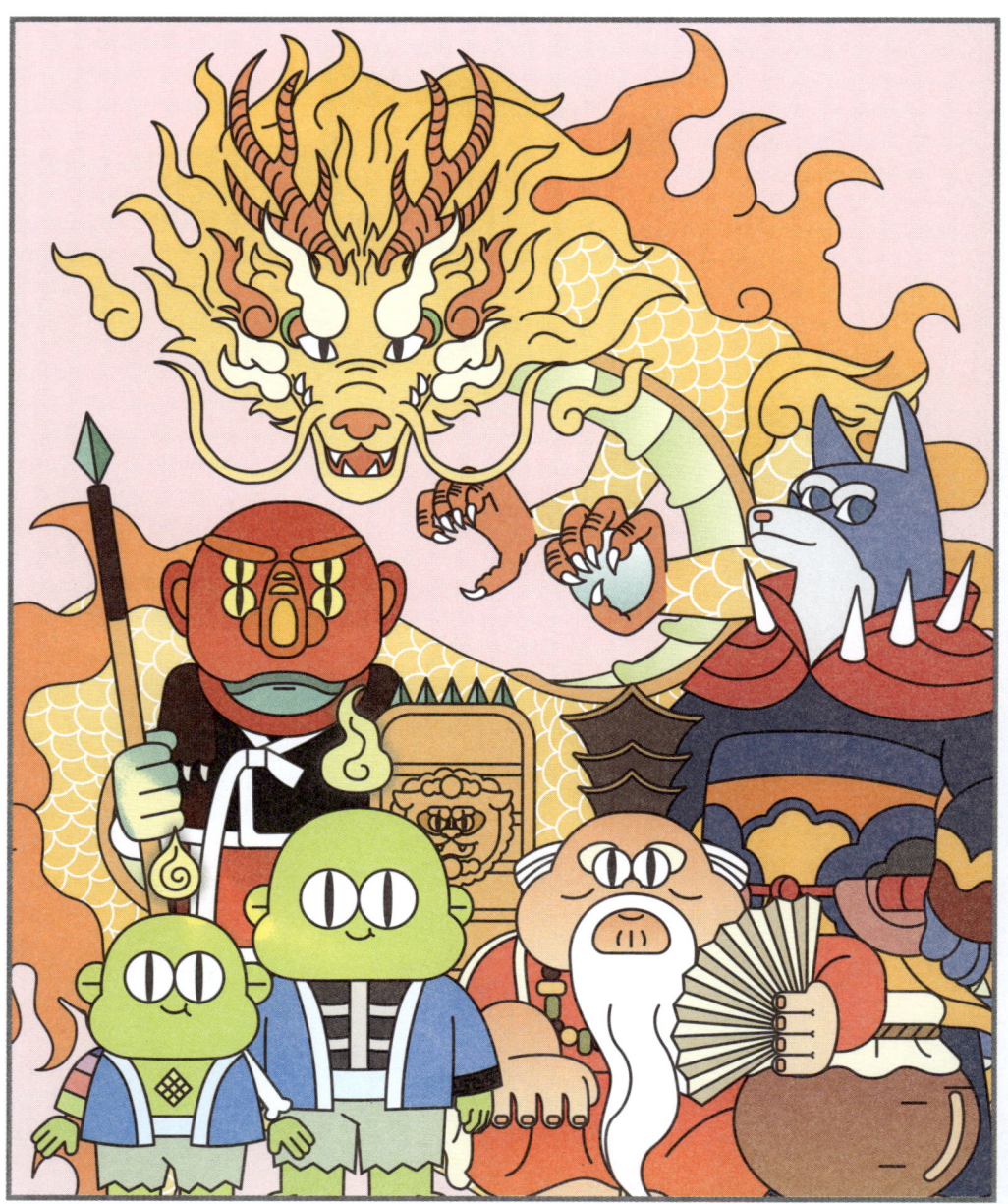

THE LEGENDS OF MeoShin'Ke™

VOLUME 1

An Illustrated Guide to Korean Monsters and Mythology

Hwa Hwa Studio
Translated from the Korean by Sung Ryu

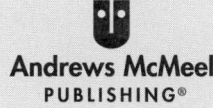

Andrews McMeel
PUBLISHING®

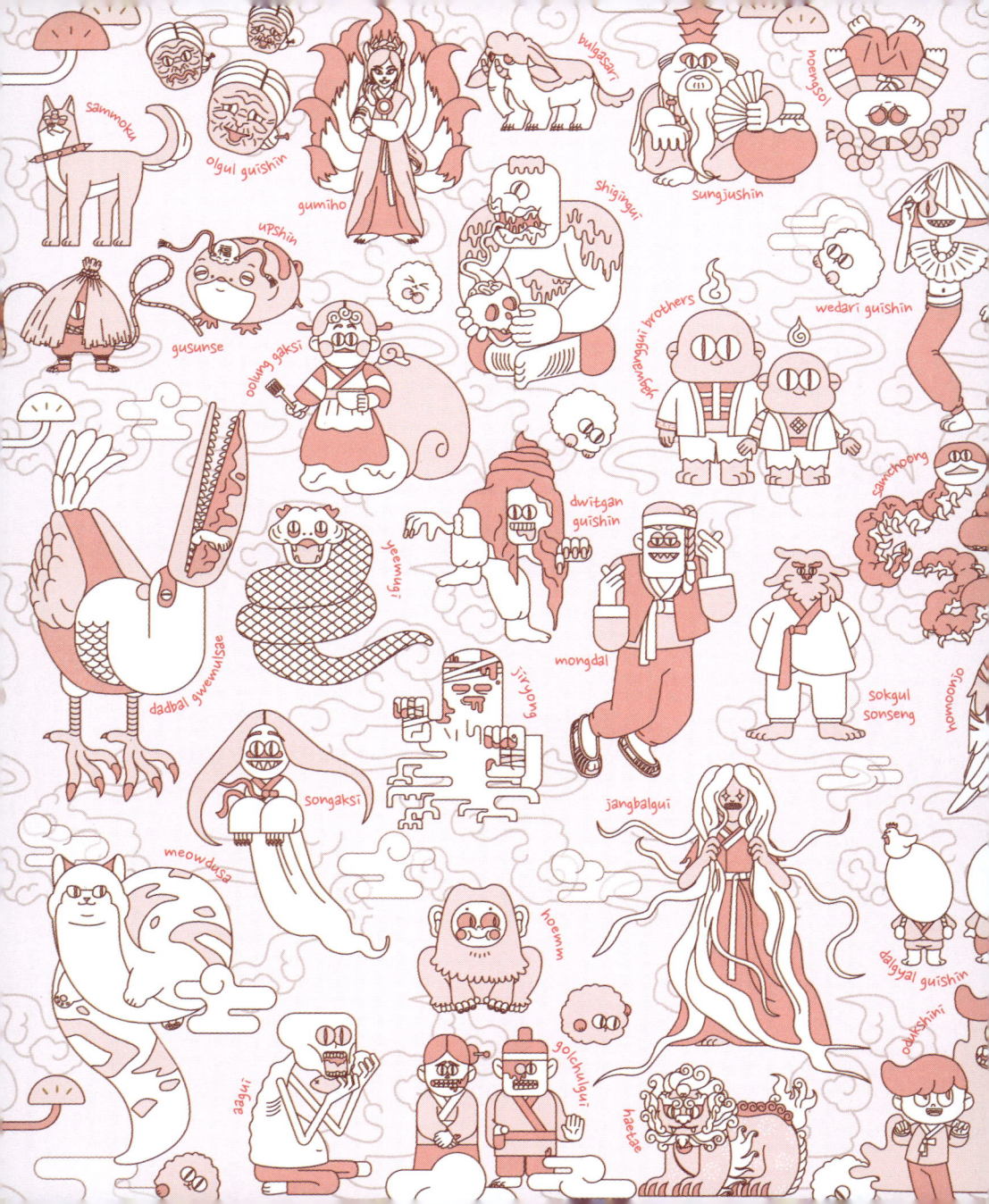

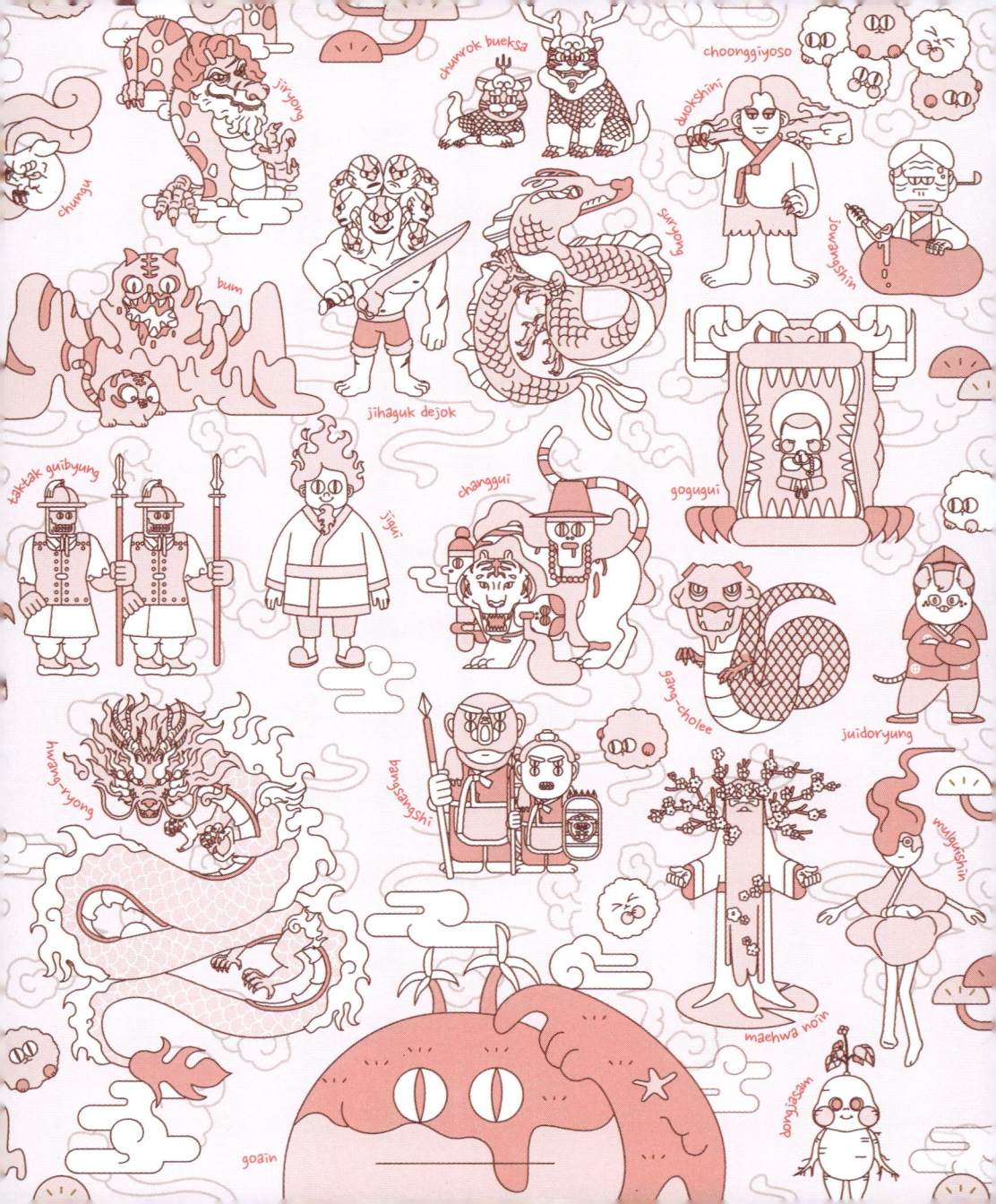

chunju

jiryong

chunrok bueksa

choonggiyoso

duokshini

suryong

jowangshin

bum

jihaguk dejok

gogugui

taktak quibyung

jigui

changgui

hwang-ryong

bangsangshi

gang-cholee

juidoryung

mulgyushin

maehwa noin

dongjasam

goain

Contents

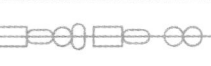 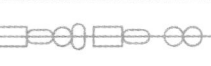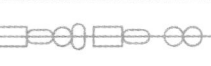

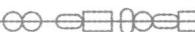

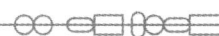

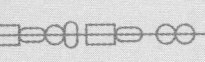
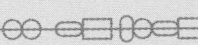

Acknowledgments

Our special gratitude to everyone who funded HWA HWA CO., LTD's yogwe project through multiple tumblbug campaigns since 2019. Thanks to your support, we published our first illustrated guide to Korean yogwe titled *Meoshi World* and launched an animation series under the rebranded name of MeoShín'Ké. Our funders are*:

Ba Sikdong   Lee Seungjun

Baek Yeongju   Kim Jahye   Reumago

BACK LYN   Hyemingyoyeong

Baek Dongcheol   Hong Myeongjin   Sejin   Yun Sujong

Ageobuk   Gwon Yongseong   Park Sangjun   Seo Jihyeon

Choi Seokhong   Jeon Suyong   Jeong Jayun   Oh Eunji

cieolo   DEWEY   E.JeongA.9102

NOOGOONA (Kim Taeheon)   Wol

---

* Listed by funding frequency and alphabetical order

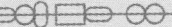
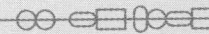

서론

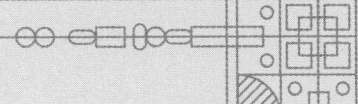

Introduction

Dear traveler, there are certain things you must know before entering the realm of MeoShín'Ké. Here we offer a little primer on MeoShín'Ké to help you understand its strange, powerful, chaotic, and ethereal inhabitants. Kindly note that we will not be responsible for whatever happens in the realm should you encounter MeoShín'Ké's masters without knowing—or should you choose to ignore—the information contained herein.

MeoShin'Ké™
A KOREAN FANTASY WORLD

This book is an illustrated guide to the fantastical realm of MeoShín'Ké and the Korean monsters, ghosts, and gods that dwell there. All our characters are inspired by Korean myth and folklore from classical texts, but we added our own twist as we developed the MeoShín'Ké universe through the books and animation series.

Since 2018, HWA HWA has been creating characters from the pantheon of mysterious beings described in ancient Korean texts, characters with which we built a fantasy world blending Eastern and Western imagination. At the Seoul Illustration Fair in July 2019, we showcased this world to audiences for the first time, calling it "Meoshi World." Then, as we got ready to launch a full-fledged animation series and introduce this quickly growing universe to overseas audiences, we renamed it "MeoShín'Ké."

The new name means "a world ruled by MeoShin," where MeoShin is the cat god that wasn't chosen as one of the twelve animal gods of the zodiac. Compared to "Meoshi World," we thought "MeoShín'Ké" had a nicer Korean ring to it that we wanted to share with international fans.

The Legends of MeoShín'Ké™ is an illustrated series that introduces you to the world and lore of MeoShín'Ké, which will be the basis for the franchise's animated works and a range of other content to come. That's why we rigorously double-checked our research for this edition and added to or revised the material, even tweaking some of our character designs to better suit animation development.

While all our characters are based on real records, we added fresh premises that are unique to MeoShín'Ké.

As you read through the guide, you might wonder about some of the characters, especially ones excavated from classical novels: Aren't the region and era associated with some of these fantastical creatures Chinese? We'd like to clarify that point here. Long ago, Koreans wrote many stories set in China, with some Korean records mentioning creatures or ghosts against the backdrop of the Tang, Song, or Ming dynasties. Just as how some Korean fantasy writers today draw on

Western fictional regions and characters with unique, hard-to-pronounce names, Koreans of old would have found the vast lands of what is present-day China a good stage on which to unleash their imagination.

Yet we hesitated to indicate the settings as such for our project amid sensitive historical debates between South Korea and its neighbors. After many discussions in which we carefully considered different approaches, we decided to accept, as is, the settings that our ancestors had dreamed up to make their tales more entertaining. A Korean novel featuring a protagonist who lives in America is still a Korean novel; likewise, the characters of MeoShín'Ké described as living in foreign regions are still Korean. Which is to say, a creature from a classical novel whose exploits take place in the Ming dynasty is a Korean one born out of a Korean author's imagination.

And so we have indicated the backgrounds of our characters exactly as described in the source texts from which we drew them. However, we have not used the modern concept of nations to specify location; rather, we used the Hangul pronunciations* of locations as indicated in the source novels, portraying them as countries that exist somewhere in the East within MeoShín'Ké.

Just as our ancestors played with the world-building of their tales, we believe it's important to see that as a kind of culture, to adapt it and to grow it.

One last thing we'd like to emphasize is HWA HWA's commitment to creating a fictional universe rooted in Korean folklore and, through MeoShín'Ké, championing Korean culture as well as Asian fantasy. We hope that many around the globe will delight in this world as we have. We are committed to this mission with unwavering passion.

Without further ado, and for the very first time, we unveil MeoShín'Ké: the weird and wondrous world of magical Korean creatures.

---

* Character names and related terms are transliterated according to HWA HWA CO., LTD.'s internal romanization rules, and all other transliterations follow the Revised Romanization system. Location names use the standard romanization for clarity.

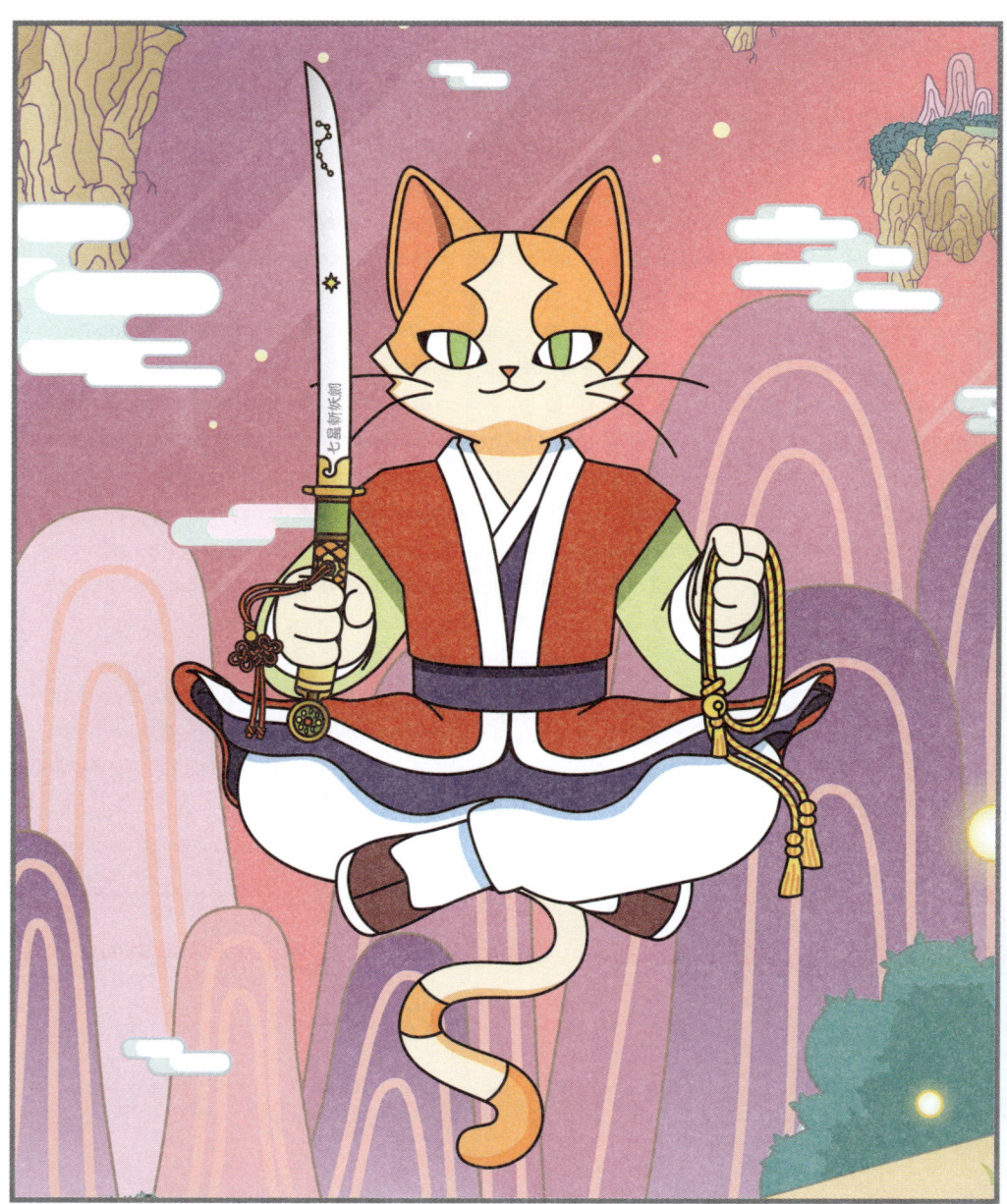

MeoShin, the Cat God

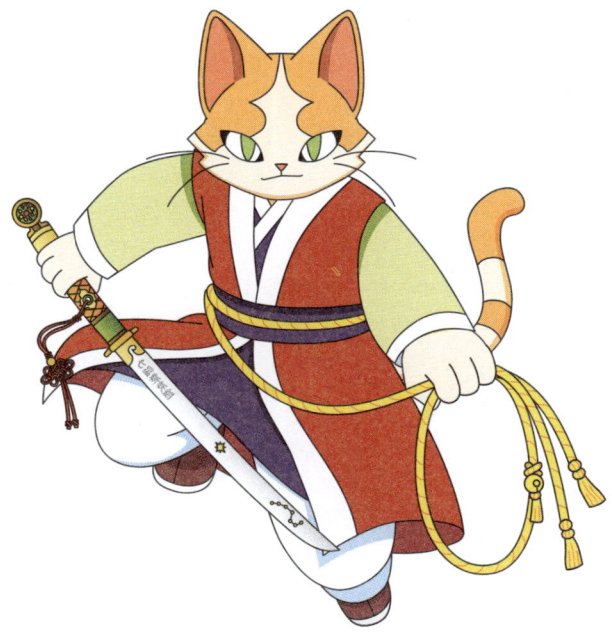

The Chinese zodiac comprises twelve animal gods, but one never made the cut: MeoShin, the cat god. Instead of protecting the earth like the zodiac guardians, this hidden thirteenth deity stewards the mystical realm of souls crawling with monsters, ghosts, and gods. Many have speculated about why the cat was left out of the zodiac, but no one knows for sure. At any rate, MeoShin took charge of the then-nameless realm of souls (not to be confused with other domains of the afterlife like Jeoseung or Hwangcheon) that has since come to be known as MeoShín'Ké.

    Cats have always had a special place beside humans, inspiring both fear and wonder. MeoShin is a cat that can see souls with unearthly clarity. But too many eons of looking after MeoShín'Ké have turned MeoShin into a permanently bored cat, unstartled and unexcited by most things it sees.

The World of ᗰᗴᗝᔕᕼᎥᑎᐠᏦᏋ™

MeoShin's realm of souls is nothing like the world people are familiar with—the world with sky and earth, a rising sun, a setting moon. Time and space, too, work differently there from the gravity-bound world of humans. MeoShín'Ké is the home of strange, special beings we call by many names.

MEOSHÍN'KÉ'S SUPERNATURAL RESIDENTS

When it comes to curious creatures that defy logic and natural laws, humans tend to group them into categories like yogwe,* ghosts, animal gods, and spirit gods. But these supernatural creatures existed long before the earliest human records and behaved in ways that are beyond mortal understanding. Since this book records their stories from a strictly human point of view, we are likely not capturing the full truth.

CATEGORIZATION

The taxonomy of MeoShín'Ké's supernatural beings works in the same way as that of natural organisms: We define and classify into groups. First, we put every MeoShín'Ké inhabitant through the following three questions:

> *How were they born or originated?*
> *What do they look like?*
> *What are their attributes?*

At the highest level, we classify a creature based on its birth or origins. We sort by its essence first, and if that alone isn't clear, we look at the background and manner of its birth. In this way, we divide all our characters into five broad categories: **mulgwe** (monstrous object), **gwesu** (animal

---

* **yogwe:** literally "eerie and strange," a broad term for monsters, spirits, and just about any supernatural beings. Comparable to the Japanese word *yōkai*.

monster), **gwein** (superhuman), **shinsu** (animal god), and **shinryung** (spirit god). We classify them further according to their appearance: For instance, gwesu that look like common monsters are labeled **typical**, while the truly bizarre-looking ones are labeled **atypical**. Gwein are also divided into either typical or atypical depending on how human they look. But appearance is a less useful criterion for shinsu and shinryung, so we use their roles and attributes instead. Finally, we sort the creatures into more detailed, trait-based subcategories if needed.

We use the descriptions pulled straight from our research to categorize most of MeoShín'Ké's creatures, but those whose appearance or traits were tweaked during character development and world-building are classified based on their adjusted profiles.

MULGWE: MONSTROUS OBJECTS

Mulgwe are objects found in homes or nature that have turned into monsters. Some can even transform into humans, but since they were originally objects, we group them under "mulgwe."

- **NATURAL:** classification given to the spirit of a naturally formed object, or to the object itself possessing special powers
- **ARTIFICIAL:** classification given to an old, human-made object that harbors a dark spirit, or to any magical item

MULGWE			
	NATURAL	ORGANIC	an organism like a flower or tree that can sustain life on its own
		INORGANIC	inorganic matter that doesn't consist of cells, such as rock, water, or soil
	ARTIFICIAL	DIRECT	an object that has itself turned into a monster
		INDIRECT	an object used as a medium to summon a monster

GWESU: ANIMAL MONSTERS

Gwesu are animals that turned into monsters. Some can transform into humans, but if they were originally animals, we consider them "gwesu."

- **TYPICAL:** classification given to an animal with special powers. It takes the form of a regular animal but for various reasons has undergone a change in essence.
- **ATYPICAL:** classification given to a monster whose shape, appearance, and characteristics are drastically different from regular animals

GWESU			
	TYPICAL	MORPHED	an animal that has morphed into a new form later in life
		MAGICAL*	an animal that can shapeshift (including into a human) or possesses magical powers
		SPECTRAL	the ghost of a dead animal
	ATYPICAL	MUTANT	an animal with physical features not found in regular animals
		HYBRID	a hybrid of different animals
		FANTASTICAL	an animal with a form or trait not found in the natural world, or one that defies other categorization

---

* Atypical gwesu can straightaway be identified as monsters by their appearance, so we didn't feel the need to create a separate "magical" category for atypical gwesu that have magical powers. But we created one for typical magical gwesu because their ability to use magic—despite looking like regular animals—is their defining trait.

GWEIN: SUPERHUMANS

Any being that was born human but has transcended the appearance and qualities of a regular human is classified under "gwein."

- **TYPICAL:** classification given to a nonhuman being that looks convincingly human
- **ATYPICAL:** classification given to a being that was born human and still is in essence but no longer looks it

GWEIN*	TYPICAL	HUMANOID	a nonhuman creature that looks human
		SPECTRAL**	the ghost of a dead person
	ATYPICAL	MUTANT	a superhuman with genetic traits entirely new to the human genome that manifest in appearance or quality
		ACCIDENTAL	a human that turned superhuman not by choice but by accident or a curse
		HYBRID	the hybrid of a human with other species

---

* Gwein don't include animal yogwe that wear human skin to impersonate people; these creatures are sorted according to their origins. Humans that trained in magic or shapeshifting are also not considered gwein.

** Not all gwein whose names have *gui* ("ghost") in them are ghosts. We classify gwein as "spectral" only when their origins suggest it.

SHINSU: ANIMAL GODS

We consider as shinsu ("animal god") any being that takes the form of an animal and protects a place, an object, or an ideal or does great good in the world.

SHINSU	ACQUIRED	an animal that has acquired the status of a god through long training or an unusual experience
	INNATE	a legendary creature born a god

SHINRYUNG: SPIRIT GODS

We view as shinryung any divine being with superhuman or supernatural powers. Compared with shinsu, shinryung look closer to humans and command more influence in human society.

SHINRYUNG	ACQUIRED	a human who has acquired the status of a god through long training or an unusual experience
	INNATE	a humanlike being born a god

ENERGY

MeoShín'Ké is a world that runs on seven types of energy. Though all these energies affect its population, each creature channels one dominant energy. We've researched every creature meticulously to connect it to a particular energy, studying its powers, disposition, and influence instead of simply referring to its habitat or appearance.

As with all things in nature, energy is diverse. MeoShín'Ké's creatures can't simply be good or evil. Their dominant energy can't explain everything about them, either. It is, however, important in understanding their essence.

In line with the concepts of yin and yang and the five agents, the seven energies that course through MeoShín'Ké are: moon, fire, water, wood, metal, earth, and sun.

SEVEN ENERGIES OF MEOSHÍN'KÉ

	MOON	moon, yin energy, darkness, curse, seduction, mystery, wisdom, prophecy
	FIRE	fire, passion, love, disaster, conflagration, sparks, change, drought, courage, lightning
	WATER	water, freezing, tsunami, purification, healing, flexibility, resuscitation, oblivion, confusion (disorder)
	WOOD	absorption, recovery, persistence, abundance, poison, inflexibility (stubbornness), obsession, anxiety (fear)
	METAL	metal, weaponry, illness, greed, wealth, strength, punishment, intelligence (reason)
	EARTH	earth, land, regeneration, decay, neutralization, life, death
	SUN	sun, yang energy, light, justice, luck, order, authority (power)

FRIENDLINESS TO HUMANS

In ways big and small, the supernatural beings of MeoShín'Ké affect human lives with unfathomable powers and behaviors. They do things that may help or harm people, acting out of love or fear or for no reason at all. Since this is essential information for people to know, we came up with a system that indicates the "friendliness" of MeoShín'Ké's residents to humans, drawing on records left throughout history. Again, the system is a human-centric one, and while we tried our best to be objective, we can't guarantee how creatures will actually react in an encounter.

-3	threatening to great masses of people on the scale of a natural disaster
-2	inflicts direct physical or mental harm on many people
-1	inflicts direct or indirect harm on a few people through tricks, terrorization, or sabotage
0	neither harmful nor helpful to humans
+1	indirectly helps a small number of people, from assisting with house chores to warding off evil
+2	directly benefits a large number of people
+3	helps great masses of people with wondrous strength and magic
★	can turn helpful or harmful depending on human behavior, so must interact with caution
▲	can be either helpful or harmful to humans

SIGHTINGS

Supernatural beings don't stay cooped up in MeoShín'Ké but venture out to many corners of the human world. They turn up at specific locations like Gaeunpo Fortress in Ulsan, Mount Namsan of Gyeongju, Gimje of North Jeolla Province, Gijang of Busan, or Mount Baekdu, their appearances and names often being recorded. On each creature's profile, we noted the places in which it has been sighted using the geographical names from the original records. Some classical Korean novels, however, point to locations with names no longer used in present-day Korea, instead mentioning places that once existed in other ancient countries. We did not specify the modern names of such countries and tried to preserve the Hangul pronunciation of names used in the source texts.

For creatures recorded as being sighted around night streets, mountain trails, valleys, and residential areas instead of specific geographic names, we noted in their profiles the general categories of such places.

SIZE AND WEIGHT

In old records, a creature's size is often left unelaborated or exaggerated. One creature is described as being so humongous that its upper lip brushes the sky, another as towering over a mountain; still another's single feather can apparently crush a house. Our storytellers of yore probably sprinkled in such outlandish details to give their tales a whimsical spark.

In our world-building for MeoShín'Ké, we determined a character's size and length by taking realistic factors into account while respecting the source descriptions as much as possible.

For animal or human characters that are bipedal, we indicated the length from the top of their head to the tip of their feet as their height. A character's accessories or headpiece wasn't included in the measurements.

For four-legged animals or lengthy creatures like snakes or dragons, we indicated their full length from head to tail, which is how biologists measure similar animals.

For creatures that can change in size, we marked their default size along with their transformed size, or used the plus (+) sign to note that they can grow bigger than what is indicated. Some shinsu and shinryung in particular have the power to expand or shrink to whatever size, in which case we added the note "(can change size)."

When there are multiple creatures of the same species, we noted their average size.

We also specified each creature's weight. The spectral gwein and gwesu—the ghosts, that is—have a special weight. When someone dies, does their soul weigh as much as their body did? Not at all. No matter how big or small a ghost is in MeoShín'Ké, it weighs twenty-one grams: the average weight of all souls. The fields we marked as "immeasurable" are for the shinsu carrying an island on their backs or the occasional creature whose weight or dimensions no one has successfully measured or who simply transcends human perception.

AGE

If you ask MeoShín'Ké's beings how old they are, how do they answer? Some remember their age exactly, but some tell you a different number every time you ask or have existed for so long that they've lost count! In such cases, we noted their ages as "unknown." If what we are profiling isn't a single creature but a species consisting of multiple entities, we indicated their age as "varies by entity."

As you read, you will find some entries that specify age but also describe a creature as being "a thousand years old" or "ten thousand years old." Here we don't mean that literally but rather are alluding to its mythically long lifespan.

On a side note, these creatures aren't governed by the laws of gravity. In fact, ever since they entered the entirely alien space-time that is MeoShín'Ké, they've stopped aging with every passing year. Age is just a fun trivia that we added in to reflect the age-conscious culture of Korea and to create an interesting dynamic between characters.

ERA

Every MeoShín'Ké character has its own era. By "era," we mean the period in which these creatures were active or were sighted. This was easy enough to identify for some creatures, but for others, the more we researched, the harder it was to say that they belonged to one particular era or country. It was especially difficult to pinpoint the era for shinsu or shinyrung found commonly across East Asian cultures, like the guardians of the four cardinal directions, or the girin (aka *qilin* or *kirin*). For such cases, we marked the era as "unknown."

POWER INDEX

In MeoShín'Ké, power doesn't simply mean muscle strength. The power index of a creature factors in its intelligence, muscle strength, spellcasting, magic, and ecokinesis abilities and compares that combined statistic across characters. For reference, humans have an average power index of 13 to 14 because we are all intelligence and muscle strength with zero powers of spellcasting, magic, and ecokinesis.

For creatures that can change size or show their true form right before devouring human prey, their power index is measured when they are transformed or are using their powers.

While it's true that creatures with a higher power index are generally stronger and more skilled than those with lower statistics, the former may not necessarily beat the latter in a battle. A creature may have a hyper-concentration of a single power, or certain attributes may prove especially lethal against an opponent's, or other situational factors could produce surprising results.

	INTELLIGENCE	wisdom and mental ability to make sense of new situations or entities and respond appropriately
	STRENGTH	power and endurance of muscular strength
	SPELLCASTING	ability to cast spells to prevent misfortune or disaster; includes the power to alter an entity's state, such as cursing or healing
	MAGIC	supernatural power to alter one's own state or perform strange feats, including prophecy, shapeshifting, and space contraction
	ECOKINESIS	ability to manipulate nature, such as water, fire, wind, and earth, but also to alter one's own nature. Nature refers not only to the mountains, rivers, seas, plants, and animals that form independently of people but also to the true essence of things. Ecokinesis is sometimes mistaken for magic.

NAME

Every MeoShín'Ké creature has a name. The names of some became famous in the human world, but some came to be called by another name based on how they looked or behaved at the time of their discovery. For instance, the name Dalgyal Guishin ("egg ghost") was coined by humans who thought the ghosts had egg-like faces, but to their MeoShín'Ké friends, they are "Dagal." Dong-jasam ("ginseng boy") got that name because humans thought the ginseng looked like a child, when actually its true MeoShín'Ké name is "GinGin." Mulguishin ("water ghost") is just a blanket term for any ghosts of people who drowned, and each of the countless Mulguishin out there has its own name. Beings that are not of this world often go by many names; their true names are hidden from human knowledge. It's important to learn the real names of MeoShín'Ké creatures to better understand them.

Classification of Supernatural Beings

GHOST

YOGWE

SHINSU

SHINRYUNG

SUPERNATURAL BEINGS BY ENERGY

MOON
 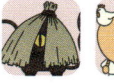

FIRE

WATER

WOOD

METAL

EARTH
 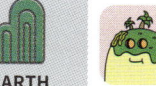 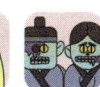 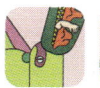

SUN

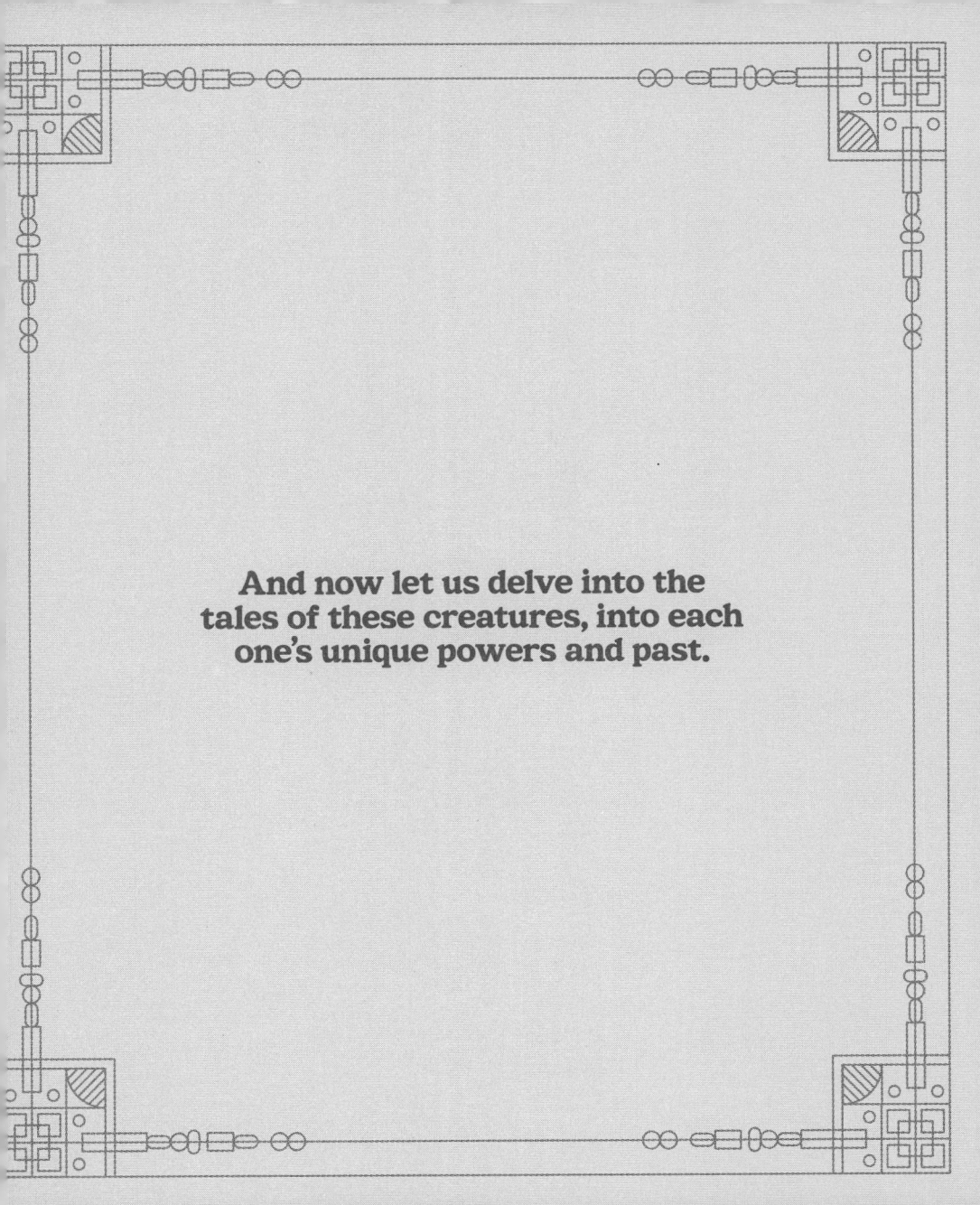

And now let us delve into the
tales of these creatures, into each
one's unique powers and past.

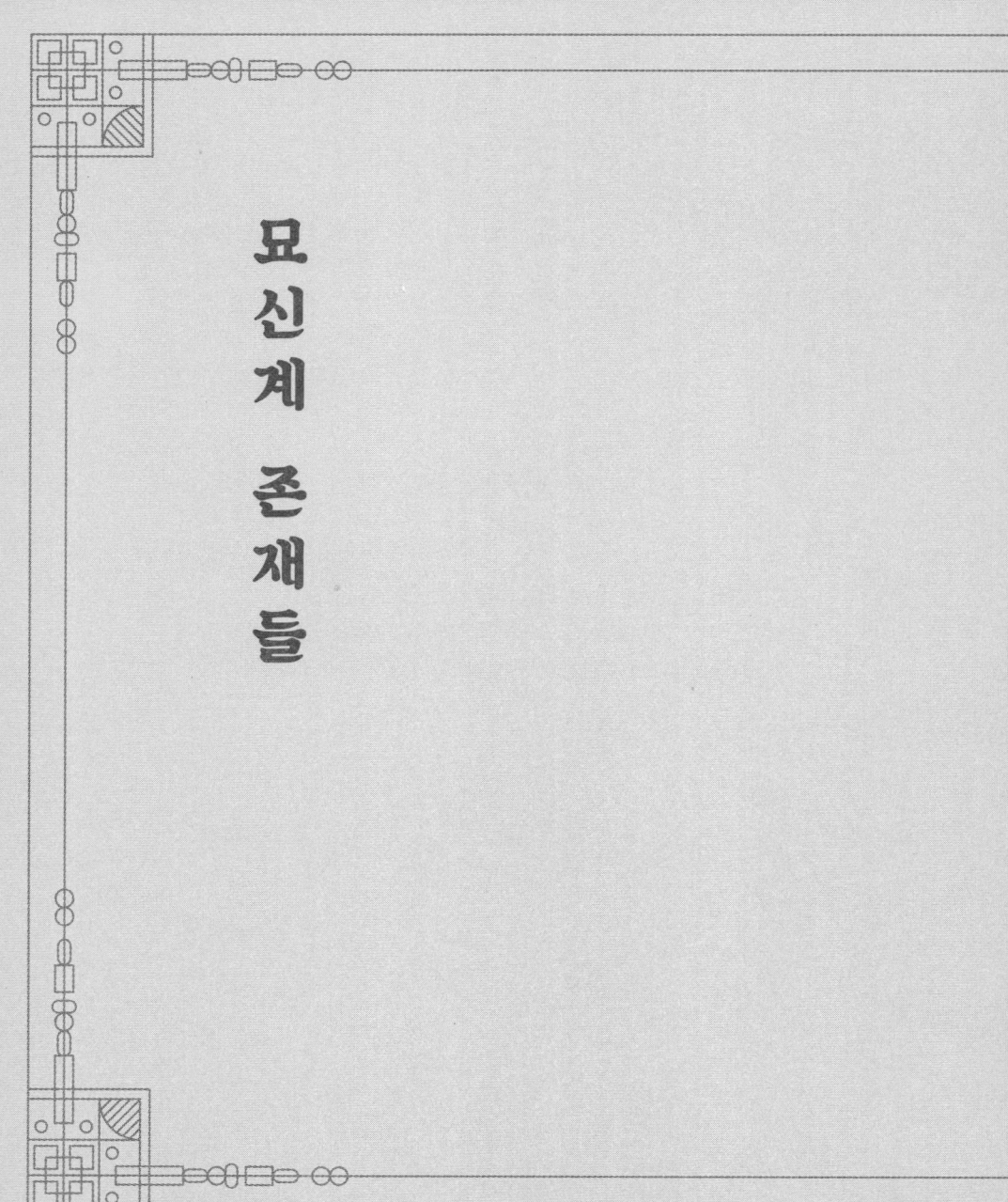

묘신계 존재들

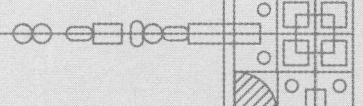

The Creatures of MeoShin'Ké™

Ghosts, monsters, mythical beasts, and gods are just some of the names people give to strange beings that fly smack in the face of nature's laws. And these marvelous oddities are what populate the realm of MeoShín'Ké. Their stories, which you are about to find in the following pages, have been taken down by human scribes and so may not always represent the true nature of things.

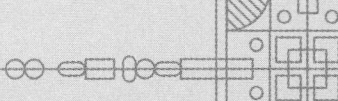

Gang-Cholee

강철이

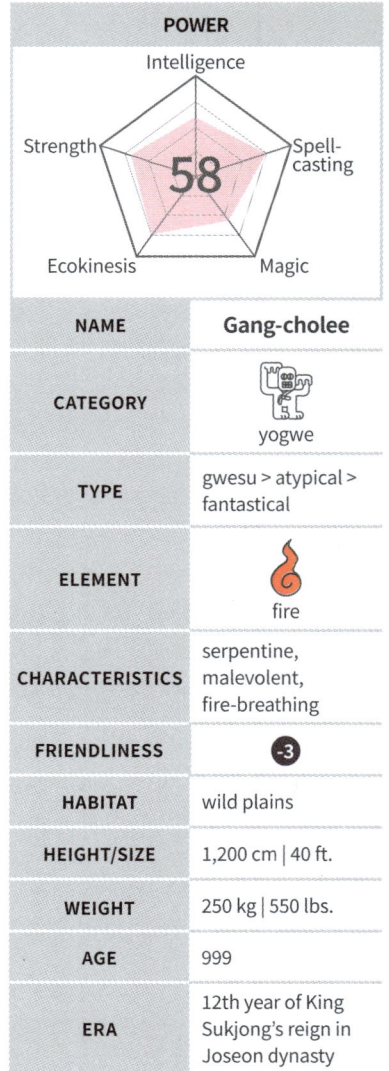

POWER	
58	

NAME	**Gang-cholee**
CATEGORY	yogwe
TYPE	gwesu > atypical > fantastical
ELEMENT	fire
CHARACTERISTICS	serpentine, malevolent, fire-breathing
FRIENDLINESS	-3
HABITAT	wild plains
HEIGHT/SIZE	1,200 cm | 40 ft.
WEIGHT	250 kg | 550 lbs.
AGE	999
ERA	12th year of King Sukjong's reign in Joseon dynasty

Gang-cholee is a malevolent Yeemugi serpent that failed to evolve into a dragon but is sometimes mistaken for one that spews poison. Even though it ended up a common yogwe instead of joining the sacred ranks of shinsu, Gang-cholee is an immensely powerful creature. Its scales are dark and murky, but its eyes and maws are a menacing red. Because it was trying to become a dragon before falling short, it has small horns on its head and sharp front claws.

All Yeemugi can manipulate water, but Gang-cholee, a degenerate form of Yeemugi, has a special affinity with fire instead. Spitting out potent blasts of fire that are hard to put out, it leaves a trail of flames wherever it goes, causing terrible droughts that dry up whole fields of crops and vegetation. Gang-cholee usually takes a snakelike or dragon-like form but in rare instances is found resembling a cow or a horse. In this form, it doesn't raise fire but rains down hails of ice that poison lands and rivers and ponds, also killing crops.

GANGCHOLGEOCHEO SUCHUYEOCHUN

Where Gang-cholee goes,
fall turns back to spring

A proverb originating from the Gang-cholee's power to ruin harvests, it refers to a nasty obstacle that ruins something about to reach fruition.

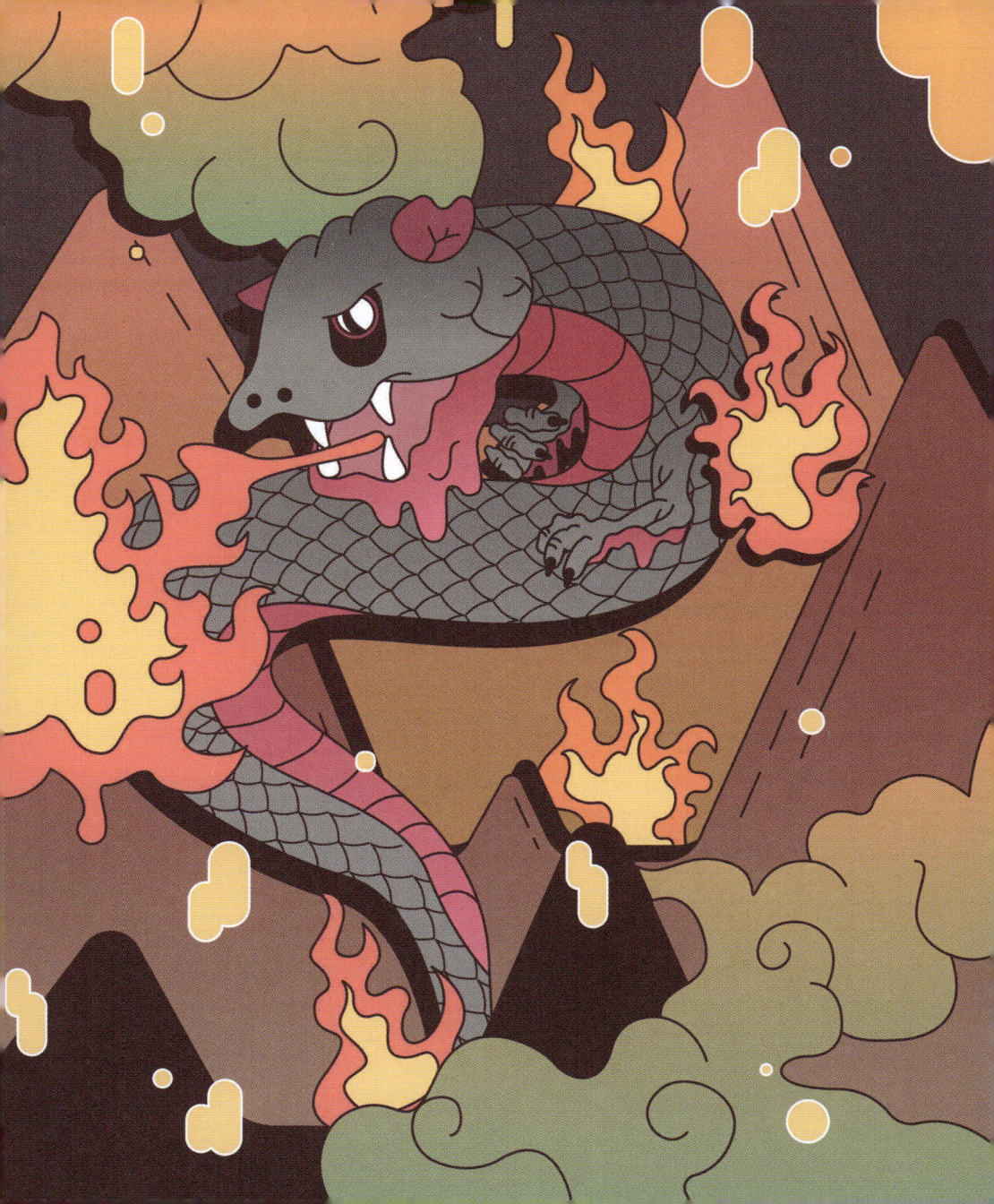

Gogugui

Gogugui has a mouth so gargantuan that when it opens its jaws to the fullest, its upper lip brushes the clouds. Its hard, massive body makes its mouth seem like a cave. It crouches, waiting in the darkness, then pounces on human prey with a flash of eyes and fangs.

But when it chances on an utterly fearless human, Gogugui transforms into Chunguidongja—literally, a "boy in blue"—and offers protection. Chunguidongja is a sweet-faced child ghost with powers of clairvoyance. Once he chooses to protect someone, he tells them everything in store for them, both good and bad, ensuring his charge a safe, successful future.

Once upon a time, a man named Munchung Shin Sukju and his friends were traveling the road when they crossed paths with Gogugui. All of his friends fled from the monster's frightful jaws, but Shin Sukju walked right into them, unfazed. Admiring his bravery, Gogugui transformed into Chunguidongja and became his guardian yogwe. Shin Sukju's extraordinary act earned him Chunguidongja's protection for the rest of his life.

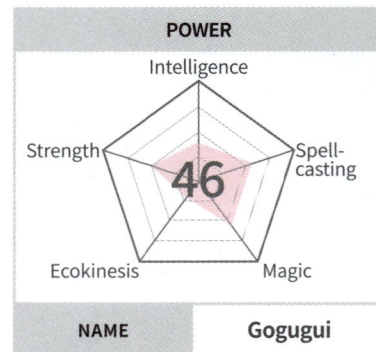

POWER

NAME	Gogugui
CATEGORY	yogwe
TYPE	gwesu > atypical > fantastical
ELEMENT	sun
CHARACTERISTICS	enormous mouth
FRIENDLINESS	▲
HABITAT	mountain paths
HEIGHT/SIZE	500 cm | 16 ft.
WEIGHT	1.3 t | 1.4 tn.
AGE	605
ERA	early Joseon period

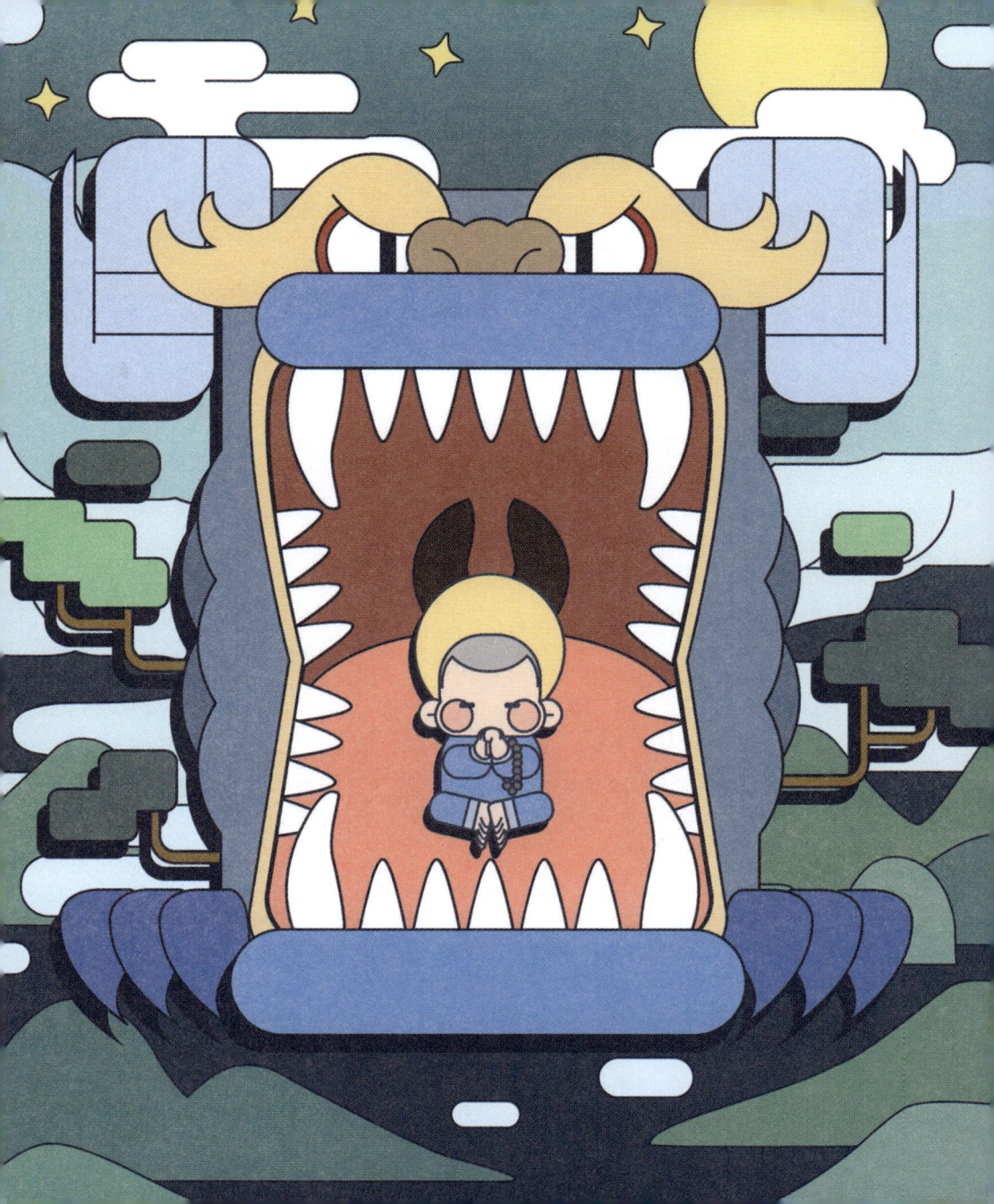

Goain

Goain are giant yogwe with a human form. They are many times bigger than humans, with some being simply too big to measure. A colorful range of Goain species exists, with some being friendly to humans while others are wanton cannibals. Exercise caution when dealing with a Goain.

GOAIN OF BIG PEOPLE KINGDOM

Living across the ocean in Daeinguk, or Big People Kingdom, is a group of one-eyed giants three to four times larger than the average human. Traveling mostly by boat, these Goain have a penchant for capturing humans and roasting them on skewers.

GOAIN OF TALL PEOPLE KINGDOM

Living across the ocean in Janginguk, or Tall People Kingdom, is a group of Goain five to six times larger than the average human. Their teeth are sharp as saws, and they have thick black hair all over their bodies. These sorts prefer animal and human meat raw.

GOAIN OF THE SEA

These sea giants roam oceans alone, never staying too long in one place. They are at least ten times the size of humans, and the largest are recorded to be as vast as a mountain. Sea Goain tend to have relatively tiny feet, which allow them to travel quickly underwater. Above ground, they are clumsy and thus rarely come up to land.

POWER

Intelligence — Strength — Spell-casting — Magic — Ecokinesis

39

NAME	Goain
CATEGORY	yogwe
TYPE	gwein > typical > humanoid
ELEMENT	earth
CHARACTERISTICS	head mistaken for island when sitting underwater
FRIENDLINESS	-2
HABITAT	unknown
HEIGHT/SIZE	6,000 cm | 197 ft.
WEIGHT	immeasurable
AGE	unknown
ERA	antiquity

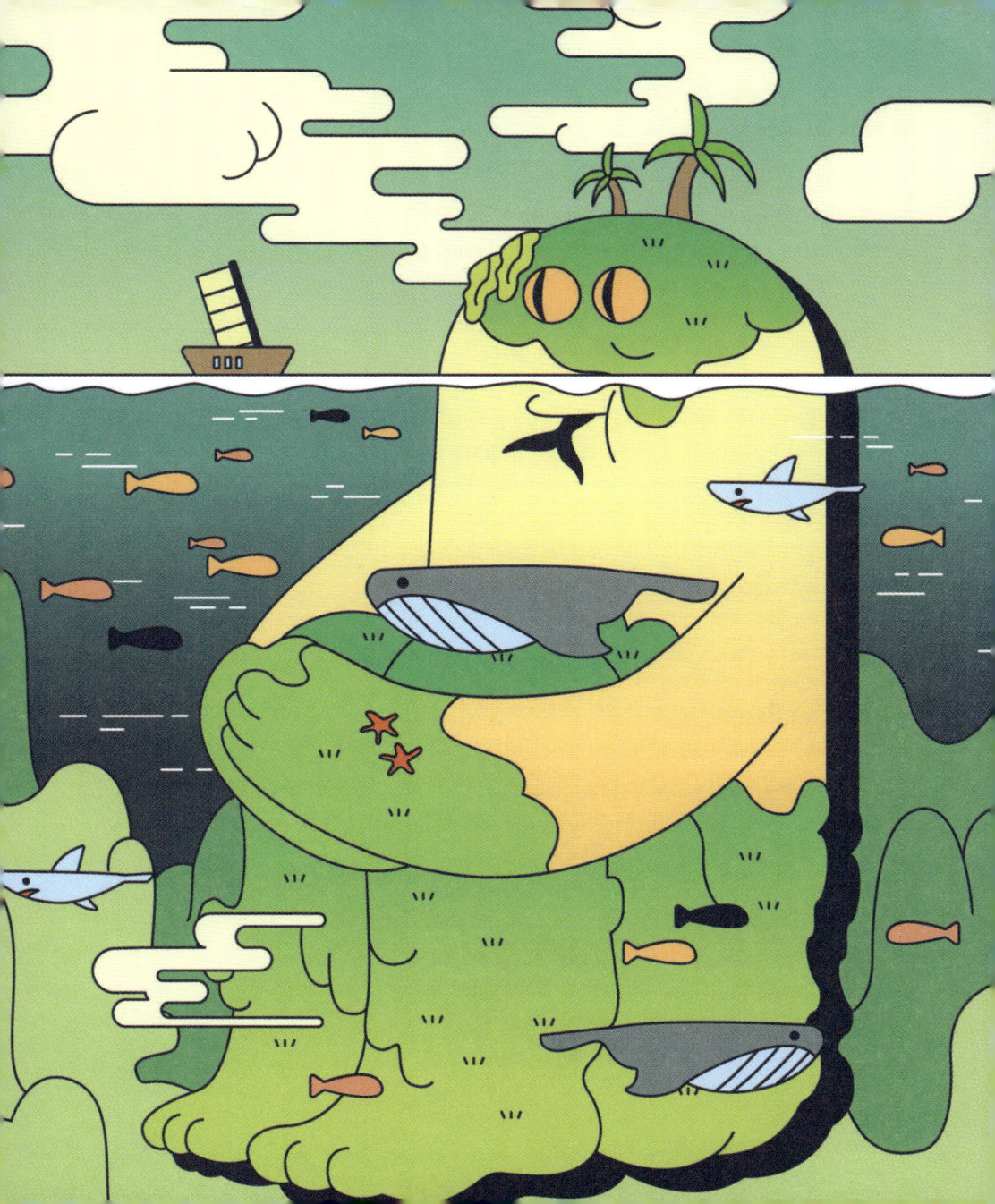

Golchulgui

Golchulgui are the ghosts of corpses that awaken underground and crawl out to fix their neglected graves. Long buried in the soil, they have pale skin almost the color of milky jade. Their bodies are decaying, with bones jutting out in places and an appendage or two missing. Curiously, their fingernails, toenails, and hair grow longer and longer like those of the living.

Since all they want is to look after their dilapidated graves, Golchulgui don't attack or harass humans. If someone happens to pass by a Gulchulgui's gravesite, it asks ever so politely, "Could you help me fix my grave?" The trouble is, most people take one look at the Golchulgui and run for their lives, some even fainting, much to the poor creature's dismay. If it does receive help from a kind passerby, it thanks them profusely before quietly climbing back into its grave to sleep.

ZOMBIES VS. GOLCHULGUI

The Western zombie and the Eastern Golchulgui may appear similar in that both are walking corpses, but they are quite different in nature. Zombies are often transformed or reanimated by a virus infection, but Golchulgui are souls reposing in graves. Zombies are mindless creatures reduced to primal, human-hunting instincts, whereas Golchulgui are rational enough to have perfectly normal conversations with people.

POWER

Intelligence / Strength / Spell-casting / Ecokinesis / Magic

13

NAME	**Golchul**
CATEGORY	ghost
TYPE	gwein > typical > spectral
ELEMENT	earth
CHARACTERISTICS	grave-keeping
FRIENDLINESS	-1
HABITAT	gravesites
HEIGHT/SIZE	140 cm | 4.6 ft.
WEIGHT	21 g | 0.05 lbs.
AGE	varies by entity
ERA	varies by entity

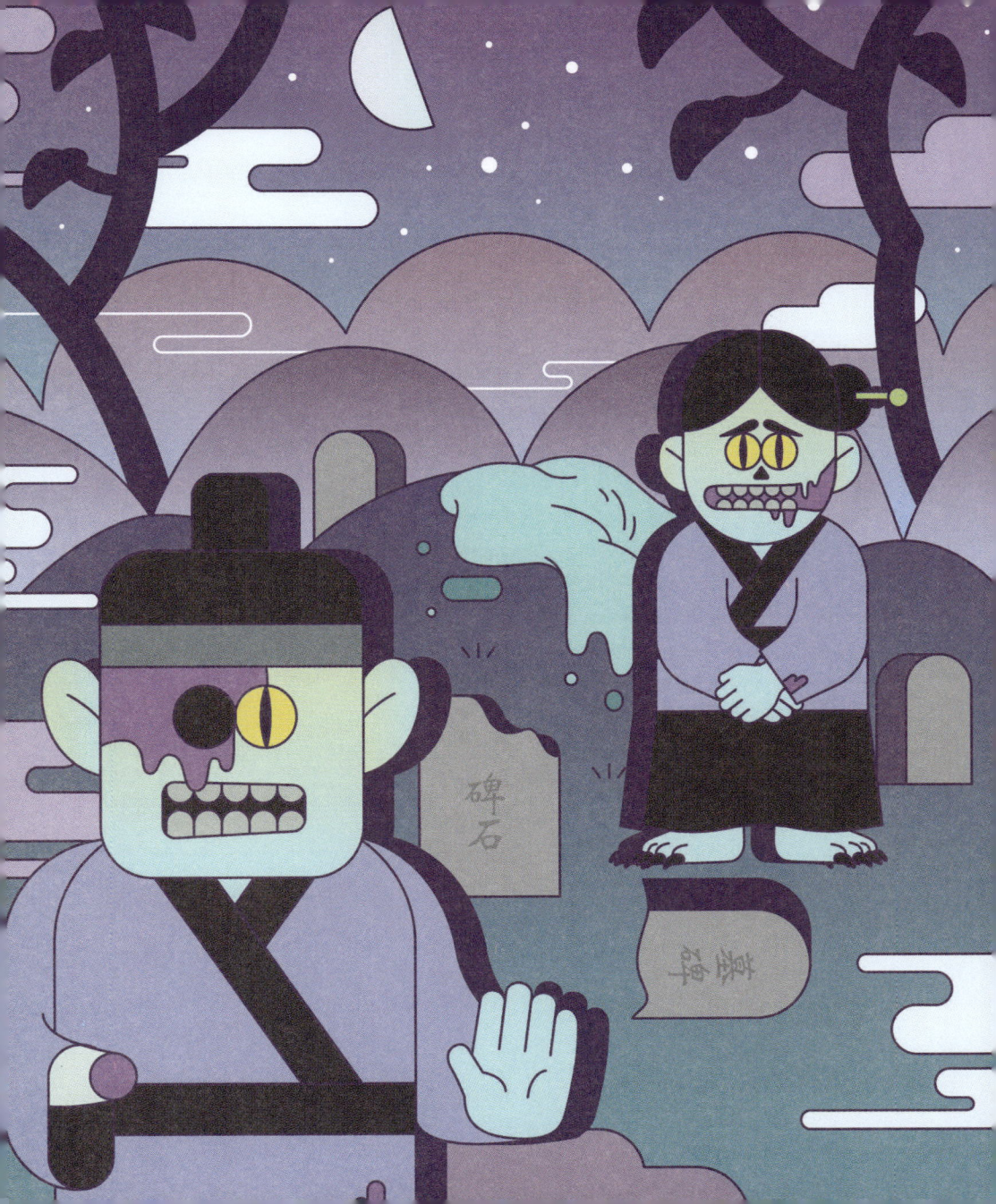

Gumiho

When a fox lives for a hundred years, it sprouts an extra tail for every century it lives thereafter, each tail bringing greater wisdom, power, and allure. A nine-hundred-year-old fox has nine tails, becoming a Gumiho, but only the cleverest few succeed. So the Gumiho is the name of a species, but this particular yogwe featured here was the first of its kind to be discovered by humans, and has since been simply dubbed "Gumiho."

Gumiho with a wicked streak feed on human liver, but there are also honest Gumiho that help humans. A Gumiho that has trained honorably for a thousand years turns into the sacred ten-tailed Cheonho* and rises up to the heavens. Most Gumiho cradle a fox orb** inside their bodies with which they perform magic. Talented shapeshifters, they blend in among humans effortlessly. In human guise, Gumiho often seduce people to suck out their life force and add it to their fox orb. Yet they have an instinctive fear of hunting dogs, trained falcons, and human hunters: all age-old predators of foxes. If they run into one, they may panic and accidentally slip back into their fox form.

---

* **Cheonho:** a golden-furred fox shinsu that serves the Jade Emperor in heaven's court

** **fox orb:** an orb in which a fox stores all its powers. Once a human claims an orb, they can learn all the secrets of the land with one downward glance and all the mysteries of the sky with one upward gaze.

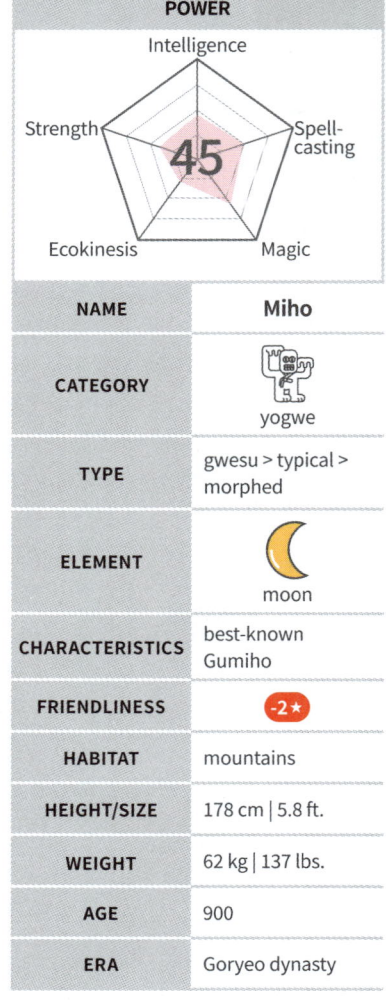

POWER	
NAME	**Miho**
CATEGORY	yogwe
TYPE	gwesu > typical > morphed
ELEMENT	moon
CHARACTERISTICS	best-known Gumiho
FRIENDLINESS	-2★
HABITAT	mountains
HEIGHT/SIZE	178 cm | 5.8 ft.
WEIGHT	62 kg | 137 lbs.
AGE	900
ERA	Goryeo dynasty

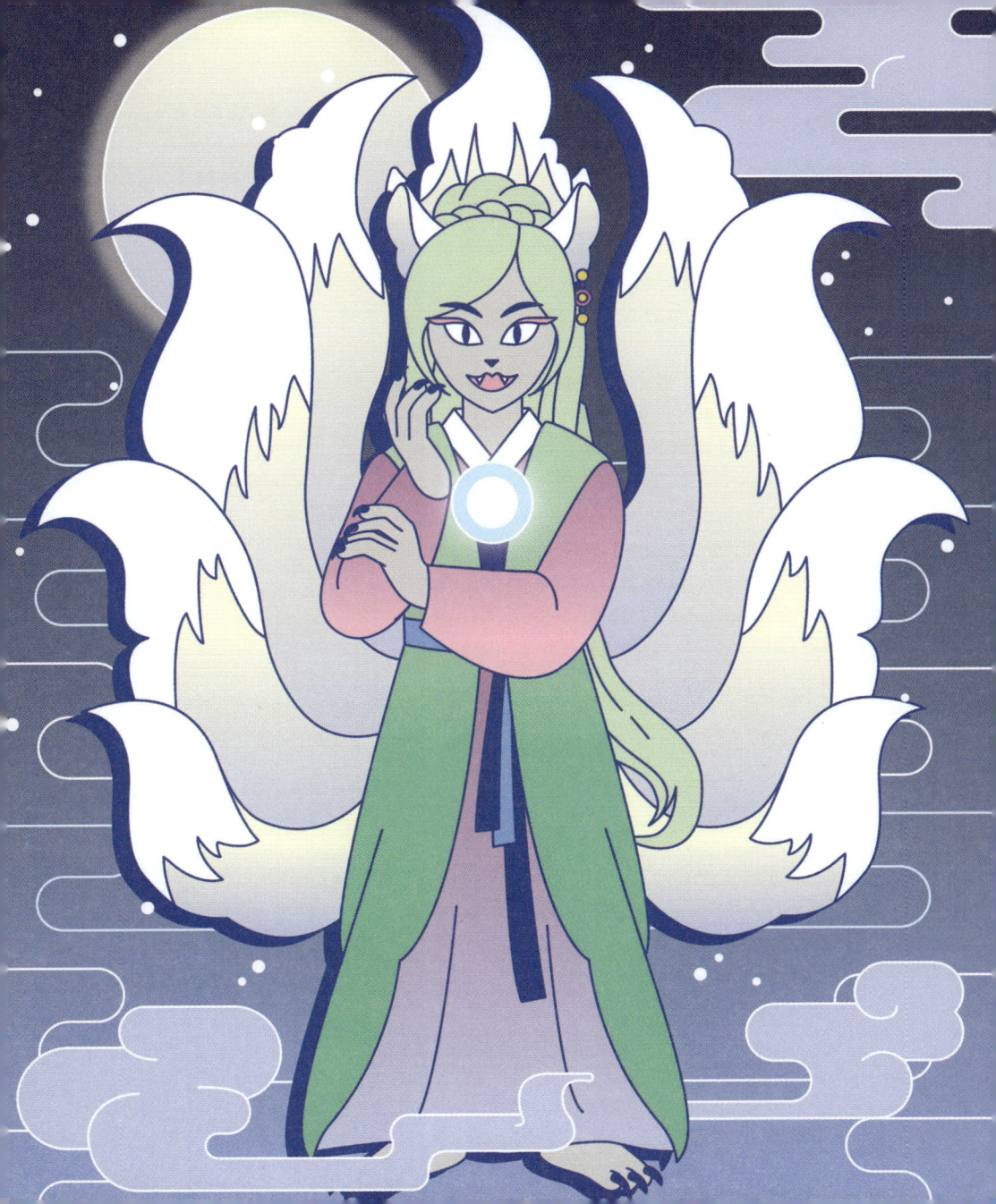

Gusunse

Sighted around Jeju Island, Gusunse is notorious for bewitching humans. It is the size of a small child and wraps itself in a straw cape to keep out rain. Appearing mostly on rainy days or gray days, it hovers in midair looking for a solo traveler.

Gusunse is a master manipulator of the mind. It targets people who are alone and draws them into eye contact. The moment they look into its gleaming eyes beneath the straw cape, their mind falls under its control; then it makes them seek the nearest rope or twine to take their own life. Since this leaves behind no traces of external harm, people don't suspect foul play. But fighting off Gusunse's mind control is actually quite simple: just talk to or distract the victim to help them snap back to their senses.

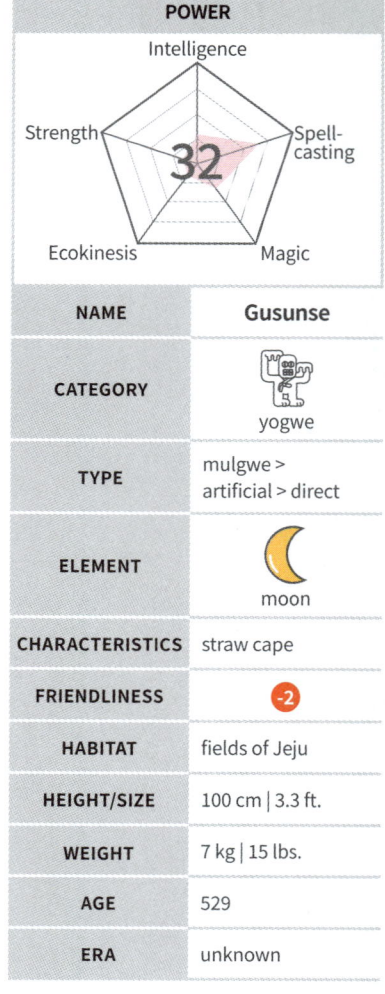

POWER

Intelligence · Spell-casting · Magic · Ecokinesis · Strength

32

NAME	Gusunse
CATEGORY	yogwe
TYPE	mulgwe > artificial > direct
ELEMENT	moon
CHARACTERISTICS	straw cape
FRIENDLINESS	-2
HABITAT	fields of Jeju
HEIGHT/SIZE	100 cm | 3.3 ft.
WEIGHT	7 kg | 15 lbs.
AGE	529
ERA	unknown

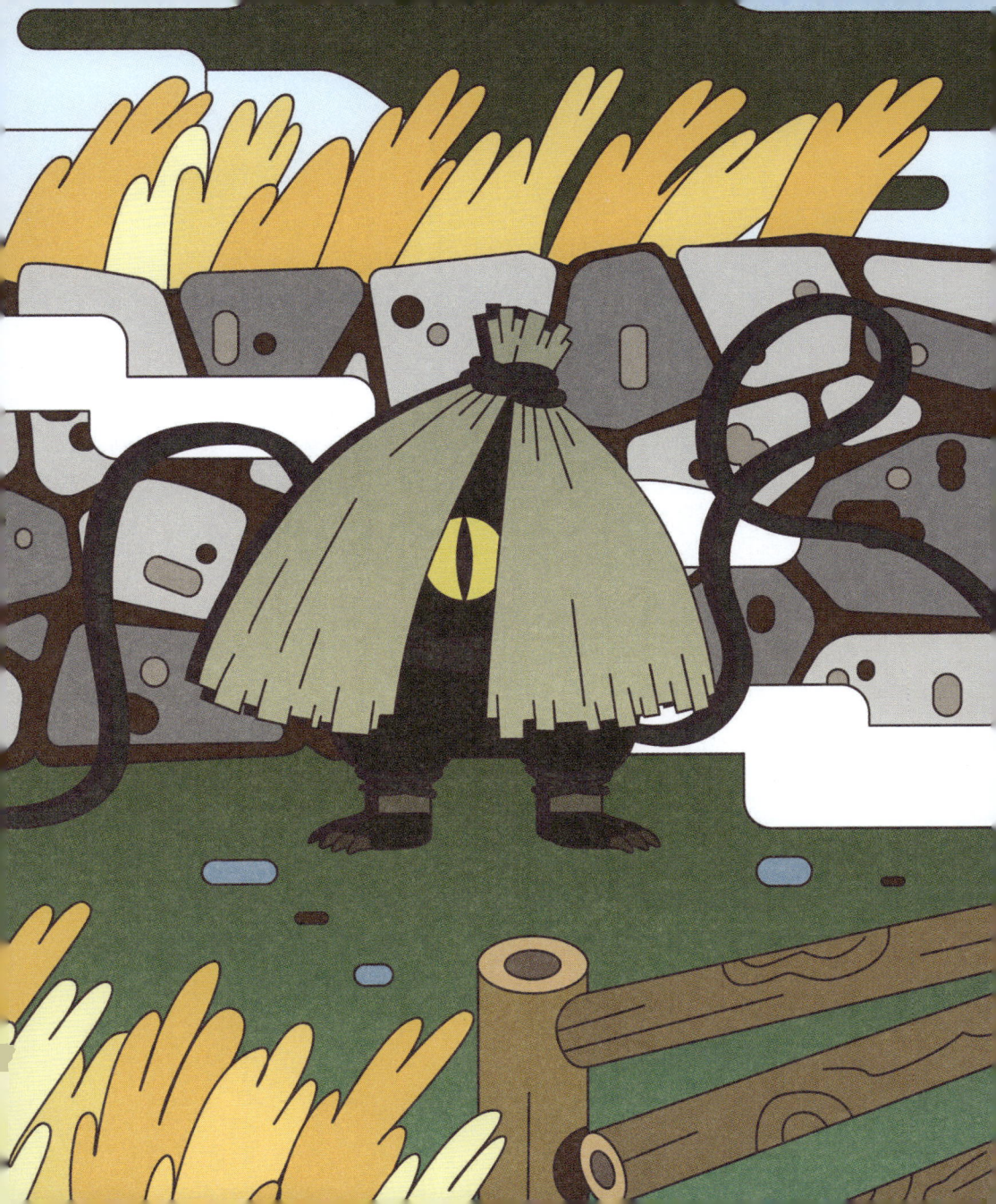

Noengsol

Although popularly known as "Noengsol," this ghost resembling a little girl likes to call herself "Ceilia." She is usually spotted inside homes, hanging upside down from the ceiling or a pillar, or levitating. She has the face of a child but the voice of an old songbird, which surprises humans when they first hear her.

Noengsol can read minds. She might use this power to play tricks or to help a household by warning its members of malicious hearts. Her other gift is searching: She knows where lost items are in the house and exactly how and why you lost them. She tells you all this with a child's earnestness but can sometimes be a tad stubborn, convinced that what she has to tell you—whether good news or bad—is always right, thank you very much.

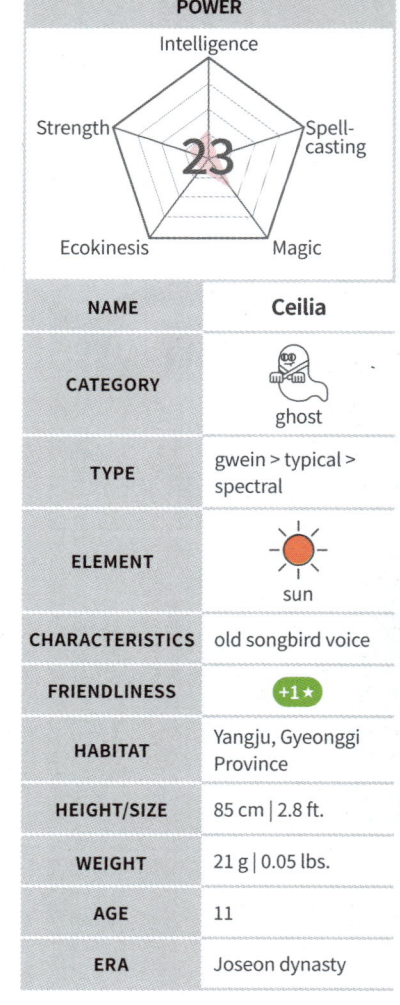

POWER	
Intelligence: 23	
NAME	**Ceilia**
CATEGORY	ghost
TYPE	gwein > typical > spectral
ELEMENT	sun
CHARACTERISTICS	old songbird voice
FRIENDLINESS	+1★
HABITAT	Yangju, Gyeonggi Province
HEIGHT/SIZE	85 cm | 2.8 ft.
WEIGHT	21 g | 0.05 lbs.
AGE	11
ERA	Joseon dynasty

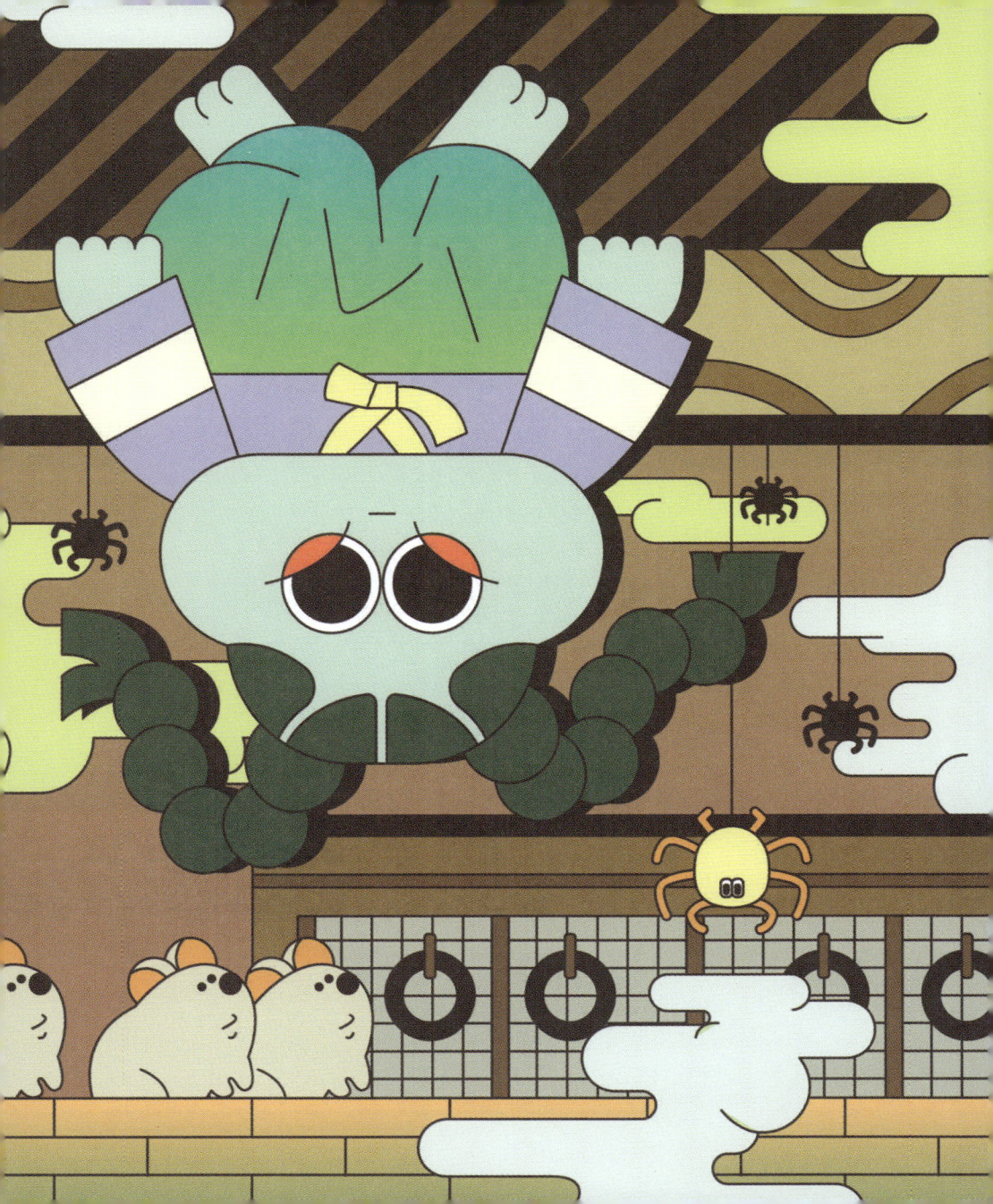

Dalgyal Guishin

Dalgyal Guishin ("egg ghost") have faces that resemble a smooth egg. Since these ghosts have no eyes, nose, or mouth to speak of, they can't see, smell, or talk. But they move as if they can see, they breathe, and they can communicate with others.

Dagal like to meander through deserted alleyways and mountain paths. Drifting from place to place, they dress humbly and carry little.

They are also fainthearted souls. Of course, humans who see them are much more frightened, the shock sometimes causing a long, drawn-out sickness that ends in death. But Dagal never attack or harm you first. Approach them without warning, though, and they may perceive this as an attack and hex you. The curse doesn't take immediate effect, unfolding slowly: After a day, your mouth disappears; the next day, your nose; and so on until you, too, become an egg-faced ghost. The curse is irreversible, so it's best to give Dagal a wide berth.

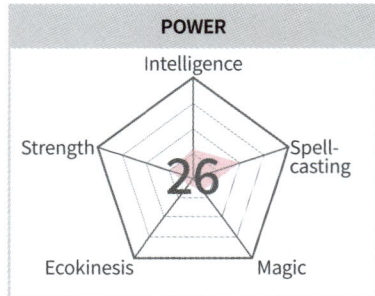

POWER	
NAME	**Dagal**
CATEGORY	ghost
TYPE	gwein > typical > spectral
ELEMENT	moon
CHARACTERISTICS	eyeless, noseless, mouthless
FRIENDLINESS	-2
HABITAT	Paju, Gyeonggi Province
HEIGHT/SIZE	72 cm | 2.4 ft.
WEIGHT	21 g | 0.05 lbs.
AGE	unknown
ERA	unknown

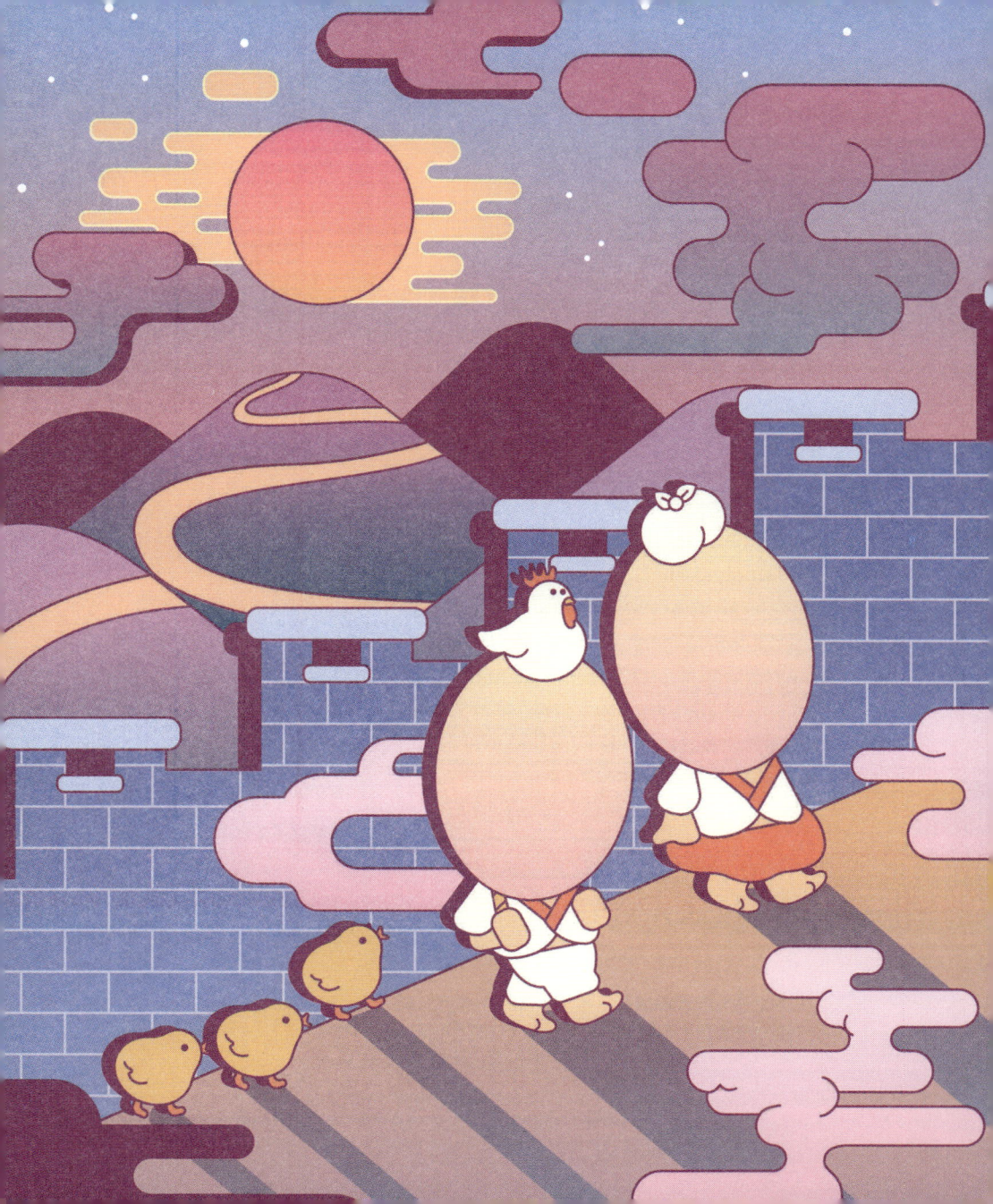

Dadbal Gwemulsae

닷발괴물새

Dadbal Gwemulsae gets its name from the fact that its beak and tail are both dadbal ("five bal") long, bal being an old unit of measure for arm span. So the front and rear ends of this monstrous bird are each a whopping five arm spans. Its green, rock-hard beak is crammed with razor-sharp teeth, and its thick, orange tail is powerful enough to bat a hapless human across the sky.

This gwesu is a carnivore, with a beak tailor-made for hunting and talons that never let go. Dadbal Gwemulsae usually hunts animals on mountains but sometimes ventures down to villages to snatch humans. Its favorite pastime is to play chef, cooking freshly caught animals or humans into soups or rice bowls—or if it's feeling fancy—steamed rice cakes. It eats large, infrequent meals that require a full day to digest. Which is why it sometimes saves what it has caught, alive in its nest, for another day's feast.

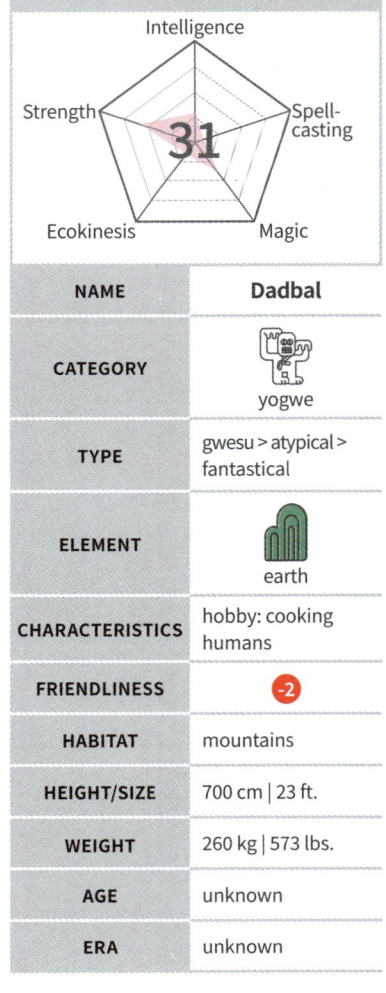

POWER	
NAME	**Dadbal**
CATEGORY	yogwe
TYPE	gwesu > atypical > fantastical
ELEMENT	earth
CHARACTERISTICS	hobby: cooking humans
FRIENDLINESS	-2
HABITAT	mountains
HEIGHT/SIZE	700 cm | 23 ft.
WEIGHT	260 kg | 573 lbs.
AGE	unknown
ERA	unknown

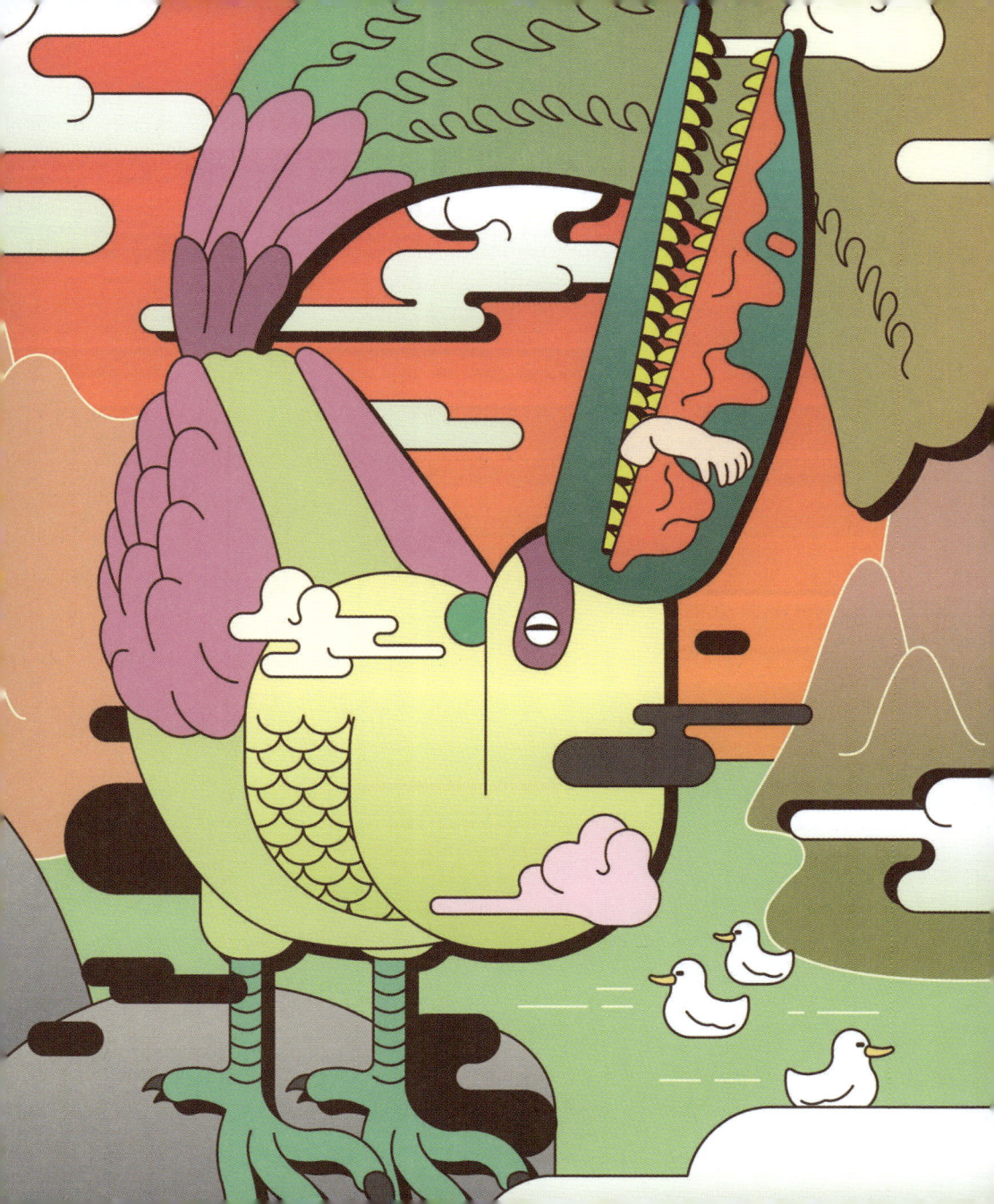

Dongjasam

A wild ginseng that has lived for over a thousand years turns into this yogwe. It is commonly called Dongjasam, or "ginseng boy," because it looks like a plump little boy and behaves like one, too. This spry, gleeful thing is called "GinGin" in MeoShín'Ké. Unfortunately, many people are out to catch it because eating it is said to cure any disease in the world. To protect itself, GinGin hides in the deepest, most secluded nooks of mountains or camouflages itself in ginseng beds. The only clue that might give it away is the magenta flower blooming atop its head or the golden sheen of its body. When not in hiding, GinGin secretly transforms into a human and struts around villages.

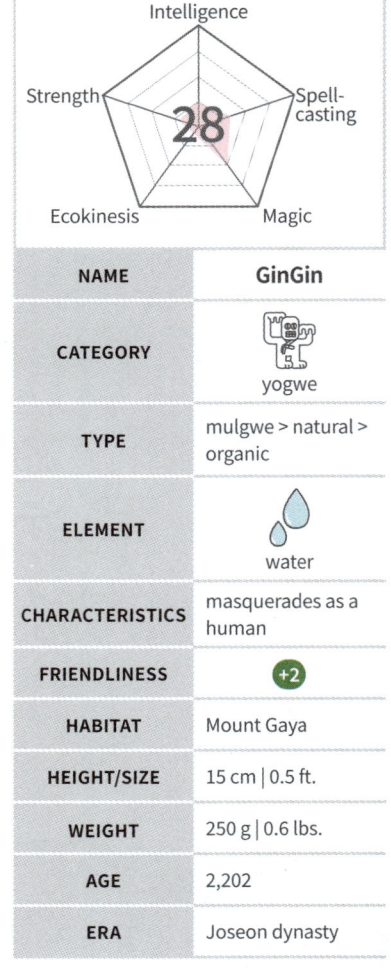

POWER	
Intelligence, Strength, Spell-casting, Ecokinesis, Magic — **28**	
NAME	**GinGin**
CATEGORY	yogwe
TYPE	mulgwe > natural > organic
ELEMENT	water
CHARACTERISTICS	masquerades as a human
FRIENDLINESS	+2
HABITAT	Mount Gaya
HEIGHT/SIZE	15 cm | 0.5 ft.
WEIGHT	250 g | 0.6 lbs.
AGE	2,202
ERA	Joseon dynasty

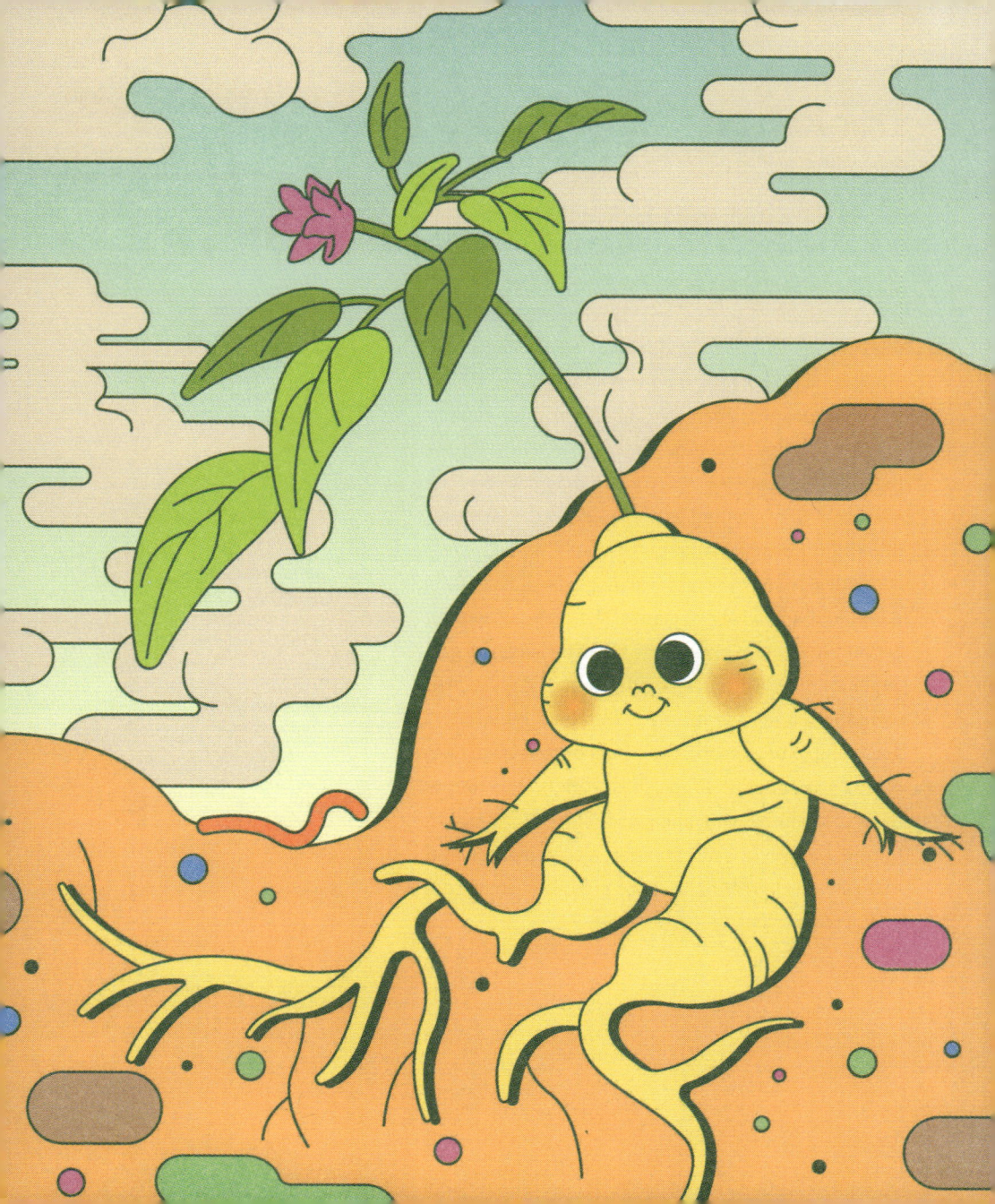

Duokshini

Duokshini is a cruel, fearsome ghost that kills humans by bashing their heads. She was originally a noble family's servant girl named Duok, who died a tragic, wrongful death. The dead girl turned into an evil spirit, then turned up at a banquet hosted by her former masters. Alarmed, they tried to throw her out, but she was so strong that even a group of burly men couldn't make her budge. She took her revenge: She smashed the heads of everyone who tried to drag her away and everyone who shouted at her and cursed everyone there with a deadly plague.

With piercing eyes and wielding a large club, Duok is formidable even at first glance. She shows up without warning in random places. She might be leading a gang of ghosts or delivering a message from the gods, inadvertently scaring the recipient with her creepy looks. According to one record, Duokshini once revealed herself to someone in all her ghastly glory and warned them of the impending Imjin War before vanishing into thin air. Duokshini is an essentially evil ghost, however, that can inflict great harm when provoked, so be careful not to cross her.

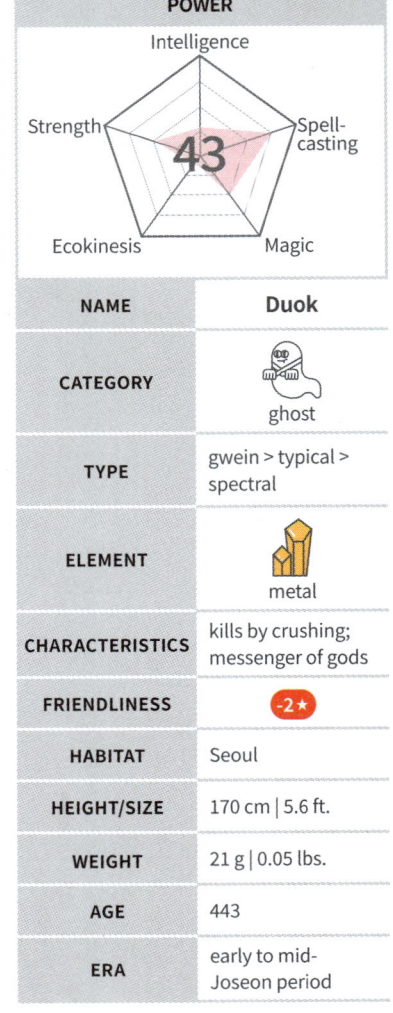

POWER	
	Intelligence
Strength	43 Spell-casting
Ecokinesis	Magic

NAME	Duok
CATEGORY	ghost
TYPE	gwein > typical > spectral
ELEMENT	metal
CHARACTERISTICS	kills by crushing; messenger of gods
FRIENDLINESS	-2★
HABITAT	Seoul
HEIGHT/SIZE	170 cm | 5.6 ft.
WEIGHT	21 g | 0.05 lbs.
AGE	443
ERA	early to mid-Joseon period

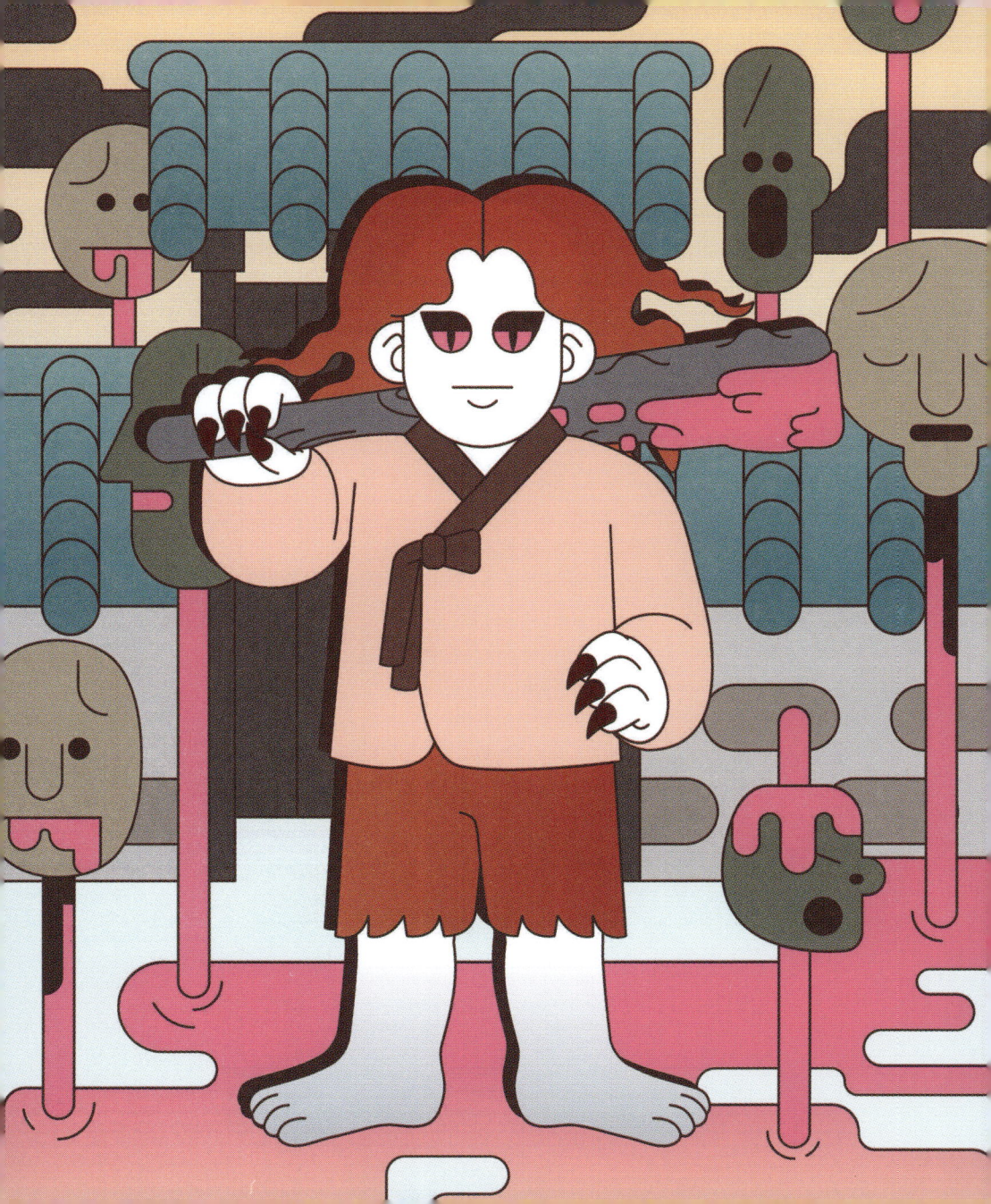

Dwitgan Guishin

Dwitgan Guishin ("outhouse ghost") is the goddess of bathrooms. Although she is a household deity presiding over the toilets of homes, she is not friendly to humans and is sometimes seen as a malevolent god or a common ghost. Taking the form of a scrawny woman with extremely long hair, she gives off a stink you can smell a mile away. Covered in gunk from head to toe, her face is sallow and dirty.

She doesn't always live in the outhouse but only stays on dates that include the number six—that is, the 6th, 16th, and 26th of every month. When at the outhouse, she usually sits on the toilet and counts her long strands of hair to kill time.

A touchy, vindictive goddess, Dwitgan Guishin is quick to lose her temper and delights in harassing or pranking humans. On most days she is content to smear gunk on you, but if you enter her domain too noiselessly, she will retaliate by pushing you right into the pit toilet.* To avoid her pranks and appease her, our ancestors sometimes made offerings of homemade rice cakes that they fittingly dubbed "poop cakes."

POWER

Intelligence
Strength
Spell-casting
Ecokinesis
Magic

34

NAME	**Chukshin**
CATEGORY	shinryung
TYPE	shinryung > acquired
ELEMENT	earth
CHARACTERISTICS	guardian of the bathroom; human hater
FRIENDLINESS	-1
HABITAT	bathroom
HEIGHT/SIZE	159 cm | 5.2 ft.
WEIGHT	42 kg | 93 lbs.
AGE	unknown
ERA	antiquity

---

* In the past, pit toilets in outhouses were quite deep and could be dangerous for young children, who sometimes fell in.

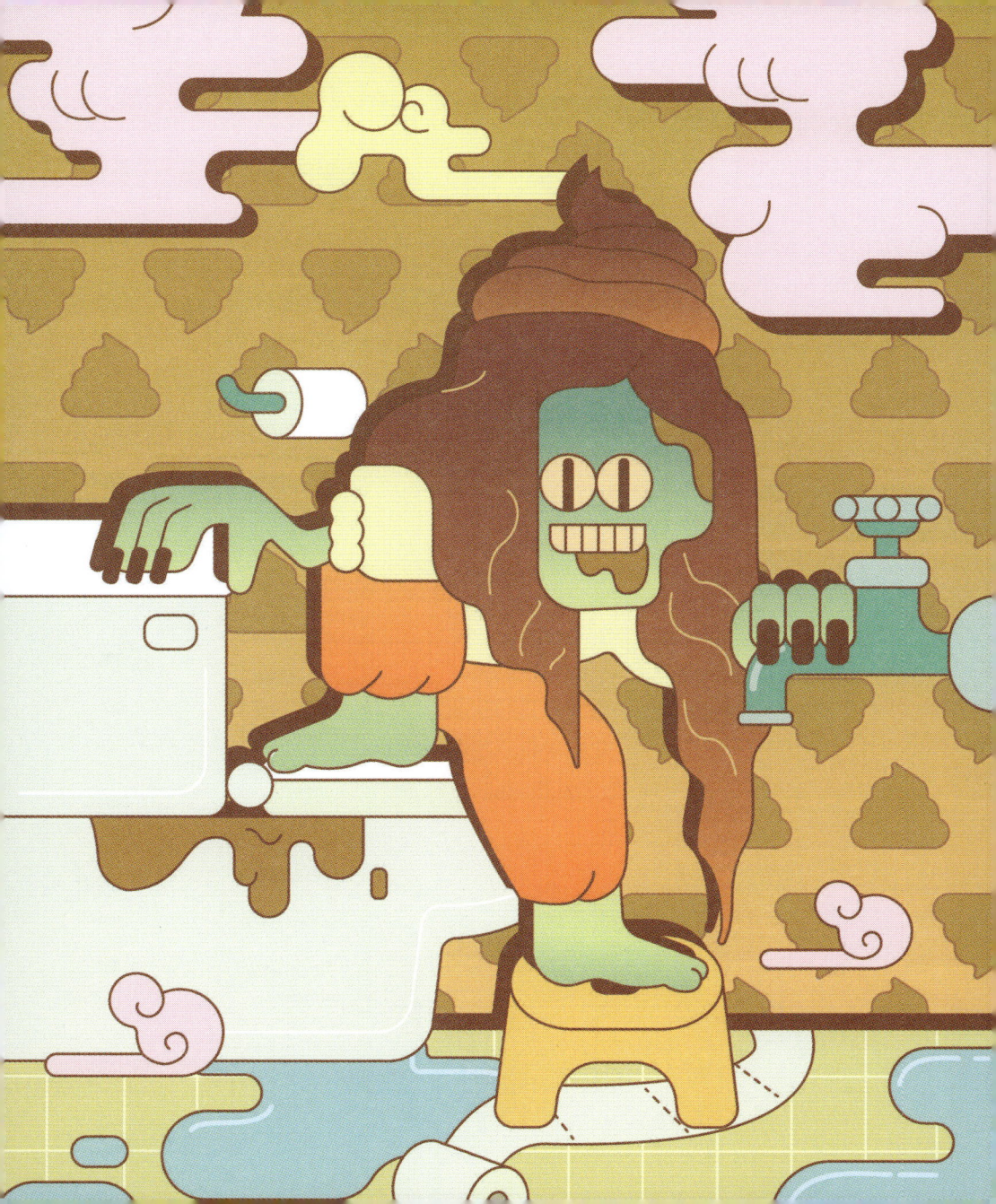

Maehwa Noin

Maehwa Noin ("plum sage") is a spirit born in an ancient plum tree. His hair and beard are abloom with beautiful plum flowers that he is very proud of. He is always dressed neatly and emanates a floral perfume. Wise as he is old, he is the leader of all trees growing in his region.

Maehwa Noin suffers when his birth tree wilts or gets hurt. Though normally mild-mannered and kind, he will give nightmares to anyone who tries to harm his tree and will curse to death any fool who dares to dry it up or cut it down.

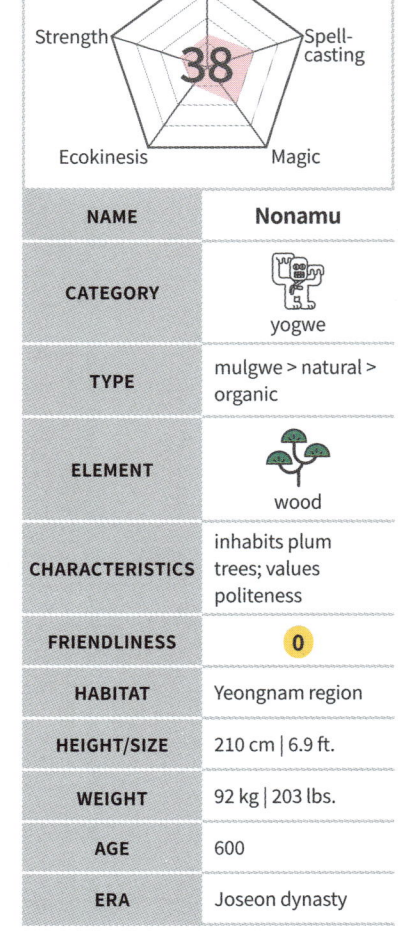

POWER	
Intelligence / Strength / Spell-casting / Ecokinesis / Magic — **38**	
NAME	**Nonamu**
CATEGORY	yogwe
TYPE	mulgwe > natural > organic
ELEMENT	wood
CHARACTERISTICS	inhabits plum trees; values politeness
FRIENDLINESS	0
HABITAT	Yeongnam region
HEIGHT/SIZE	210 cm | 6.9 ft.
WEIGHT	92 kg | 203 lbs.
AGE	600
ERA	Joseon dynasty

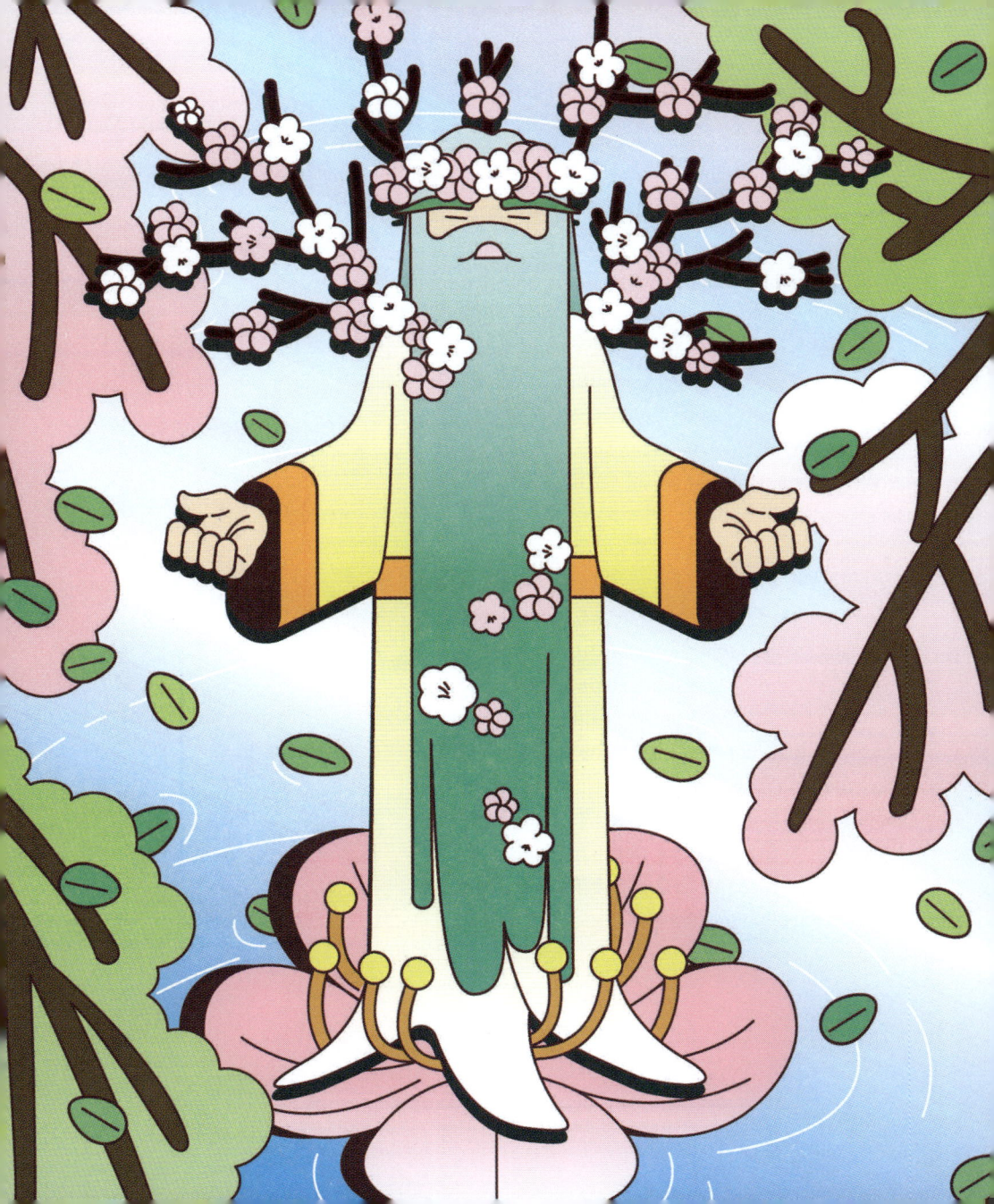

Mongdal

Mongdal is a man who died of a broken heart. Having been hopelessly in love with someone who didn't love him back, he died bitter and unmarried, only to return as a ghost.

Lovesick even after death, Mongdal haunts single women and showers them with affection, sometimes even making misguided attempts to stop them from getting married. When he gets spiteful, he tries to steal a woman away from her actual partner, so he needs to be chased away quickly.

SPIRIT WEDDING

A spirit wedding marries two souls together. Shamans or the deceased's family throws a wedding for men and women who died single and unhappy. Spirit weddings aren't too different from regular weddings. The shaman checks for the compatibility of a ghost couple, and if it is a good match, the wedding is held on an auspicious date. Dolls dressed as a bride and groom stand in for the couple. At the ceremony, the dolls are made to bow to each other, then placed in a room for the newlyweds to spend the night together.

POWER

Radar chart with axes: Intelligence, Spell-casting, Magic, Ecokinesis, Strength. Value: 22

NAME	Mongdal
CATEGORY	ghost
TYPE	gwein > typical > spectral
ELEMENT	fire
CHARACTERISTICS	besotted bachelor ghost
FRIENDLINESS	-1
HABITAT	residential areas
HEIGHT/SIZE	175 cm | 5.7 ft.
WEIGHT	21 g | 0.05 lbs.
AGE	30
ERA	Joseon dynasty

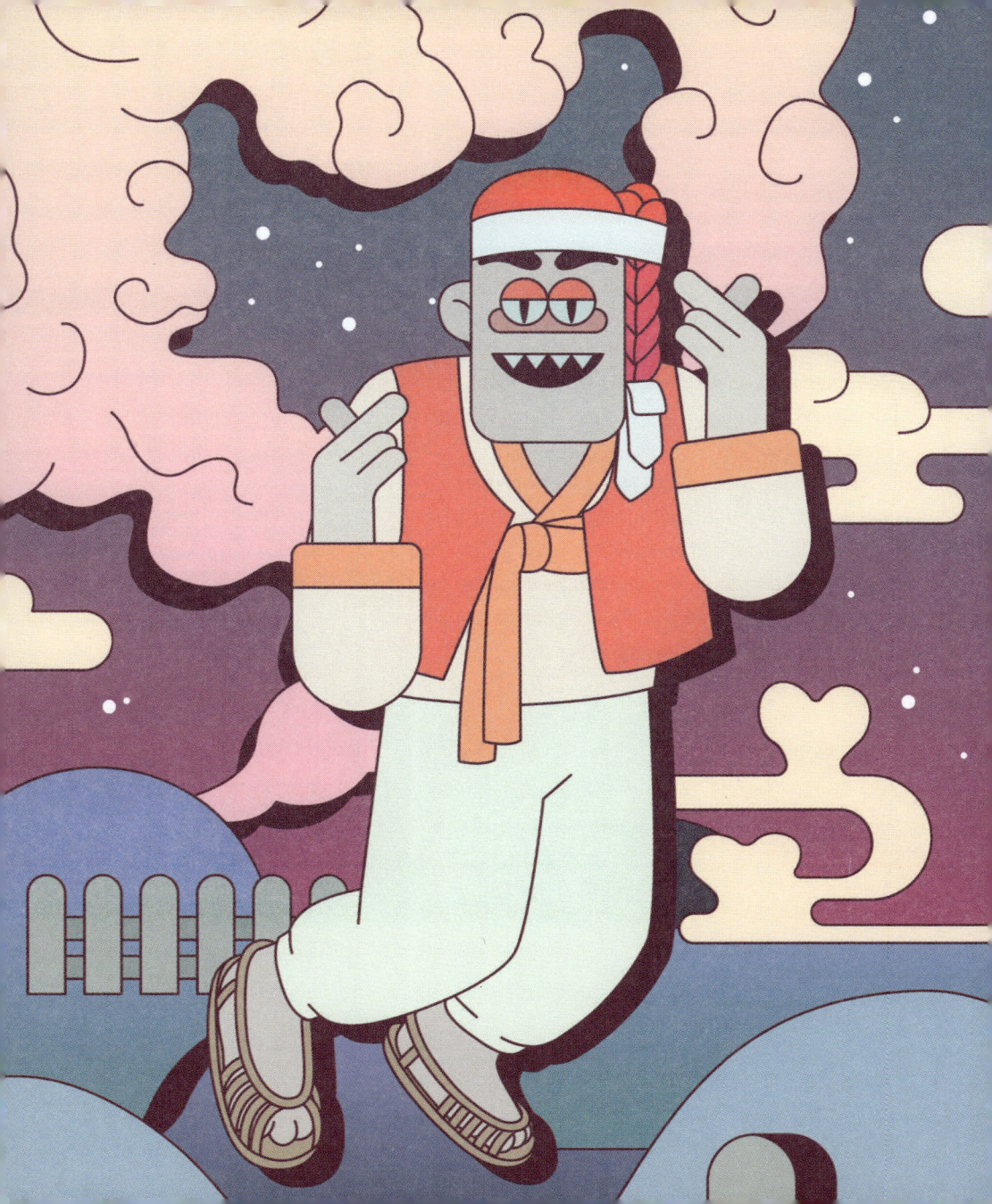

Meowdusa

Meowdusa is a yogwe with the head of a cat and the body of a snake. Its numerous vertebrae allow it to move freely and swiftly, while it can also walk or run on four extremely cute paws. Meowdusa spends most of its time on a mountain close to a village, in a snake den guarded by animals it bosses around. It is a simple, affable creature that loves to eat and will never attack unless it's provoked.

When in a good mood, Meowdusa breathes blue vapor from its mouth. Because this vapor heals sickness and cleanses bad energy, Meowdusa gets a good deal of human and animal visitors. Being particularly fond of human food, Meowdusa will gift its blue vapor to humans who feed it: Everybody wins!

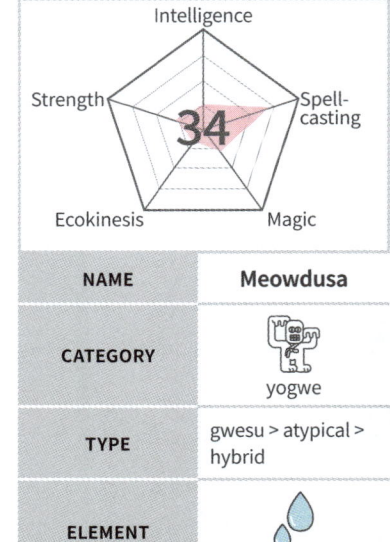

POWER

34

NAME	Meowdusa
CATEGORY	yogwe
TYPE	gwesu > atypical > hybrid
ELEMENT	water
CHARACTERISTICS	releases medicinal blue vapor
FRIENDLINESS	+2
HABITAT	Jangdun-gun, Jinseo-myeon
HEIGHT/SIZE	170 cm | 5.6 ft.
WEIGHT	80 kg | 176 lbs.
AGE	513
ERA	Goryeo dynasty

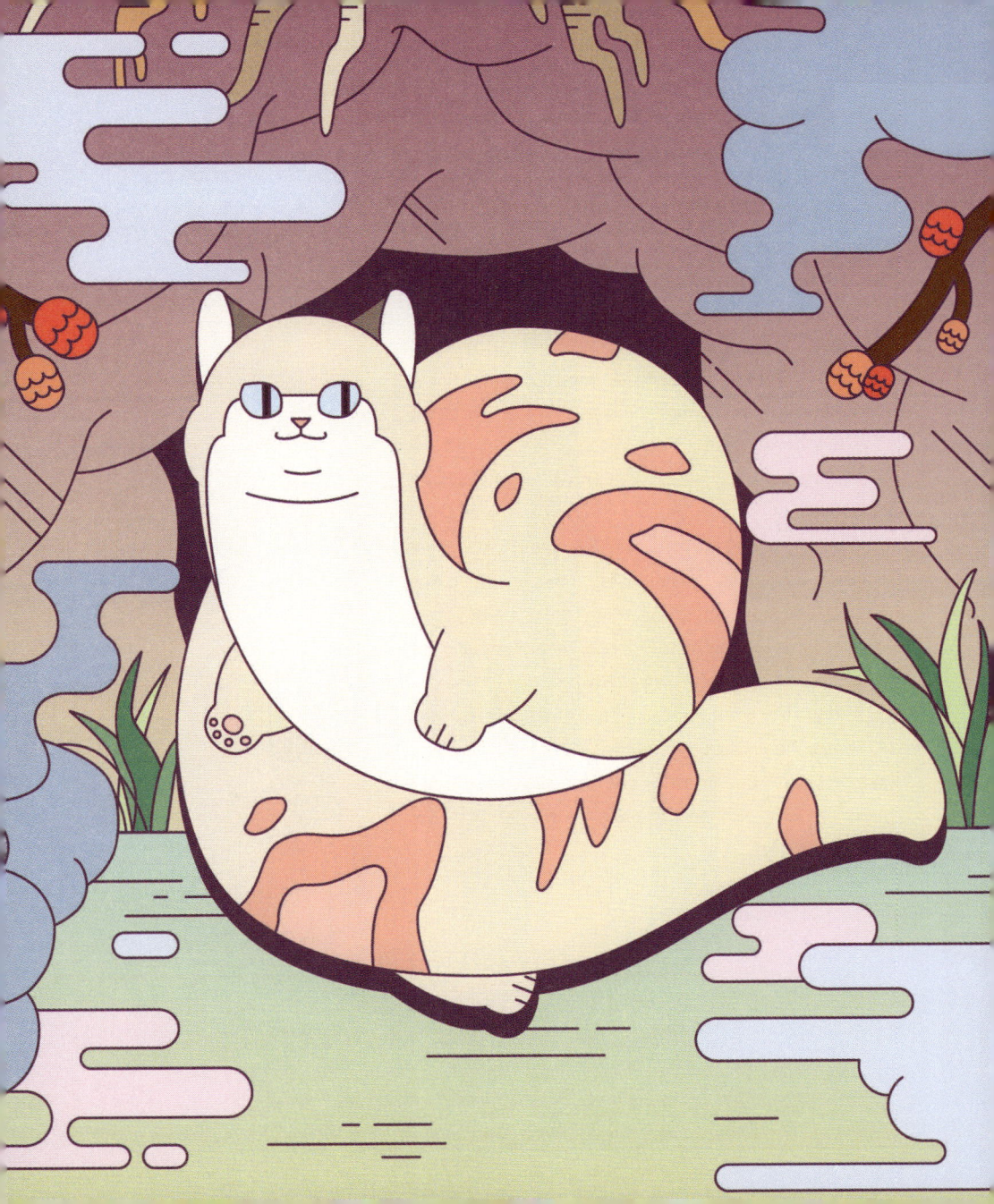

Mulguishin

Mulguishin ("water ghost") are ghosts of people who drowned. These ghosts can never leave the body of water in which they drowned; if anything, they attempt to lure more people into it and have them suffer the same fate. These ghosts prowl about mostly at night, while by day they wander the watery depths. Sooyoung, one of many Mulguishin out there, is the ghost of a drowned woman. Since she spends a lot of time underwater, she has bluish skin and gives off a strong fishy smell.

Swimmers and people near the water's edge are common targets for a Mulguishin, who usually grabs them by the ankle and drags them under. Once you're caught, escaping can be tricky. Your feet might also get tangled up in the ghost's seaweedy hair.

Mulguishin are not fans of gold and silver, so they make excellent repellents when you have to cross a lake or ocean. But to be on the safe side, best avoid rivers, ravines, and deeper parts of the sea that just scream *sinister*.

POWER

Intelligence / Strength / Spell-casting / Ecokinesis / Magic

26

NAME	**Sooyoung**
CATEGORY	ghost
TYPE	gwein > typical > spectral
ELEMENT	water
CHARACTERISTICS	pulls people into water
FRIENDLINESS	-2
HABITAT	waterside*
HEIGHT/SIZE	165 cm | 5.4 ft.
WEIGHT	21 g | 0.05 lbs.
AGE	24
ERA	Joseon dynasty

---

*   includes shores of seas, rivers, and ponds

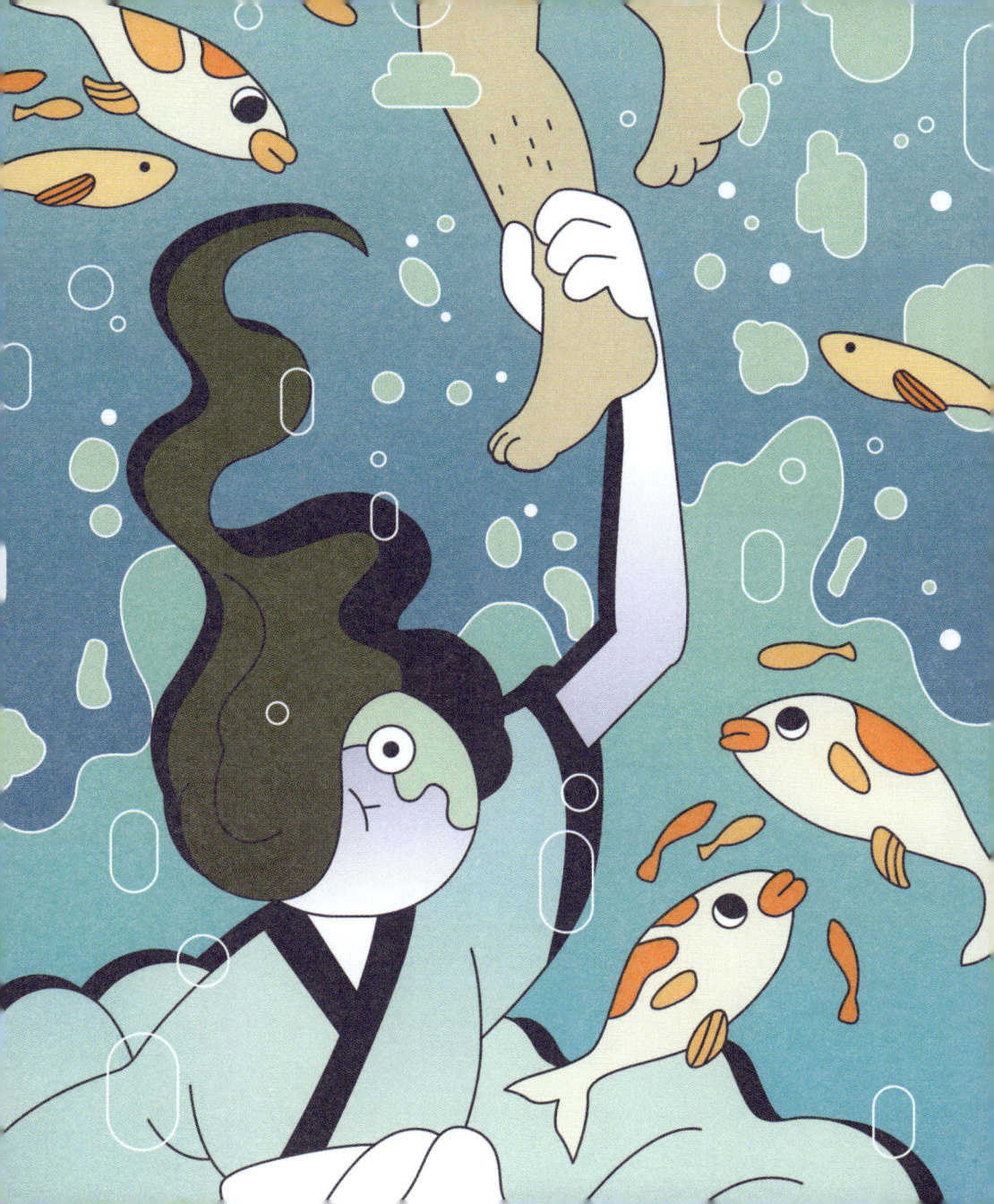

Bangsangshi

Bangsangshi is a guardian god that has warded off evil spirits at funerals and narye* rituals from as early as the Goryeo period. It famously has four golden eyes and always wears red masks. In its right hand it holds a sharp spear to battle unwelcome ghosts, and in its left a golden square shield embossed with a lion. Bangsangshi leads the funeral procession, brandishing its weapons in a fierce dance until it arrives at the burial plot. There, it drives a spear into all four corners to block any ghosts from entering.

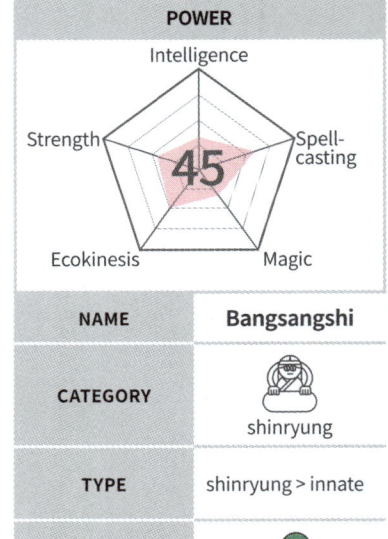

POWER

NAME	**Bangsangshi**
CATEGORY	shinryung
TYPE	shinryung > innate
ELEMENT	earth
CHARACTERISTICS	ghost-proofs funerals
FRIENDLINESS	+1
HABITAT	funeral homes
HEIGHT/SIZE	150 cm | 4.9 ft.
WEIGHT	45 kg | 99 lbs.
AGE	1,500
ERA	Goryeo dynasty

* **narye:** a ritual once held in homes and the royal palace to banish evil spirits and ghosts on Lunar New Year's Eve

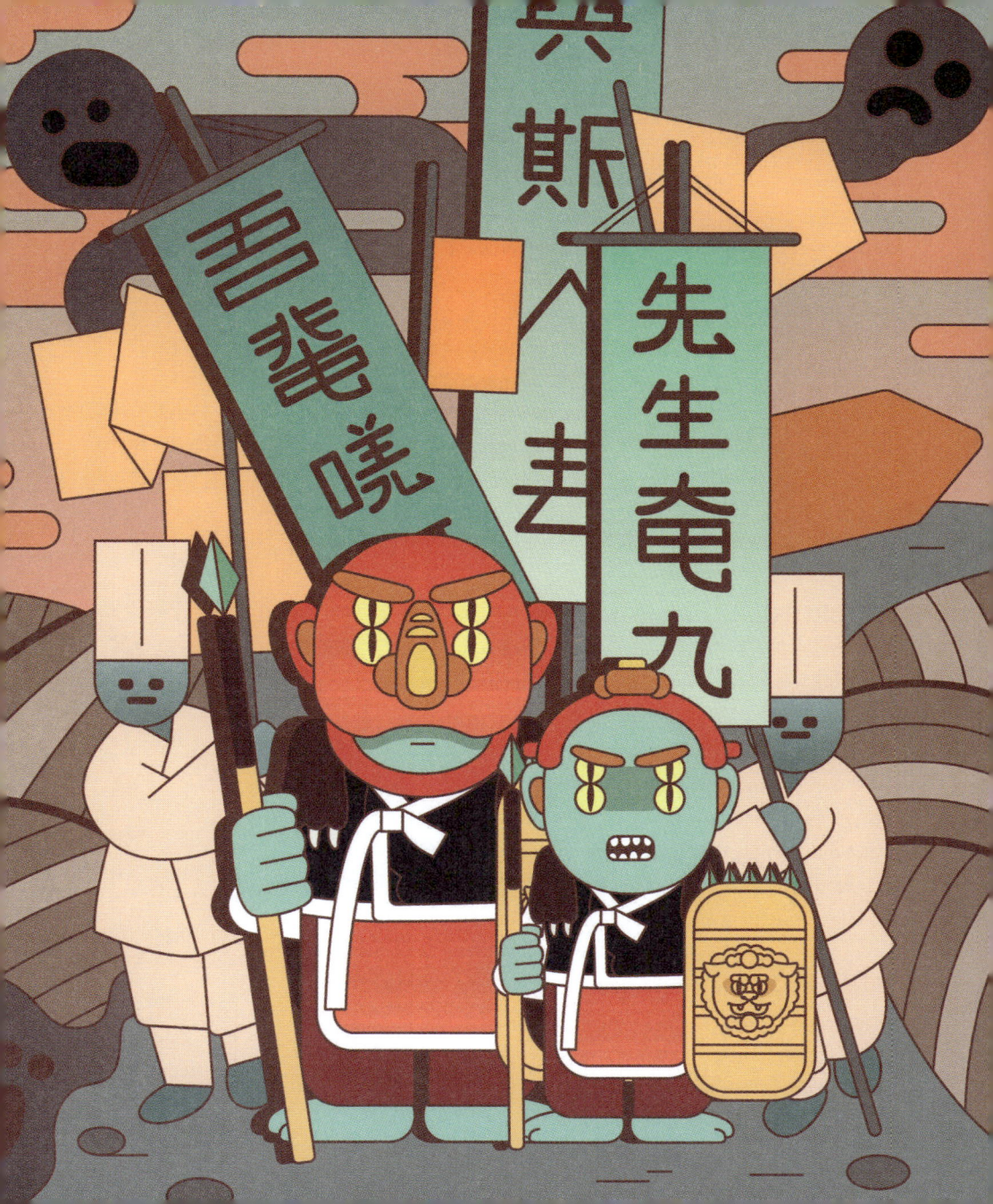

Bum

범

Bum is a yogwe that looks like a tiger. When it is weak with hunger from roaming the mountains or wants to ensnare a human, it transforms into a tiny kitten. The adorable puss makes unsuspecting humans come cooing, then devours them in a flash. That's when it reveals its true, terrible form: glinting eyes, mouth expanding monstrously like an alien's, stacks of sharp teeth. Towering over its victim, it wobbles and melts into myriad forms. Bum can imitate the voice and appearance of whomever it eats, which it uses to trick and eat even more humans.

THE BROTHER AND SISTER WHO BECAME THE SUN AND MOON

In the old folktale of the siblings that became the sun and moon, was the villainous tiger really a tiger? It could talk and act like a human. It could even sound like the siblings' mother after gobbling her up, trying to fool the poor children with her voice. And don't forget that it didn't know how to climb up a tree! Any normal tiger would've known how. Could it be that the tiger in the tale was actually Bum pretending to be one?

JANGSANBUM

A tiger yogwe known to live on Mount Jang. Covered in white, velvety long fur, it imitates human voices to trick and hunt prey.

POWER

Intelligence · Strength · Spellcasting · Magic · Ecokinesis

34

NAME	Bum
CATEGORY	yogwe
TYPE	gwesu > atypical > fantastical
ELEMENT	moon
CHARACTERISTICS	rice cake fiend
FRIENDLINESS	-2
HABITAT	mountain paths
HEIGHT/SIZE	38–400 cm | 1–13 ft.
WEIGHT	5–1,000 kg | 11–2,205 lbs.
AGE	unknown
ERA	antiquity

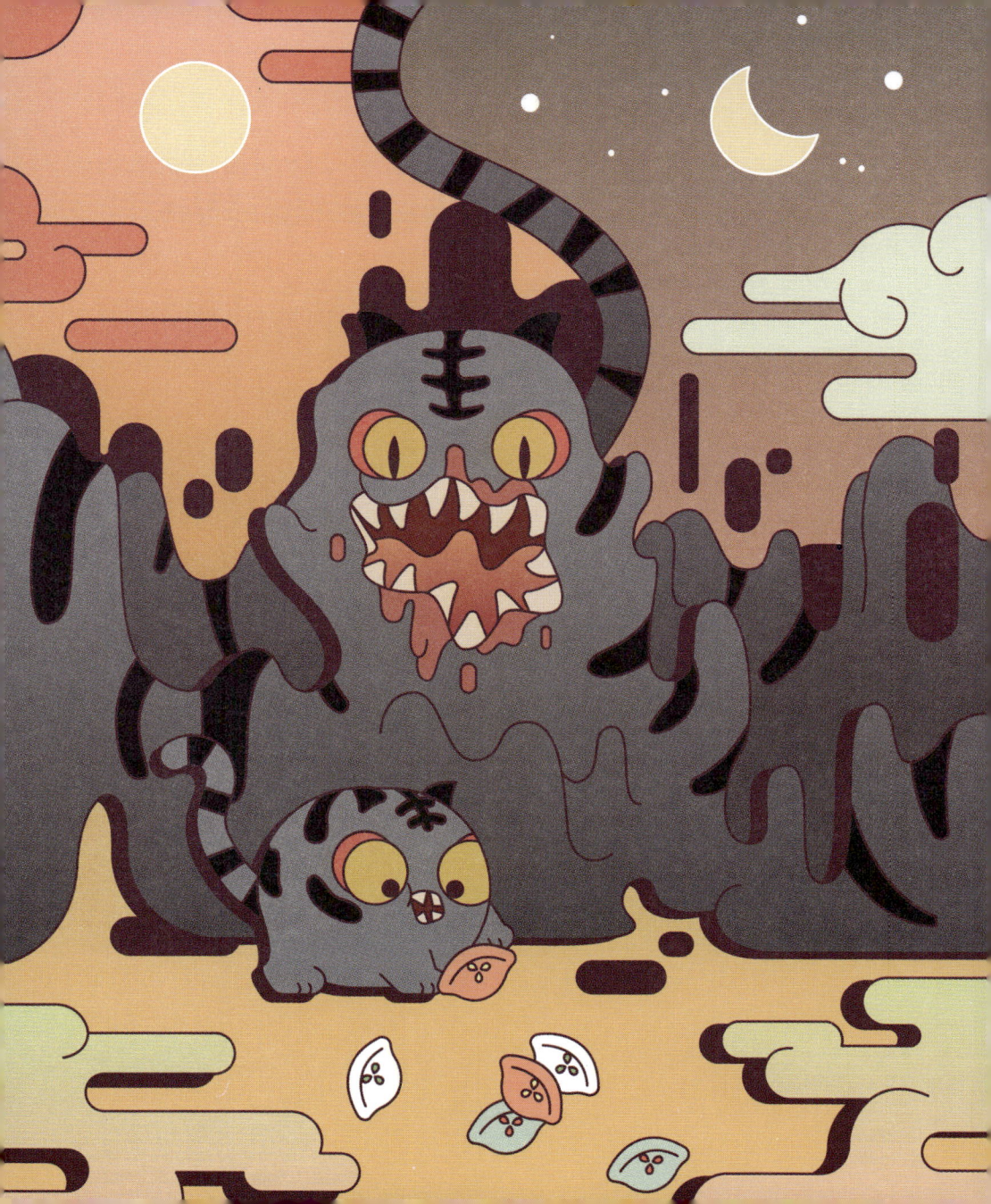

Bulgasari

Bulgasari—or Bulgasa-li according to some records—means "unkillable." This yogwe looks like a peculiar elephant with a shiny coat of blue fur. When it munches on steel and other metals, it expands. Then its hide toughens into a steely armor unpierceable by the sharpest spear or sword, effectively making it indestructible. Perhaps due to its diet, Bulgasari produces hard little turds that can cut through raw jade. Yet even the strongest creatures have a weakness: For Bulgasari, it's fire. Some people believe the name Bulgasari actually means "killable by fire." Bulgasari has the ability to chase away nightmares. It helps people it is indebted to and good, honest folks to dream away in peace.

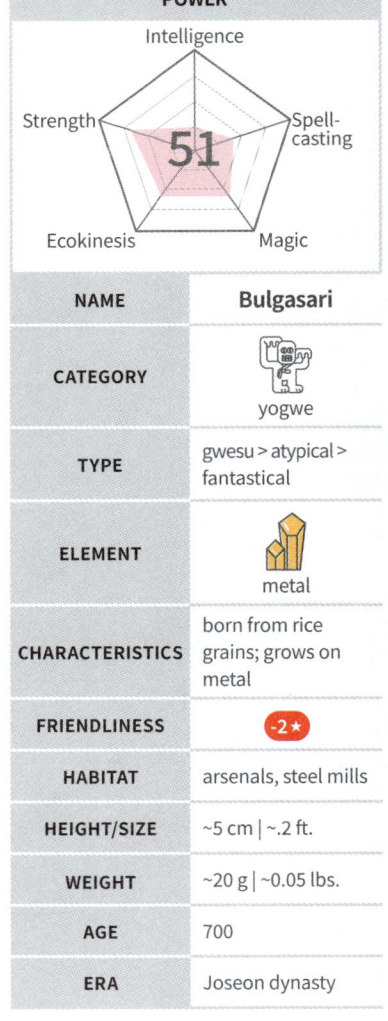

POWER	
NAME	**Bulgasari**
CATEGORY	yogwe
TYPE	gwesu > atypical > fantastical
ELEMENT	metal
CHARACTERISTICS	born from rice grains; grows on metal
FRIENDLINESS	-2 ★
HABITAT	arsenals, steel mills
HEIGHT/SIZE	~5 cm	~.2 ft.
WEIGHT	~20 g	~0.05 lbs.
AGE	700
ERA	Joseon dynasty

POWER radar chart: Intelligence, Spell-casting, Magic, Ecokinesis, Strength — 51

38

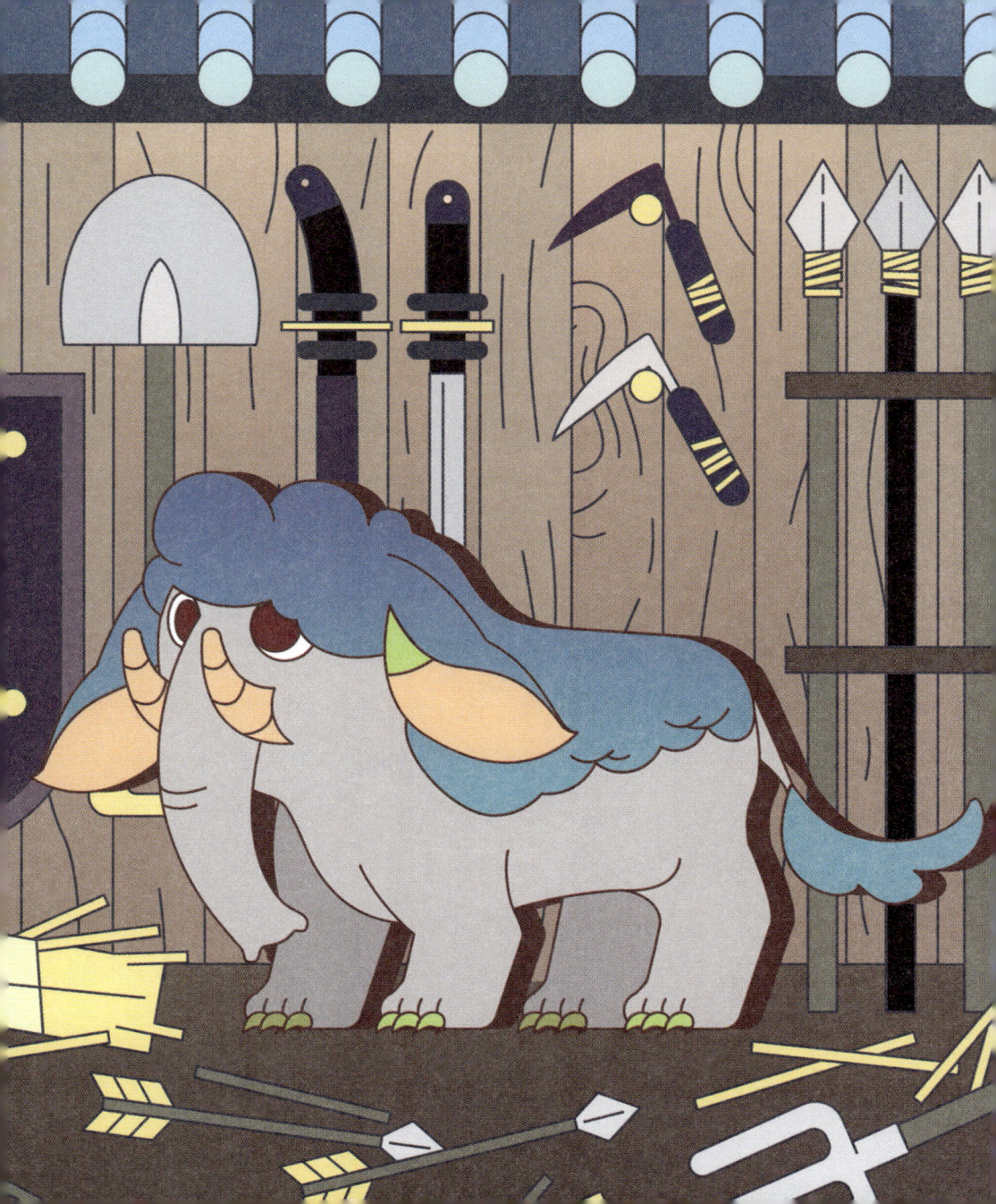

Sammoku

Sammoku shields people from disaster, evil spirits, and miscellaneous ghosts. It assumes the form of a three-eyed dog, but its real identity is the guard of Hell's gate: King Sammok the Great. The valiant king was reduced to a common pooch as part of its exile to the human world.

Sammoku can return to the afterworld only after living among people for three years, receiving and giving kindness. That's why Sammoku is an extremely loyal dog that barks away major misfortunes for the family it serves. Back in the Goryeo period, a man in Hapcheon County by the name of Lee Geo-in took Sammoku under his wing for three years. Years later when the man died and reached the afterworld, he was greeted by none other than King Sammok the Great. The king repaid the man's kindness by granting him his wish to complete the Tripiṭaka Koreana,* or so the legend goes.

---

* **Tripiṭaka Koreana:** A collection of Buddhist texts carved on 81,258 woodblocks. The project began on the twenty-third year of King Gojong of Goryeo (1236) and was completed on the thirty-eighth (1251) to call on the Buddha's strength to fight off foreign invaders. The full collection is now housed in the temple of Haeinsa in Hapcheon County.

POWER	
	Intelligence
Strength	Spell-casting
	55
Ecokinesis	Magic

NAME	**Sammoku**
CATEGORY	shinryung
TYPE	shinryung > innate
ELEMENT	moon
CHARACTERISTICS	guardian king of Hell's gate
FRIENDLINESS	+2
HABITAT	gate to afterworld
HEIGHT/SIZE	120 cm | 4 ft. (2 m or 6.6 ft. in human form)
WEIGHT	20 kg | 44 lbs. (98 kg or 216 lbs. in human form)
AGE	1,178
ERA	King Munseong's reign in Silla dynasty

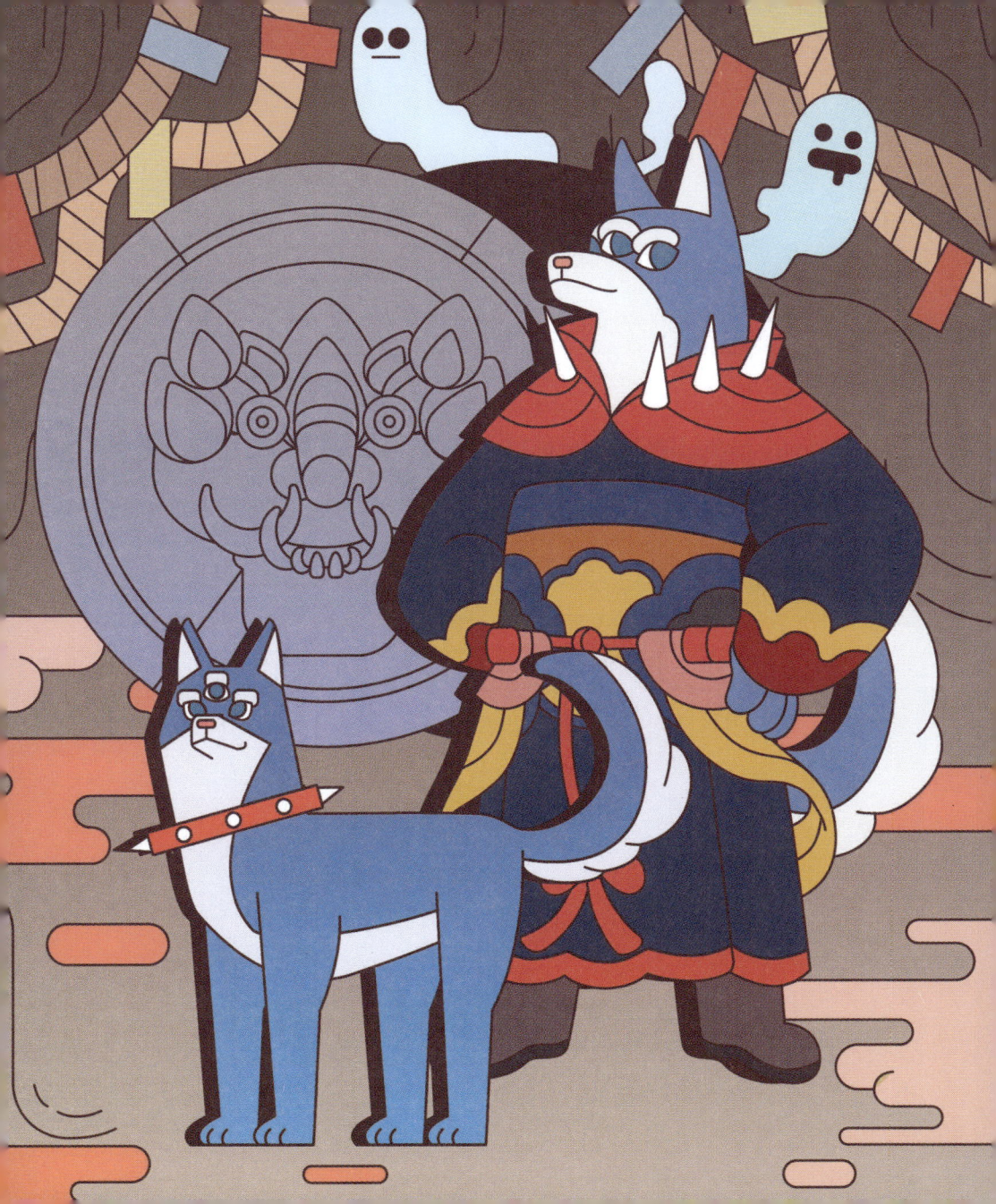

Samchoong

Samchoong are parasitic monster bugs that live in human bodies. They are a trio: The upper bug nests in a person's head, the middle bug in their stomach, and the lower bug in their feet. They are called Pango, Pangjil, and Panggyo, respectively. Like centipedes, they have long bodies with frightfully many legs. These tiny pests sneak into a human body and cause sickness, insomnia, and greed, slowly sucking life out of their host. Every sixty days, they fly up to the heavens to tattle on their host's wrongdoings to the Jade Emperor, who further reduces the human's lifespan as punishment. If Samchoong infiltrate your body, that point of entry will itch unbearably. Luckily, there is a simple way to get rid of them: Expose your itchy skin to the smoke of a burning mimosa tree branch, or easier yet, eat pomegranates.

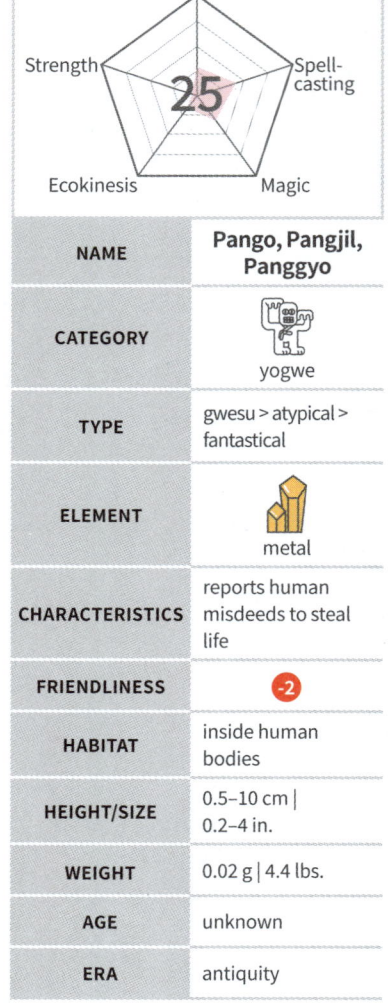

POWER	
	25

NAME	Pango, Pangjil, Panggyo
CATEGORY	yogwe
TYPE	gwesu > atypical > fantastical
ELEMENT	metal
CHARACTERISTICS	reports human misdeeds to steal life
FRIENDLINESS	-2
HABITAT	inside human bodies
HEIGHT/SIZE	0.5–10 cm | 0.2–4 in.
WEIGHT	0.02 g | 4.4 lbs.
AGE	unknown
ERA	antiquity

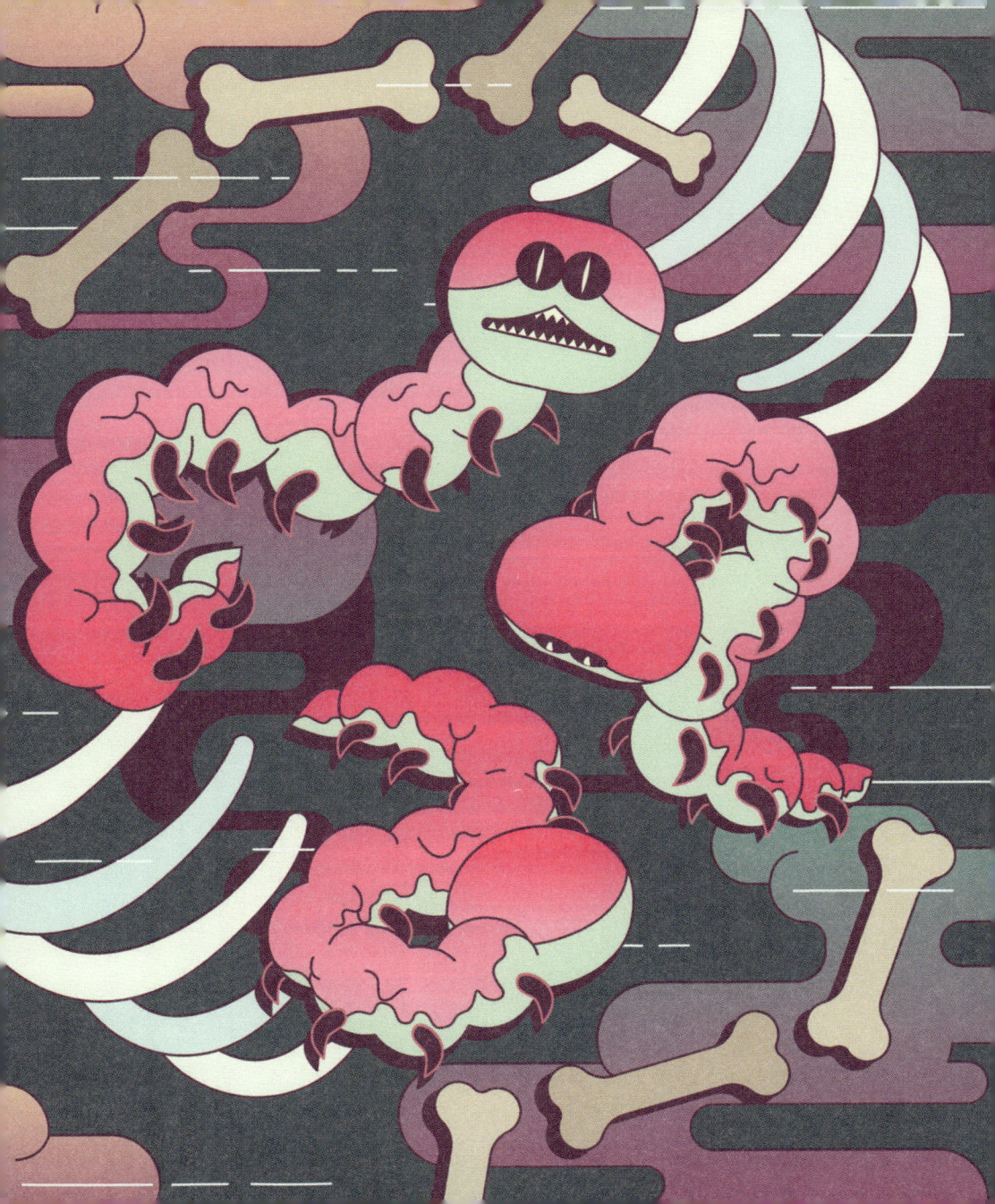

Sokgul Sonseng

석굴선생

Sokgul Sonseng ("cave master") is a mysterious gwein living in a lonely mountain cave. We don't know when or why it took up residence there, but long years of meditation have made it a wise, patient master. Always dressed in clean training robes, Sokgul Sonseng is the picture of strength and endurance.

Thick, red fur covers the gwein from head to toe. It may have started growing facial fur from staying out of the sun for too long. Ages ago, it was shunned by people for its unusual appearance. But that has never stopped it from embracing people who come to it for help, exhausted from life. The master listens to their worries and teaches them the ways of the universe. Sokgul Sonseng uses a boat in the cave to travel or escort visitors. The boat doesn't need steering: It finds its own way to visitors and transports them back to the master. The exact whereabouts of Sokgul Sonseng are unknown, but there have been sightings on Mount Jiri.

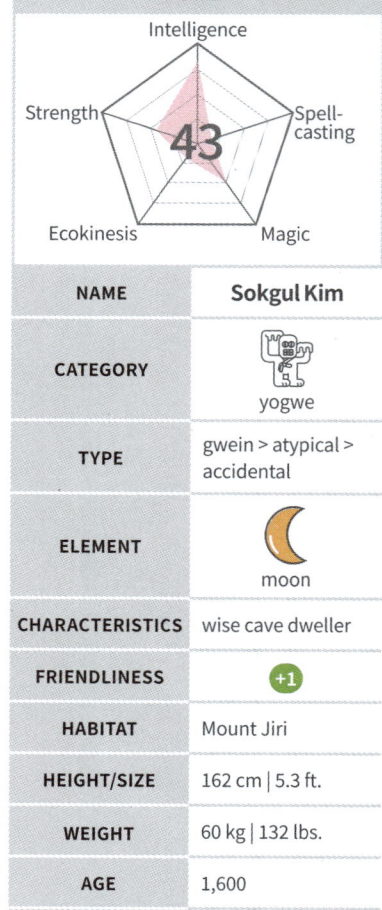

POWER

Intelligence
Strength
Spell-casting
Ecokinesis
Magic

43

NAME	**Sokgul Kim**
CATEGORY	yogwe
TYPE	gwein > atypical > accidental
ELEMENT	moon
CHARACTERISTICS	wise cave dweller
FRIENDLINESS	+1
HABITAT	Mount Jiri
HEIGHT/SIZE	162 cm	5.3 ft.
WEIGHT	60 kg	132 lbs.
AGE	1,600
ERA	Joseon dynasty

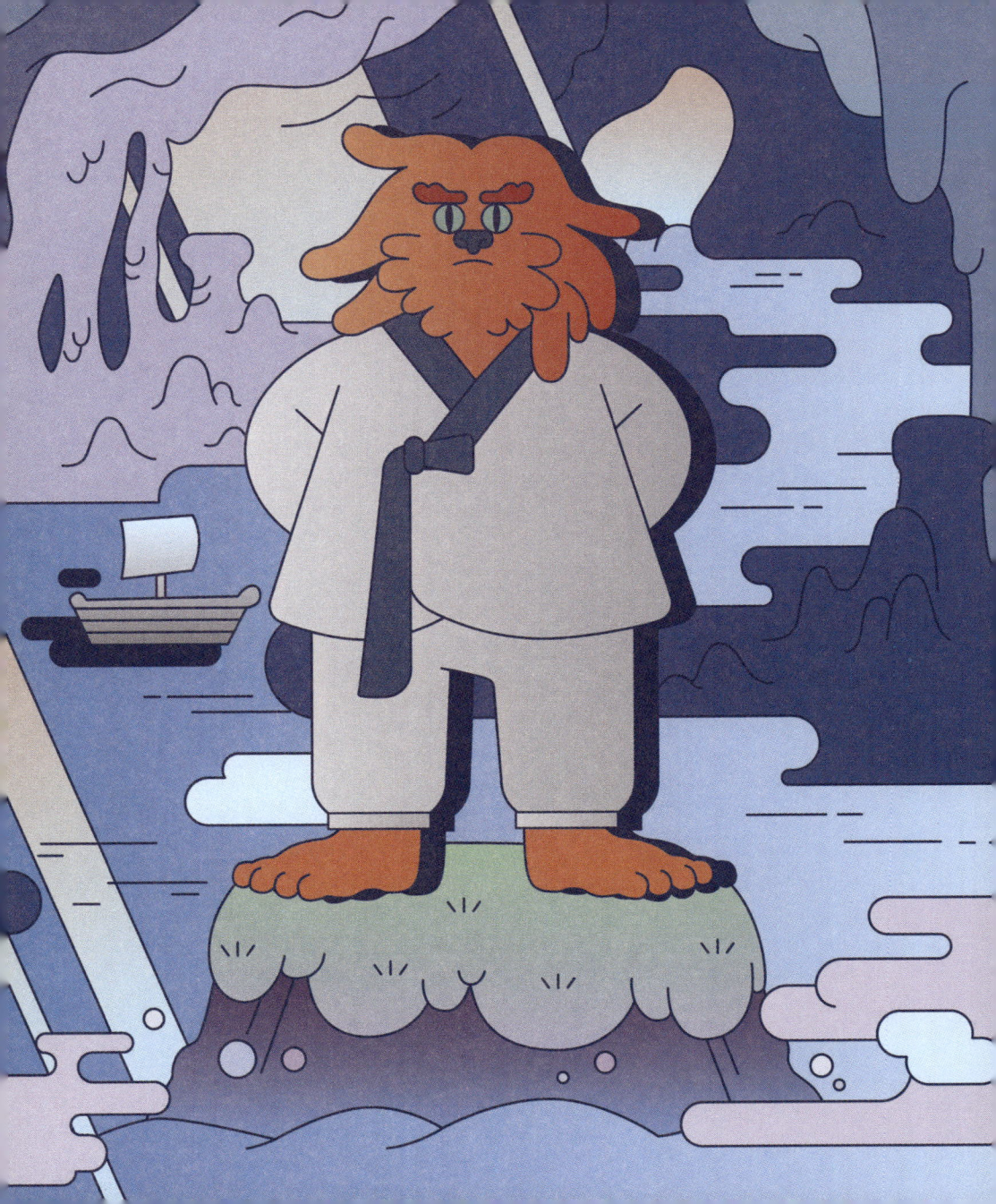

Sungjushin

Sungjushin is the protector of houses and the strongest of the household deities. Dressed in a lavish red, the god has a kindly face with an impressive white beard. He is said to have slid down bamboo—straight down from the sky—and taught early humans to chop trees and build houses. He exists everywhere around the house as its guardian, stopping the most rabid, cunning of ghosts from setting even a toe inside.

The god channels his power from the grains stored in a designated clay pot called the Sungju Pot. The grains are replaced every October with freshly harvested ones. If you neglect the Sungju Pot or if something foul happens in your home, the god will promptly rob the house of all its energy and leave. A household abandoned by Sungjushin will go to ruin, so the Sungju Pot must be tended to with care.

HOW TO TELL YOUR FAMILY FORTUNE WITH A SUNGJU POT

If the rice looks stale or has a messy pattern, it is an ill omen for the household. If the rice looks good, everything will be peaceful.

WHAT TO DO WITH A SUNGJU POT WHEN YOU MOVE

Take out and eat the rice or barley, then bury the pot in a nearby mountain before you leave.

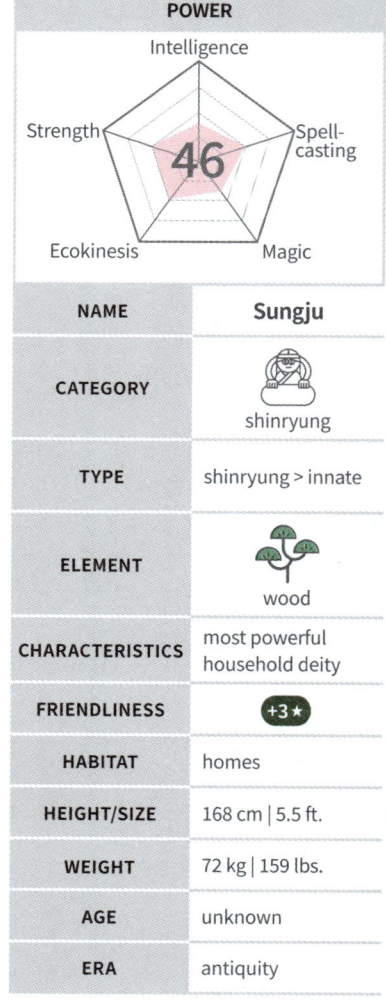

POWER	
	Intelligence, Spell-casting, Magic, Ecokinesis, Strength — 46

NAME	Sungju
CATEGORY	shinryung
TYPE	shinryung > innate
ELEMENT	wood
CHARACTERISTICS	most powerful household deity
FRIENDLINESS	+3★
HABITAT	homes
HEIGHT/SIZE	168 cm | 5.5 ft.
WEIGHT	72 kg | 159 lbs.
AGE	unknown
ERA	antiquity

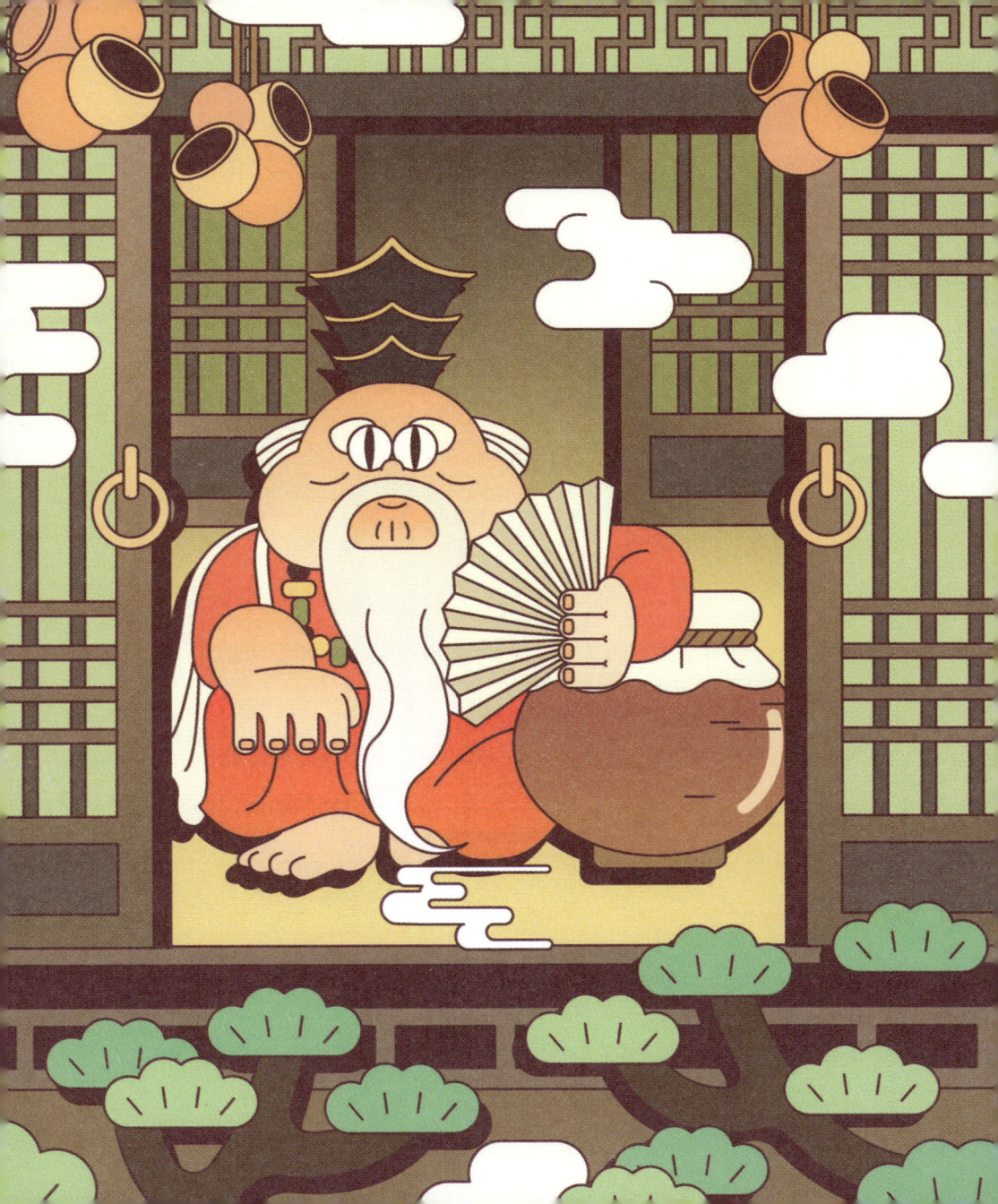

Songaksi

A-lang Son is a famed maiden ghost commonly known as Songaksi. After dying unhappily single, she turned into a vengeful spirit that wanders the earth in her signature white dress and long, wild hair.

She usually appears before the person she loved (or hated) when she was alive. Sometimes she haunts eligible bachelors and demands them to marry her or schemes to ruin the romantic prospects of other women around her age. She can even invade your dreams, in which she will harass you or beg you to listen to her grievances. The scary part is that once she sets her sights on you, she will visit you and only you until her heart finds peace. The only way to make her leave is to help avenge her. According to *Joseon Musokgo* (*A Study of Joseon Shamanism*), "Of all the vengeful spirits in Korea, the Songaksi is the most terrible." Her resentment runs deep. When she is near you, you will feel a powerful dark aura radiating from her and a chill that makes your breath mist. Don't get tangled up with this dangerous ghost.

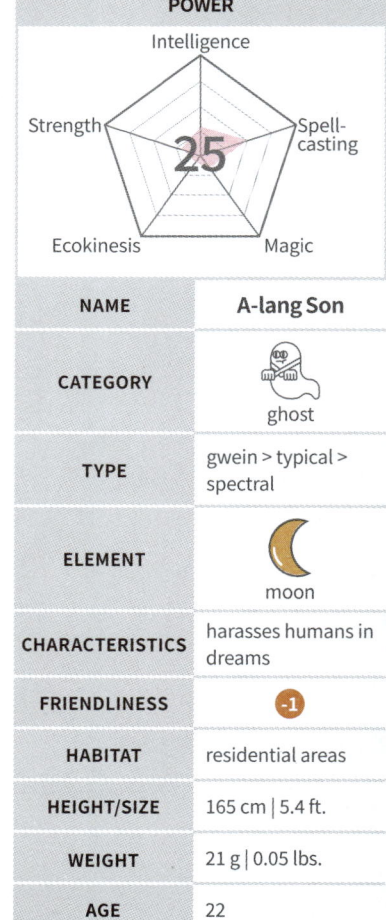

NAME	**A-lang Son**
CATEGORY	ghost
TYPE	gwein > typical > spectral
ELEMENT	moon
CHARACTERISTICS	harasses humans in dreams
FRIENDLINESS	-1
HABITAT	residential areas
HEIGHT/SIZE	165 cm | 5.4 ft.
WEIGHT	21 g | 0.05 lbs.
AGE	22
ERA	Joseon dynasty

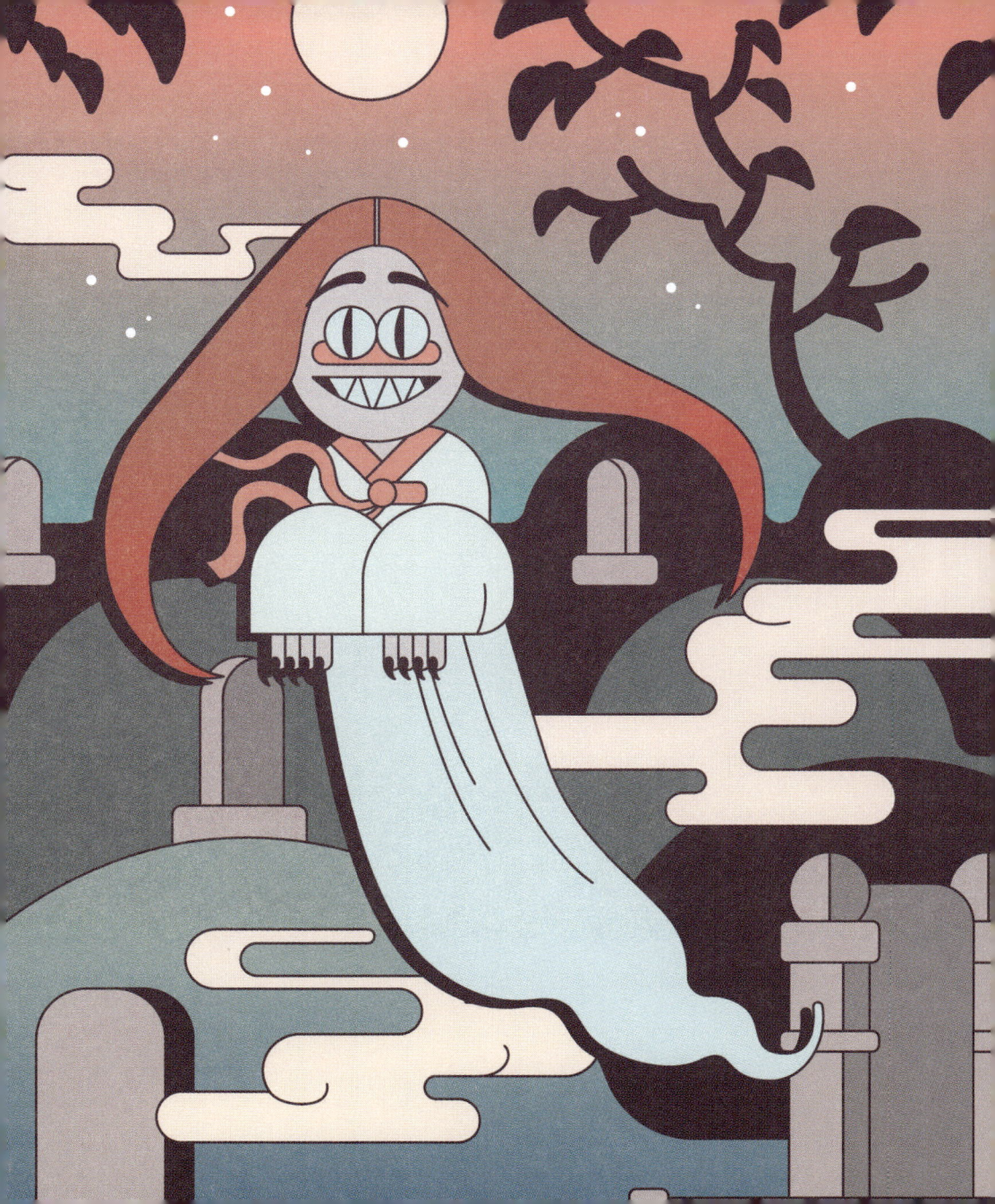

Suryong

Suryong is a dragon that rules over every body of water on the earth. Its gift for water manipulation surpasses that of all other dragon species.

This sacred creature is sheathed in sky-blue scales, which makes it a powerful swimmer free from friction. The jade-hued fins on its back and tail help it slither through the water with easy agility. With talons sharp as a falcon's, Suryong drives malicious intruders away from its domain.

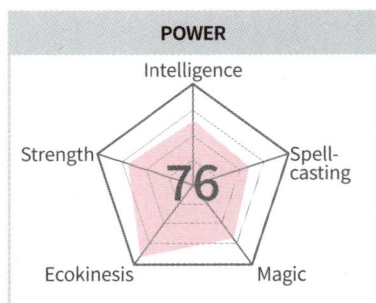

POWER

76

Intelligence · Strength · Spell-casting · Ecokinesis · Magic

NAME	Suryong
CATEGORY	shinsu
TYPE	shinsu > innate
ELEMENT	water
CHARACTERISTICS	controls all water on the earth
FRIENDLINESS	+3★
HABITAT	sea
HEIGHT/SIZE	6,000 cm | 197 ft. (can change size)
WEIGHT	1.2 t | 1.3 tn.
AGE	unknown
ERA	antiquity

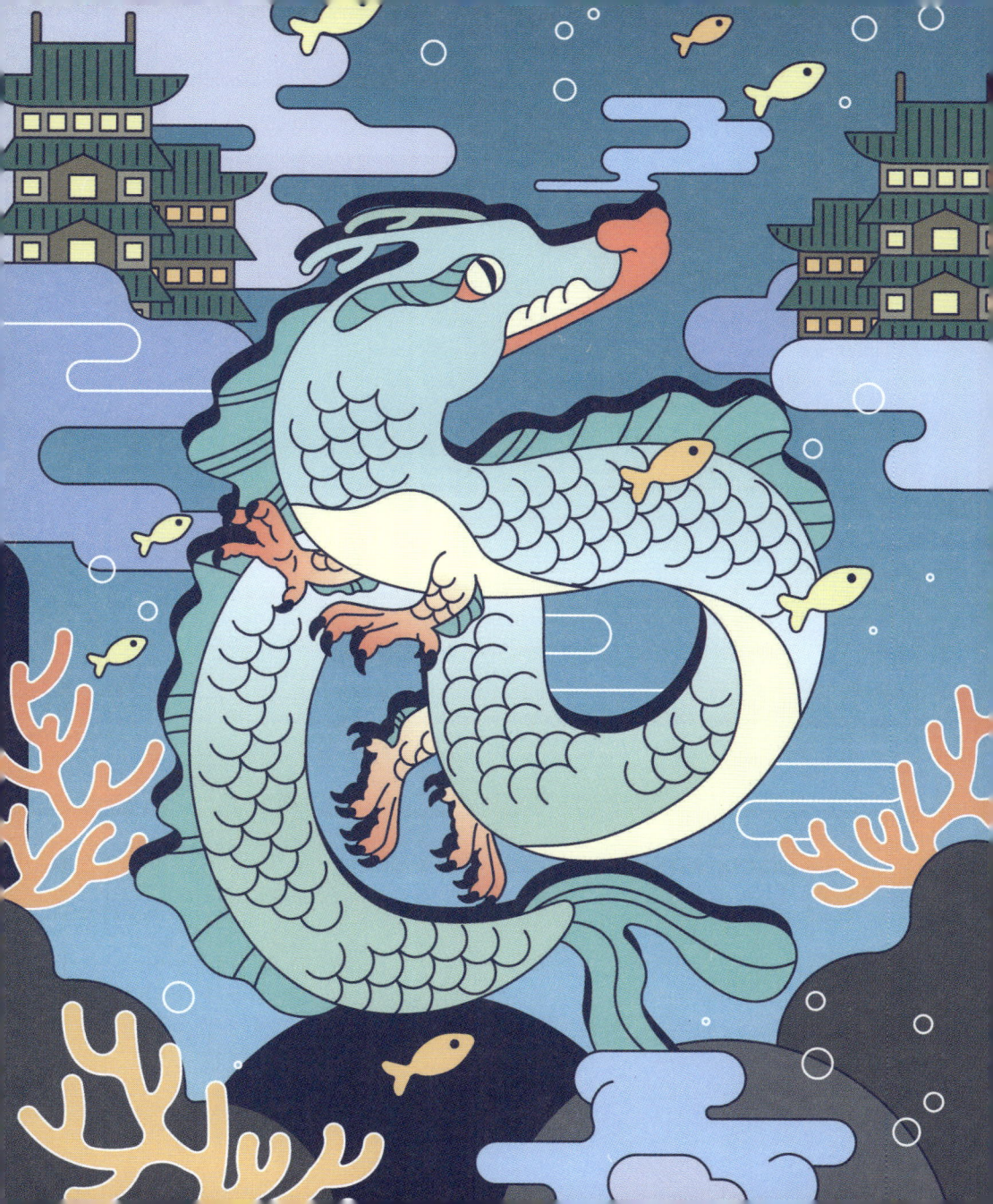

Shigingui

Shigingui is a ghost that eats humans—dead humans, to be exact. It especially likes to suck the bone marrow out of corpses, using its strong teeth and thick hands to cleave heads. That's why Shigingui is usually found in battlefields strewn with dead bodies. Once it has had its fill, it gleefully hops around the bodies, mouth dripping with blood.

And it sure looks atrocious: Shigingui is a great hulk of over six feet, with tufts of green fur blotching its red skin, and a crumpled face with a single eye and deadly teeth. It enjoys destruction and is as hot-tempered as they come but surprisingly simple and stupid. A skittish thing, it will completely lose its head when caught by surprise. In fact, there is an old record of a man who, about to be eaten by Shigingui, gave up playing dead and sprang to his feet, whacking its mouth with a rock. It scrammed.

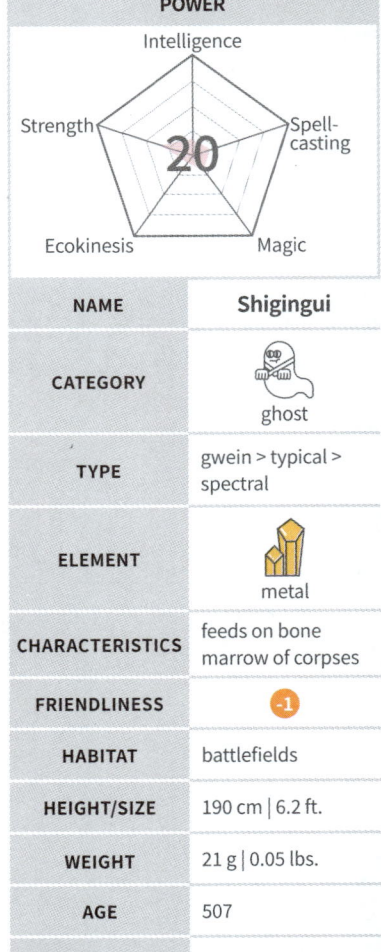

POWER

Intelligence
Strength
Spell-casting
Magic
Ecokinesis

20

NAME	Shigingui
CATEGORY	ghost
TYPE	gwein > typical > spectral
ELEMENT	metal
CHARACTERISTICS	feeds on bone marrow of corpses
FRIENDLINESS	-1
HABITAT	battlefields
HEIGHT/SIZE	190 cm | 6.2 ft.
WEIGHT	21 g | 0.05 lbs.
AGE	507
ERA	Early Qing dynasty

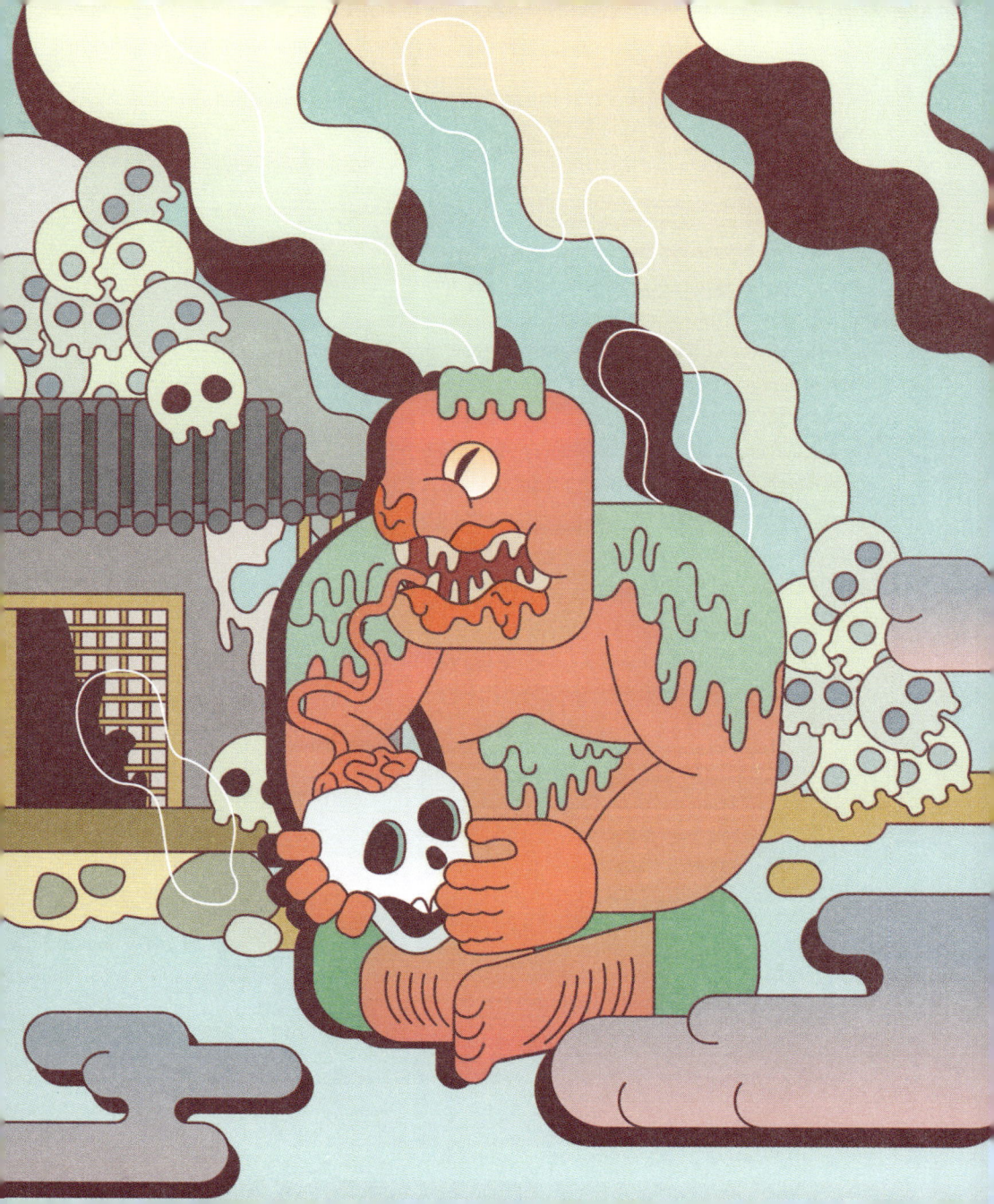

Aagui

Aagui are ghosts of people who were greedy in life. They look human but have bellies swollen up like balloons and are bone-thin everywhere else. They have abnormally skinny necks and narrow throats, which prevent them from eating anywhere close to their fill. Constantly hungry, their eyes chase and their hands grab at only one thing: food.

They exist as ghosts but occasionally possess people to satisfy their appetite. An Aagui-possessed person never stops eating, and if left unfed, they start hitting or harming those around them. Some people are reported to have gone bankrupt from trying to indulge their possessed loved one's cravings.

POWER

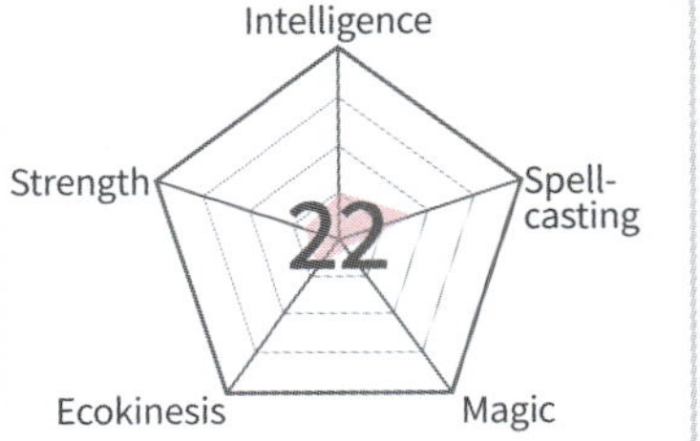

Intelligence / Strength / Spell-casting / Magic / Ecokinesis

22

NAME	Aagui
CATEGORY	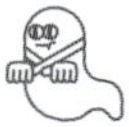 ghost
TYPE	gwein > typical > spectral
ELEMENT	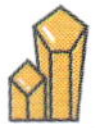 metal
CHARACTERISTICS	forever hungry
FRIENDLINESS	-1
HABITAT	good restaurants everywhere
HEIGHT/SIZE	162 cm | 5.3 ft.
WEIGHT	21 g | 0.05 lbs.
AGE	varies by entity
ERA	varies by entity

54

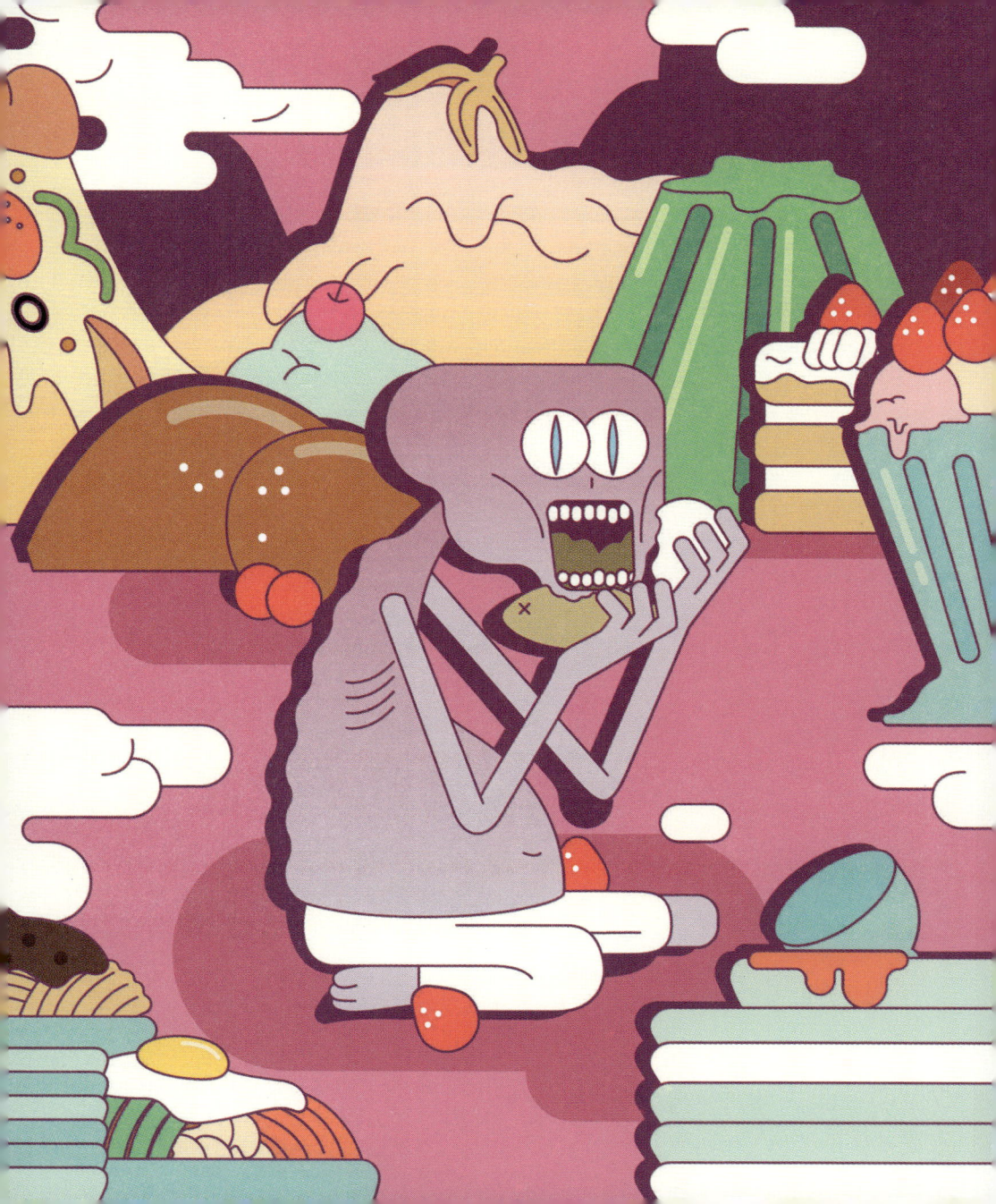

Yagwanggui Brothers

The Yagwanggui Brothers, also known as Yagwangy or Yagwangshin, or Lumino Ghosts in MeoShín'Ké, are nocturnal ghosts that glow brightafter nightfall. Their radiance is easily recognizable in the pitch dark, even from a distance. They have green skin and round, cute features but, like many ghosts, have an exposed bone or two.

The Yagwanggui Brothers love to descend on the human world and steal footwear, especially children's shoes. Victims lose not only their shoes but also their luck for that whole year. To prevent your pair from getting nabbed, hang a sieve outside your house. When they spot holes, Yagwanggui start counting compulsively and lose track of time. Then, at daybreak, they will have no choice but to flee empty-handed.

NAME	Yangy (older brother)	Gwangy (younger brother)
CATEGORY	ghost	ghost
TYPE	gwein > typical > spectral	gwein > typical > spectral
ELEMENT	moon	moon
CHARACTERISTICS	loves shoes; glows in the dark	loves shoes; copies his brother
FRIENDLINESS	-1	-1
HABITAT	residential areas	residential areas
HEIGHT/SIZE	100 cm | 3.3 ft.	90 cm | 3 ft.
WEIGHT	21 g | 0.05 lbs.	21 g | 0.05 lbs.
AGE	320	200
ERA	unknown	unknown

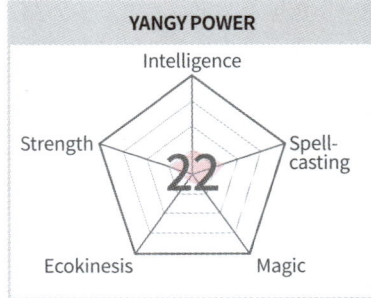

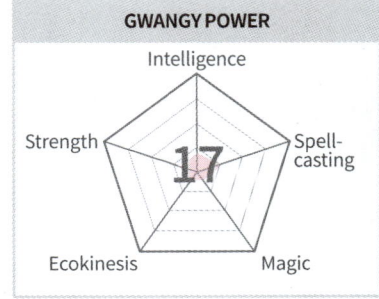

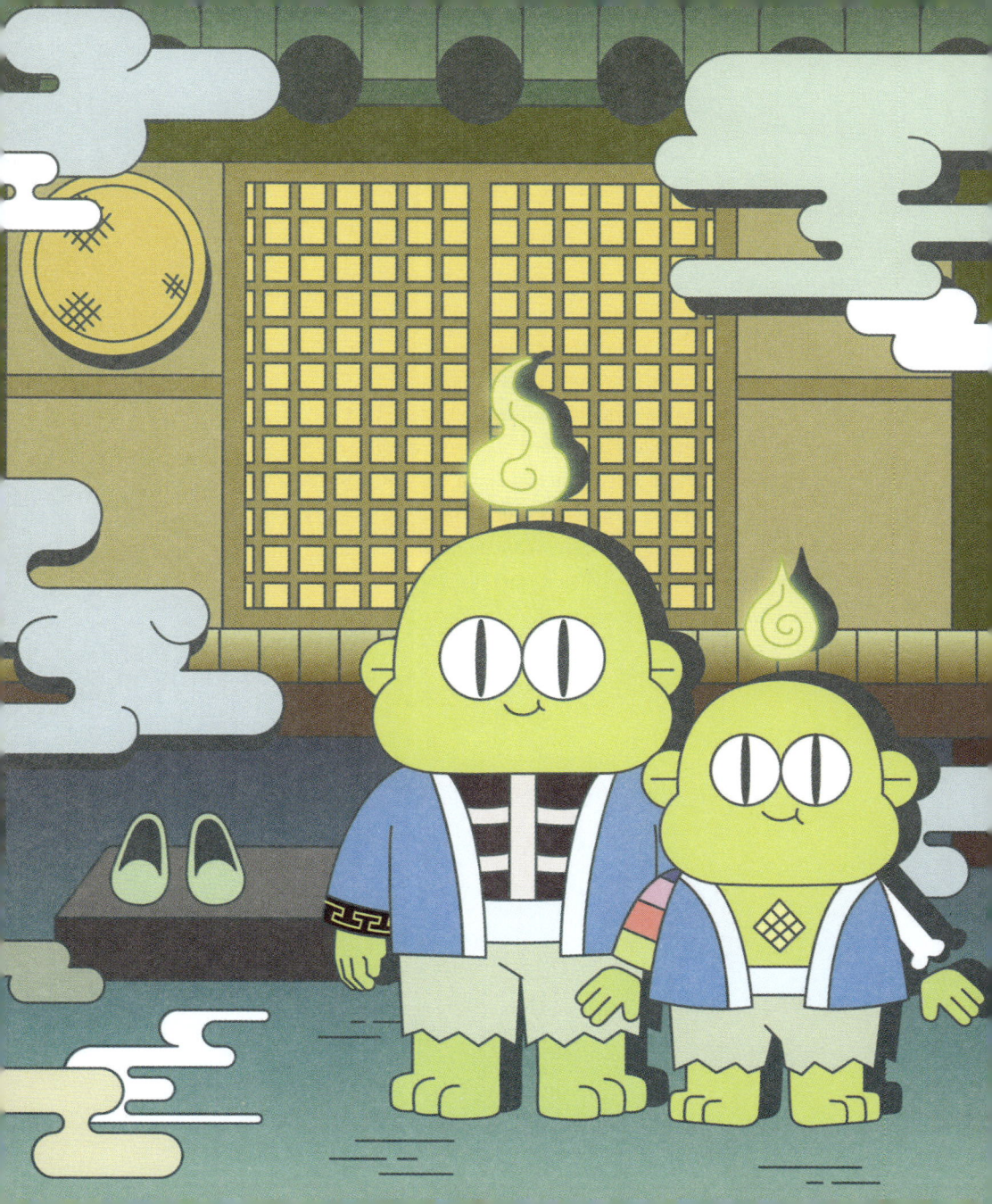

Odukshini

어둑시니

This ghost feeds on human fear. It goes by "Dimdim" in MeoShín'Ké, but humans often call it "Odukshini," a compound of *oduk* ("darkness") and *shini* ("ghost"). True to that name, the phantom appears only in the dark of night, along forest trails or mountain paths.

Odukshini totters around in the form of a small child until it attracts someone's attention, then tags along. What seems like harmless behavior at first soon turns into a creepy pursuit. The moment you feel afraid, the child inflates into a massive, fanged monster. A transformed Odukshini is difficult to escape, so the number one rule is to let go of your fear. When it can't feast on fear, Odukshini will shrink back into a tot.

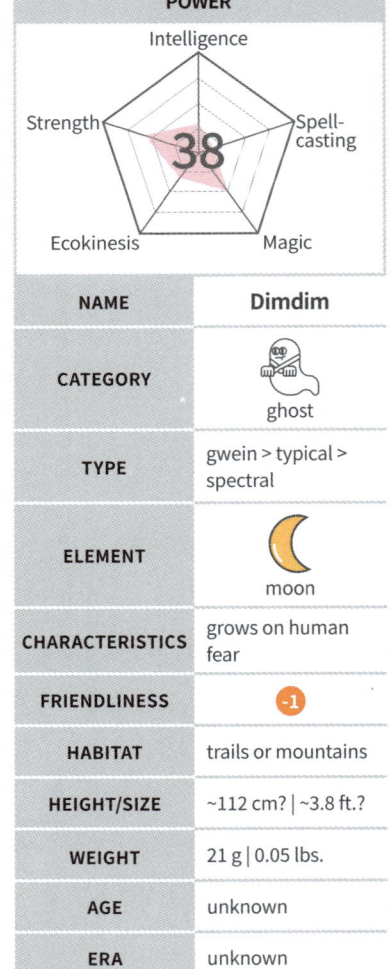

POWER	38
NAME	**Dimdim**
CATEGORY	ghost
TYPE	gwein > typical > spectral
ELEMENT	moon
CHARACTERISTICS	grows on human fear
FRIENDLINESS	-1
HABITAT	trails or mountains
HEIGHT/SIZE	~112 cm? | ~3.8 ft.?
WEIGHT	21 g | 0.05 lbs.
AGE	unknown
ERA	unknown

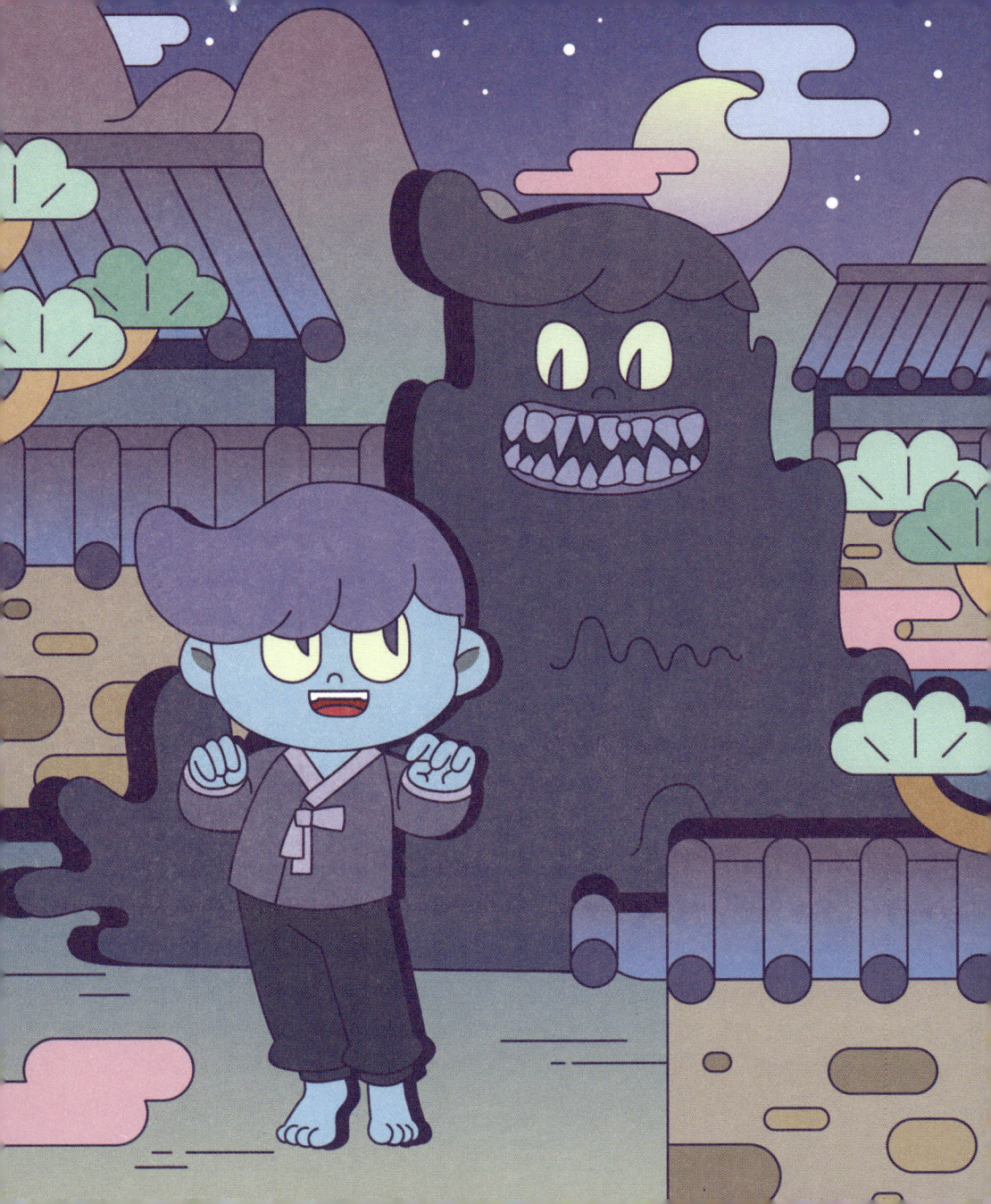

Olgul Guishin

Olgul Guishin ("face ghost") is a ghost with no body. Its face is much larger than a human's, with layers upon layers of wrinkles that sag around its eyes and mouth. Its silvery hair is done up in a haphazard bun.

Nothing excites Olgul Guishin more than playing pranks on humans. One it never tires of is to hide behind a wall or fence and call out to a passing human, showing just a bit of its face. It uses the human's pet name or childhood nickname to lure them over and . . . SURPRISE! When it peeks out from behind a fence, Olgul Guishin looks like a regular grandma, and sounds like one, too, so humans fall for the trick time and again.

Another one of its old favorites is playing ball. Olgul Guishin pretends to be a ball and rolls over in the dark to an unsuspecting passerby, who, attempting to kick the ball back to its owner, glances down and screams. If they kick without looking down, Olgul Guishin bellows at them in midair in a last-ditch effort to scare.

POWER

Radar chart with axes: Intelligence, Spell-casting, Magic, Ecokinesis, Strength. Value: **16**

NAME	Ulknee
CATEGORY	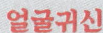 ghost
TYPE	gwein > typical > spectral
ELEMENT	moon
CHARACTERISTICS	disembodied face
FRIENDLINESS	-1
HABITAT	fences of houses
HEIGHT/SIZE	45 cm | 1.5 ft.
WEIGHT	21 g | 0.05 lbs.
AGE	411
ERA	King Seongjeong of Joseon's reign

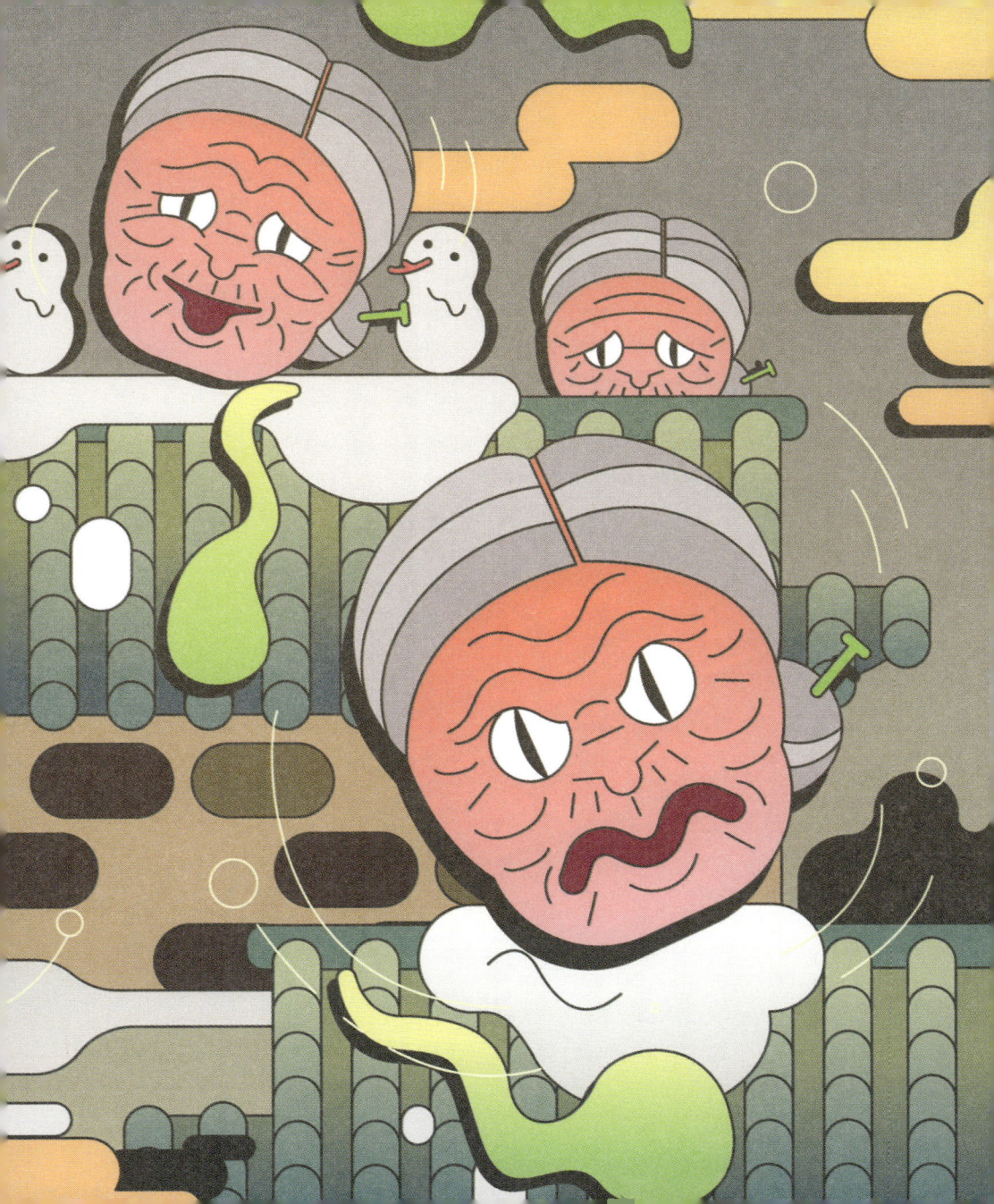

Upshin

업신

Upshin is the god of wealth that calls riches and abundance into homes. Unlike other household deities, this god has a tangible form, which is often a toad. It sometimes appears as other animals like a serpent or weasel. The nursery rhyme that goes "Hey toad, hey toad, I'll give you my house, build me a new one" originates from the custom of praying to Upshin for luck and money.

The god comes by homes of virtuous people, usually settling under the veranda of the house. If you are foolish enough to not recognize the god and chase it out or even harm it, boy, are you in trouble. Even if you do recognize it, you must never tell another soul or boast.

HEY TOAD, HEY TOAD

Hey toad, hey toad, I'll give you my
house, build me a new one
Hey toad, hey toad, draw up some
water, I'll build you a house
Hey toad, hey toad, your house is on fire
Grab a pitchfork and hop on over

Hey toad, hey toad, I'll give you my
house, build me a new one
Hey toad, hey toad, draw up some
water, I'll build you a house
Hey toad, hey toad, your house is on fire
Grab a pitchfork and hop on over

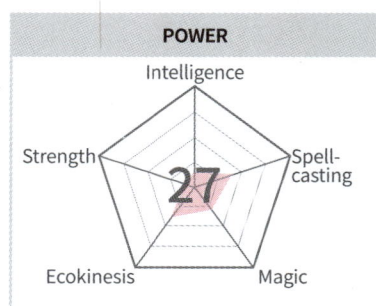

POWER

27

NAME	**Luckshin**
CATEGORY	shinryung
TYPE	shinryung > innate
ELEMENT	metal
CHARACTERISTICS	blesses families with wealth
FRIENDLINESS	+2★
HABITAT	storage rooms
HEIGHT/SIZE	20 cm	0.7 ft.
WEIGHT	1.3 kg	2.9 lbs.
AGE	unknown
ERA	antiquity

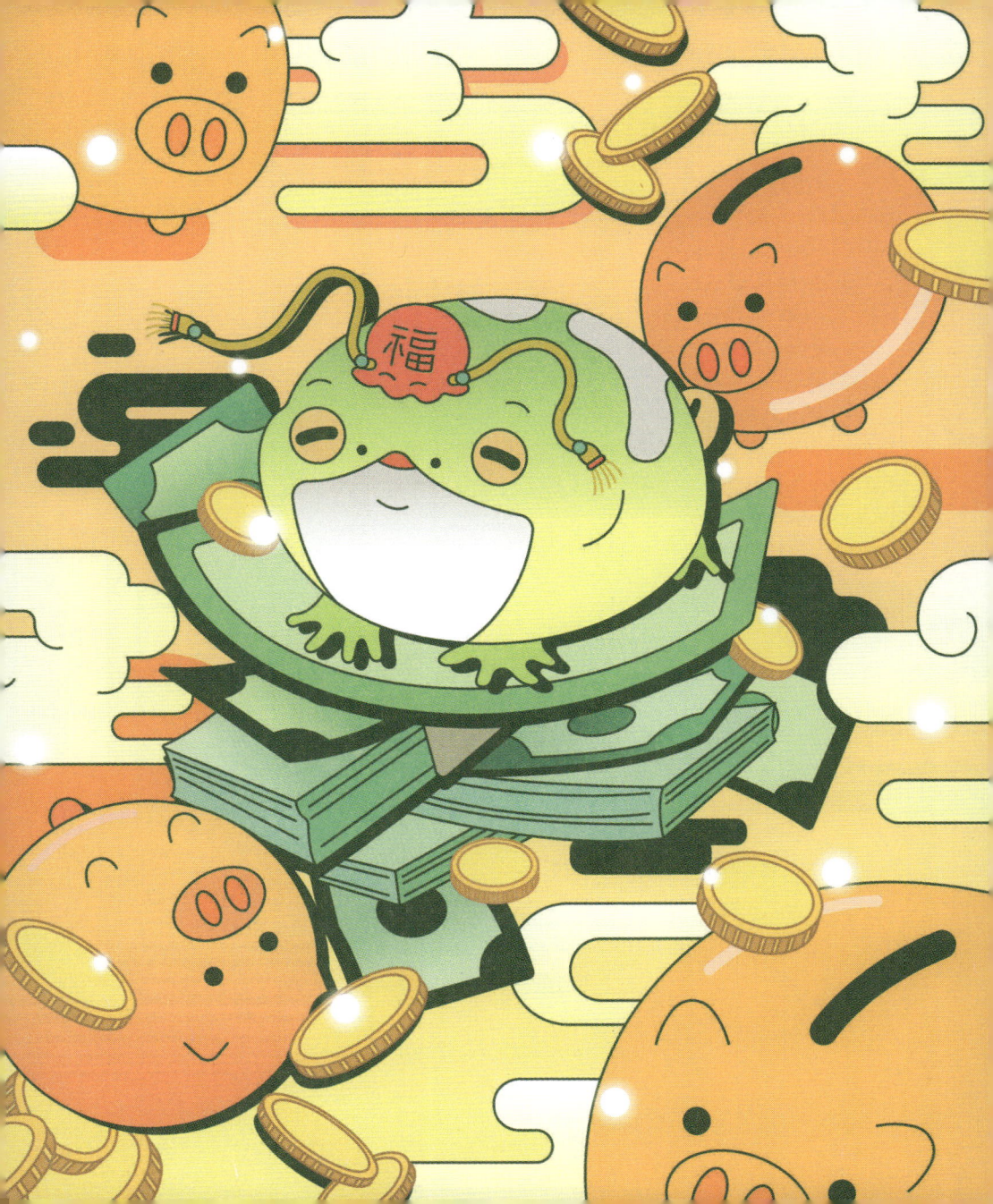

Wedari Guishin

외다리귀신

Wedari Guishin ("one-legged ghost") is a grim, baleful creature that stands on one abnormally long leg. Also known as "Dokgakgui," it goes around in a shoulder cape of straw and a matching straw hat, hopping on its single leg faster than most two-legged humans can run. It can even jump up to the roofs of houses in one bound.

The ghost often turns up on gloomy or rainy days to spread disease. Someone always falls sick if Wedari Guishin is nearby. If you have to fend it off, don't avoid its eyes because it hates a defiant stare.

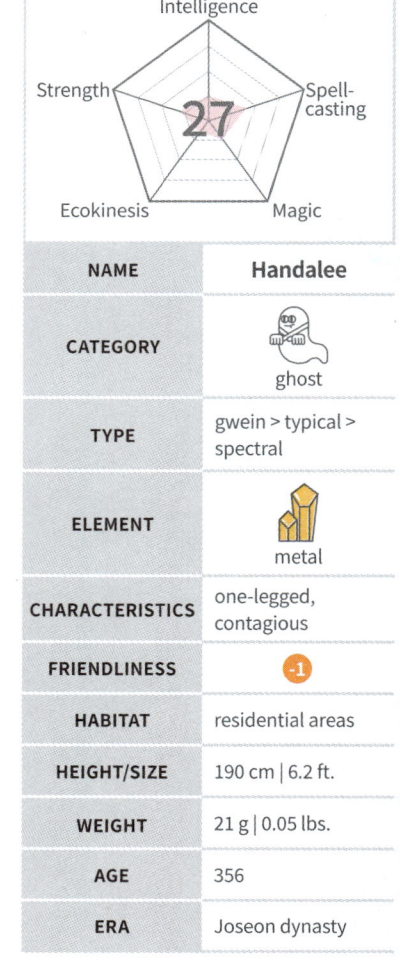

POWER	Intelligence / Strength / Spell-casting / Ecokinesis / Magic — 27
NAME	**Handalee**
CATEGORY	ghost
TYPE	gwein > typical > spectral
ELEMENT	metal
CHARACTERISTICS	one-legged, contagious
FRIENDLINESS	-1
HABITAT	residential areas
HEIGHT/SIZE	190 cm | 6.2 ft.
WEIGHT	21 g | 0.05 lbs.
AGE	356
ERA	Joseon dynasty

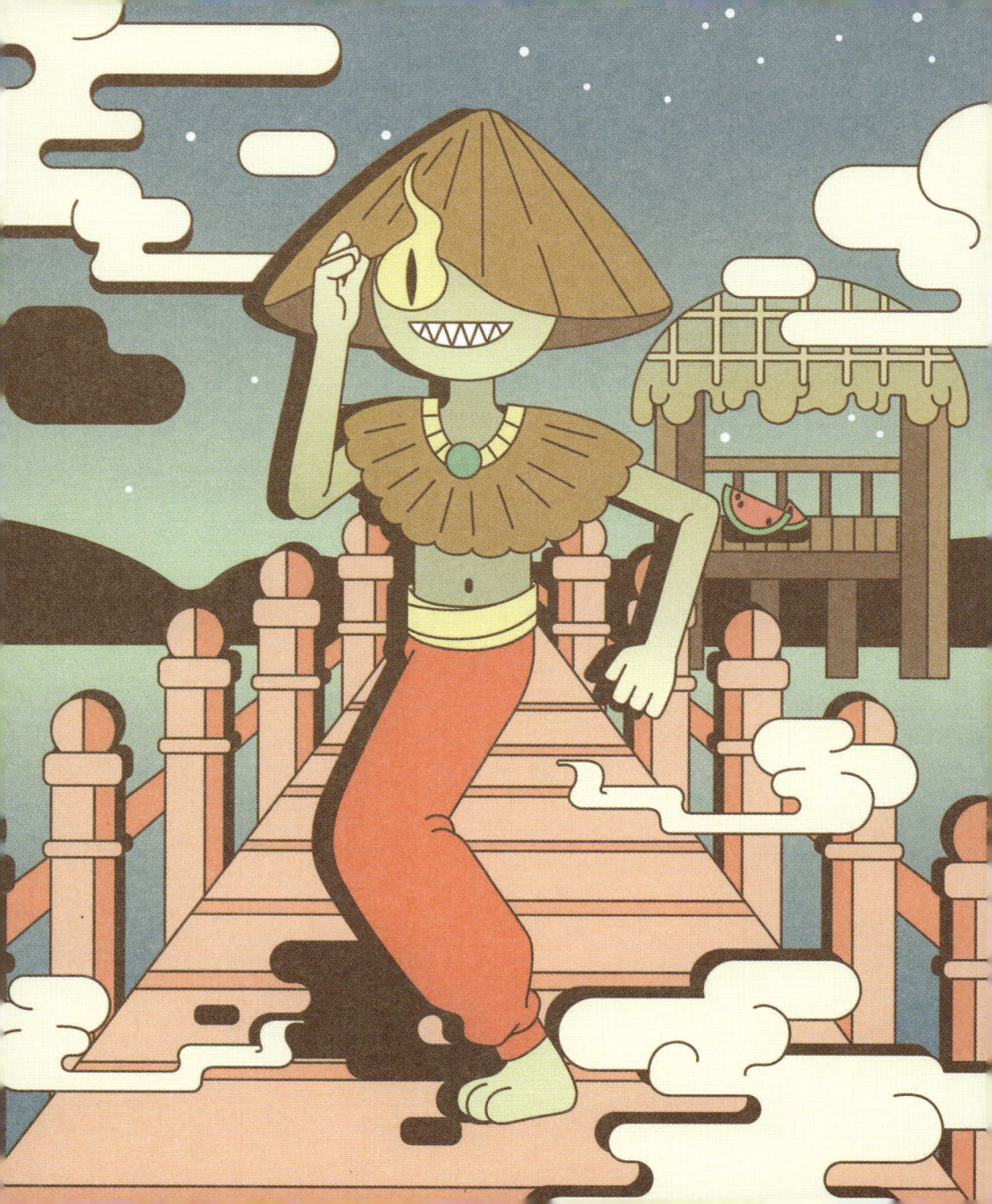

Oolung Gaksi

우렁각시

A sentient river snail that lived a very long life has gained reason and wisdom. It can transform into a human now and even help keep house. Its name is Oolung Gaksi ("snail bride"), and it has a male counterpart called Oolung Doryung ("snail groom").

When Oolung Gaksi finds a human she fancies, she talks them into taking her home. Normally she rests inside her hard shell, but when no one is around, she turns into a human and does the house chores. Careful not to reveal her identity, she stays hidden when she isn't working. In her human form, she is beautiful and dresses in comfortable work clothes. Once she spends some time in a home, she becomes fully human and is free to marry.

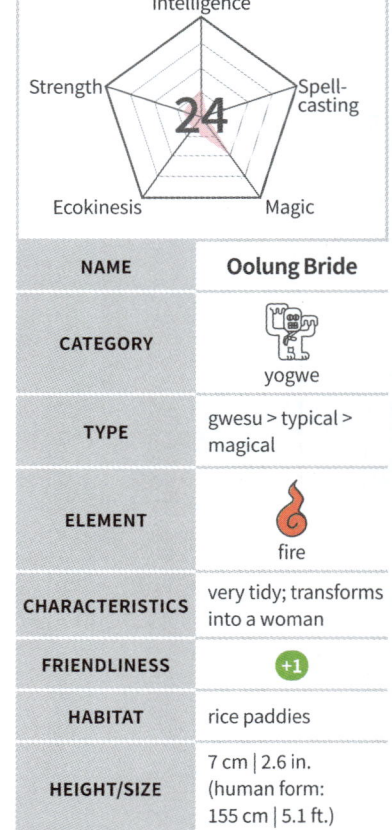

	POWER
	Intelligence
	Strength — Spellcasting
	24
	Ecokinesis — Magic

NAME	**Oolung Bride**
CATEGORY	yogwe
TYPE	gwesu > typical > magical
ELEMENT	fire
CHARACTERISTICS	very tidy; transforms into a woman
FRIENDLINESS	+1
HABITAT	rice paddies
HEIGHT/SIZE	7 cm | 2.6 in. (human form: 155 cm | 5.1 ft.)
WEIGHT	20 g | 0.04 lbs. (human form: 45 kg | 99 lbs.)
AGE	422
ERA	Joseon dynasty

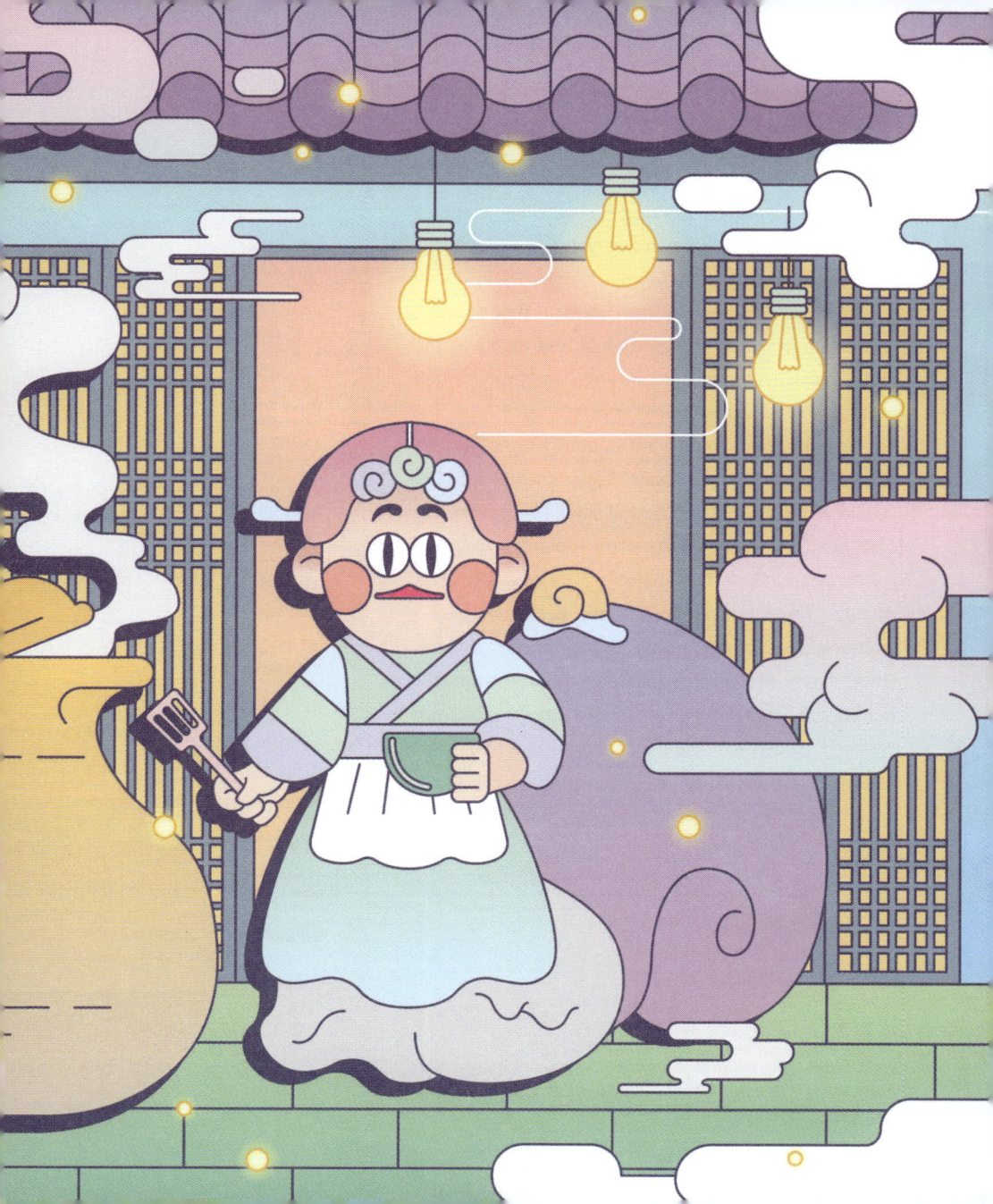

Yeemugi

Yeemugi are yogwe aspiring to become dragons. When a snake lives five hundred years, it turns into a Yeemugi, and when that lives five hundred years more in glacial water, it evolves into a dragon that wields a crystal dragon ball.* The entity featured here was the first one discovered by humans and was simply named Yeemugi, after the name of its species.

Yeemugi resembles a giant serpent, having lived for five long centuries as a snake. Scales the color of soil cover every inch of its body, and small horns poke out of its head as it prepares to morph into a dragon.

A lake, pond, or river sheltering Yeemugi will never dry up. The freshwater creatures that live there—anything that swims—serve this powerful serpent. Other types of Yeemugi exude light that entrances humans. It is said that consuming jerky made from Yeemugi meat** can cure leprosy or give you great beauty.

POWER

Intelligence

Strength

Spell-casting

42

Ecokinesis

Magic

NAME	**Yeemugi**
CATEGORY	yogwe
TYPE	gwesu > typical > morphed
ELEMENT	water
CHARACTERISTICS	five-century-old snake
FRIENDLINESS	0
HABITAT	fresh water
HEIGHT/SIZE	1,000 cm	33 ft.
WEIGHT	200 kg	441 lbs.
AGE	601
ERA	unknown

---

* **dragon ball:** an orb containing a dragon's magic. Any person who possesses it will be granted their heart's desire.
** **Yeemugi jerky:** cure for leprosy

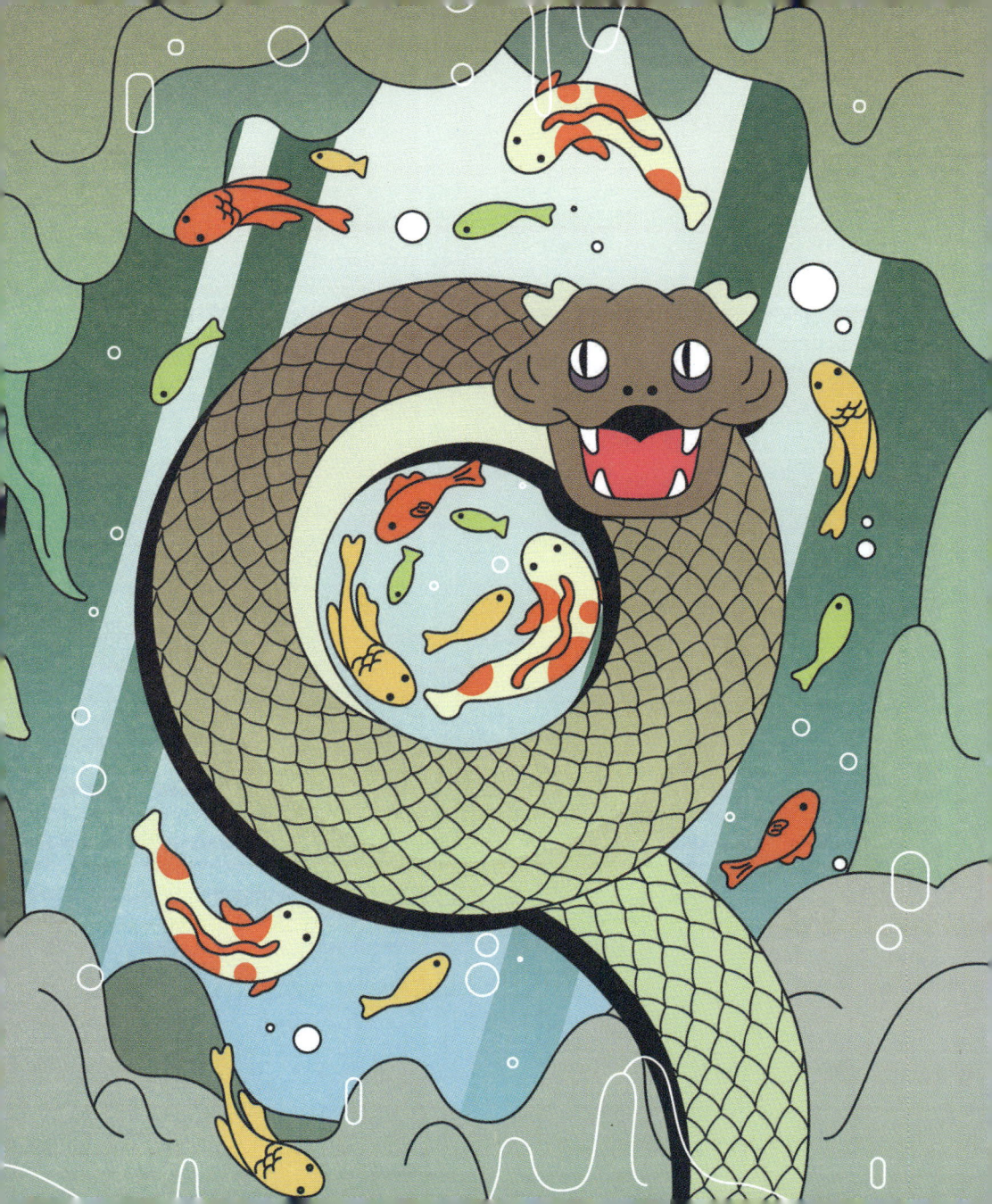

Jangbalgui

Jangbalgui is a ghost with long, long hair. It is also intimidatingly tall. It appears with its telltale reek of brackish water, its curtain of hair revealing glimpses of bright, burning eyes that attempt to lock with yours and render you immobile.

The hair moves as if it has a life of its own. It absorbs the terror of a victim and grows longer and more potent, twisting itself around them in a tight bind. If you ever find yourself in this situation, cut that hair: Jangbalgui is extremely precious about its tresses and will stand dumbstruck, staring at its snipped strands. Your second defense is to yell. The creature is surprisingly sensitive to sound and can be shouted away.

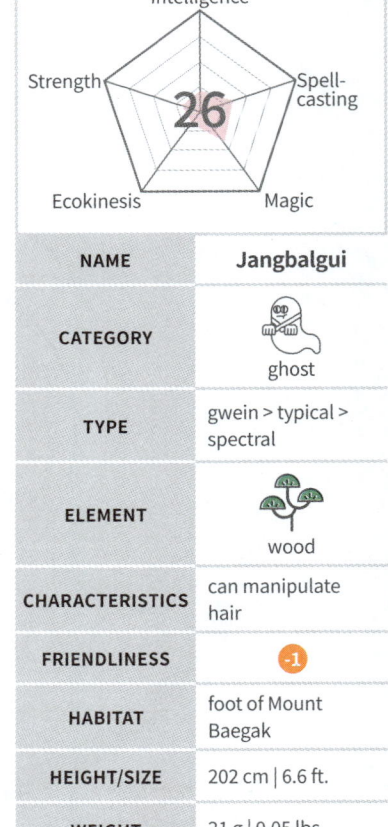

POWER

NAME	**Jangbalgui**
CATEGORY	ghost
TYPE	gwein > typical > spectral
ELEMENT	wood
CHARACTERISTICS	can manipulate hair
FRIENDLINESS	-1
HABITAT	foot of Mount Baegak
HEIGHT/SIZE	202 cm | 6.6 ft.
WEIGHT	21 g | 0.05 lbs.
AGE	629
ERA	Joseon dynasty

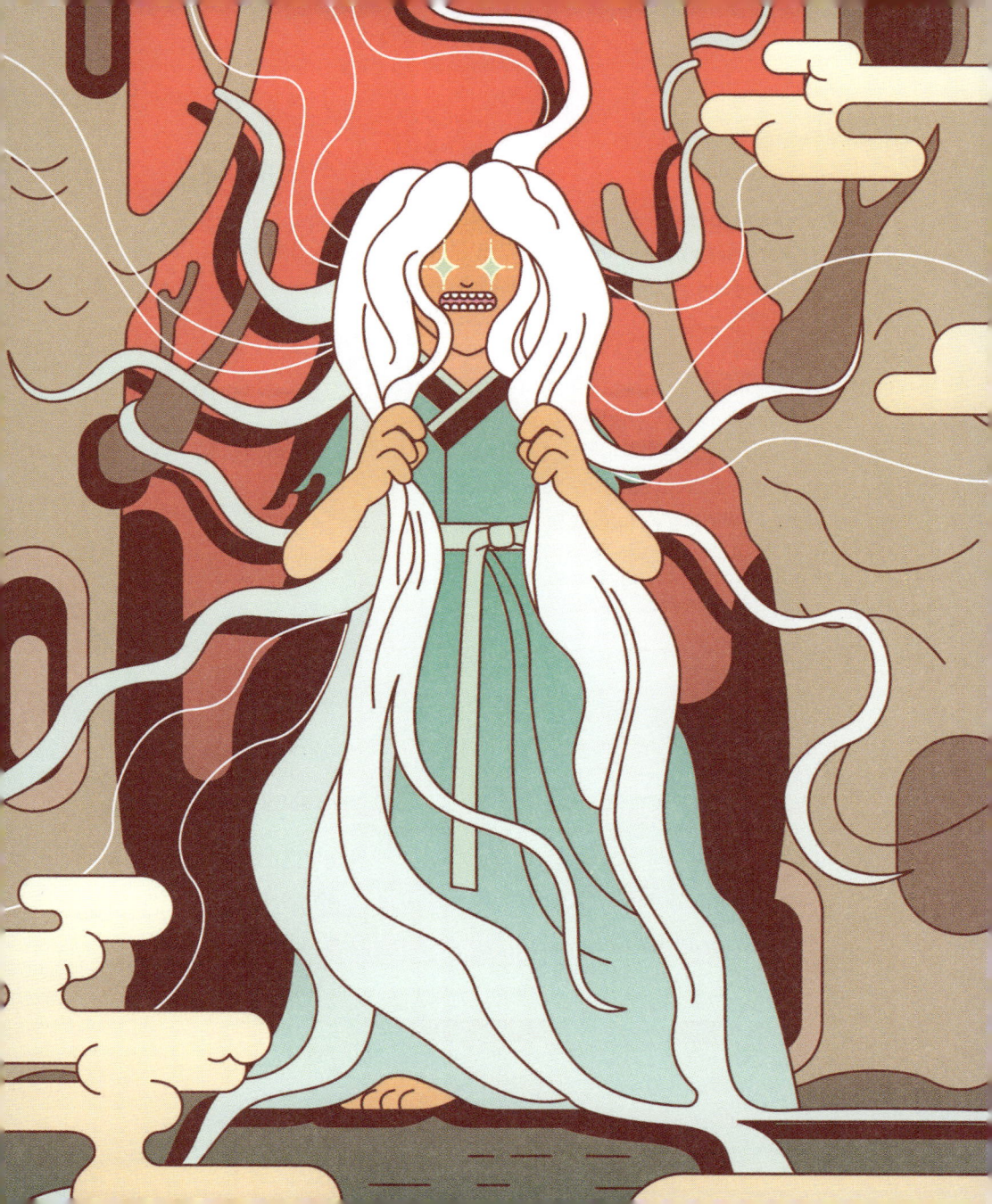

Jowangshin

조왕신

Jowangshin is the goddess of fire and the kitchen. She manifests as an ancient, snowy-haired woman with a stern, wrinkly face and piercing eyes. She dwells in the hearth. Because she and the toilet goddess Dwitgan Guishin detest each other, the kitchen and toilet have traditionally been built far apart.

The goddess also keeps a firm hand on the running of the household, ensuring the peace of the family and the health of its children. An untended kitchen and hearth can cause the family's fortune to wane, so manage them diligently.

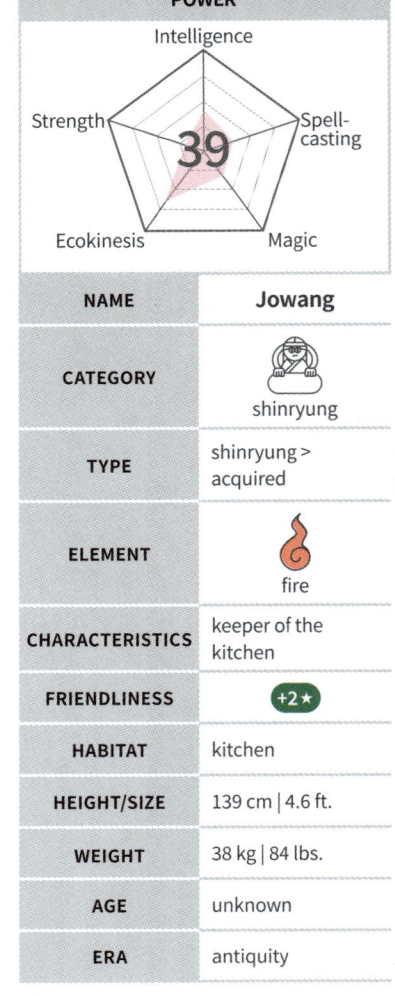

POWER

39

- Intelligence
- Spell-casting
- Magic
- Ecokinesis
- Strength

NAME	Jowang
CATEGORY	shinryung
TYPE	shinryung > acquired
ELEMENT	fire
CHARACTERISTICS	keeper of the kitchen
FRIENDLINESS	+2 ★
HABITAT	kitchen
HEIGHT/SIZE	139 cm | 4.6 ft.
WEIGHT	38 kg | 84 lbs.
AGE	unknown
ERA	antiquity

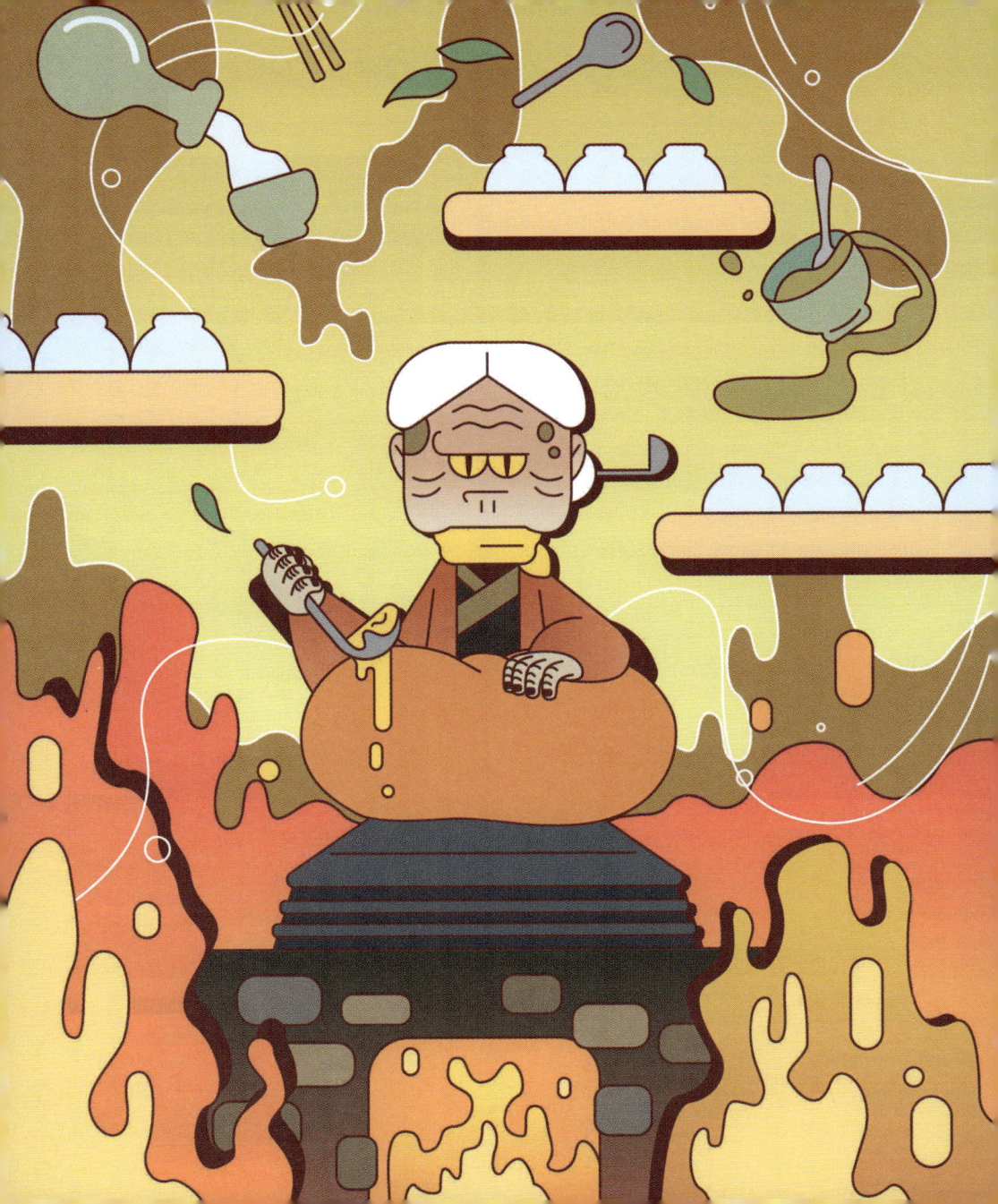

Juidoryung

쥐도령

Juidoryung ("rat boy") is a yogwe that lusts after the lives of humans. Known as "Copy-G" in MeoShín'Ké, it can turn itself into a human by nibbling on human fingernails or toenails. It masquerades as that person and steals their life, its transformation so perfect that it can fool even their family and get that person kicked out.

The scariest part is that Juidoryung doesn't simply copy your appearance but absorbs your background and knowledge. It is wilier and more clever than you, and an identity it robs is hard to get back. In fact, there is only one solution. Since Juidoryung is essentially a rat, it is terrified of cats. Thrust a cat at the phony rodent, and it will scamper away at once.

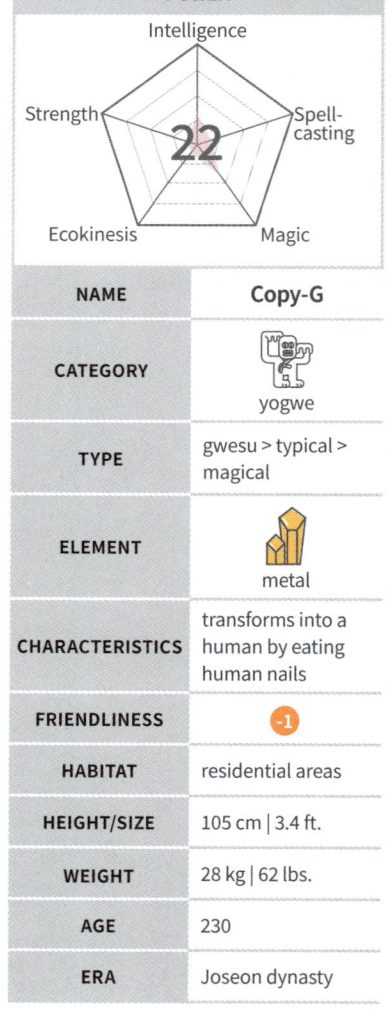

POWER	
Intelligence, Strength, Spell-casting, Ecokinesis, Magic — 22	

NAME	Copy-G
CATEGORY	yogwe
TYPE	gwesu > typical > magical
ELEMENT	metal
CHARACTERISTICS	transforms into a human by eating human nails
FRIENDLINESS	-1
HABITAT	residential areas
HEIGHT/SIZE	105 cm | 3.4 ft.
WEIGHT	28 kg | 62 lbs.
AGE	230
ERA	Joseon dynasty

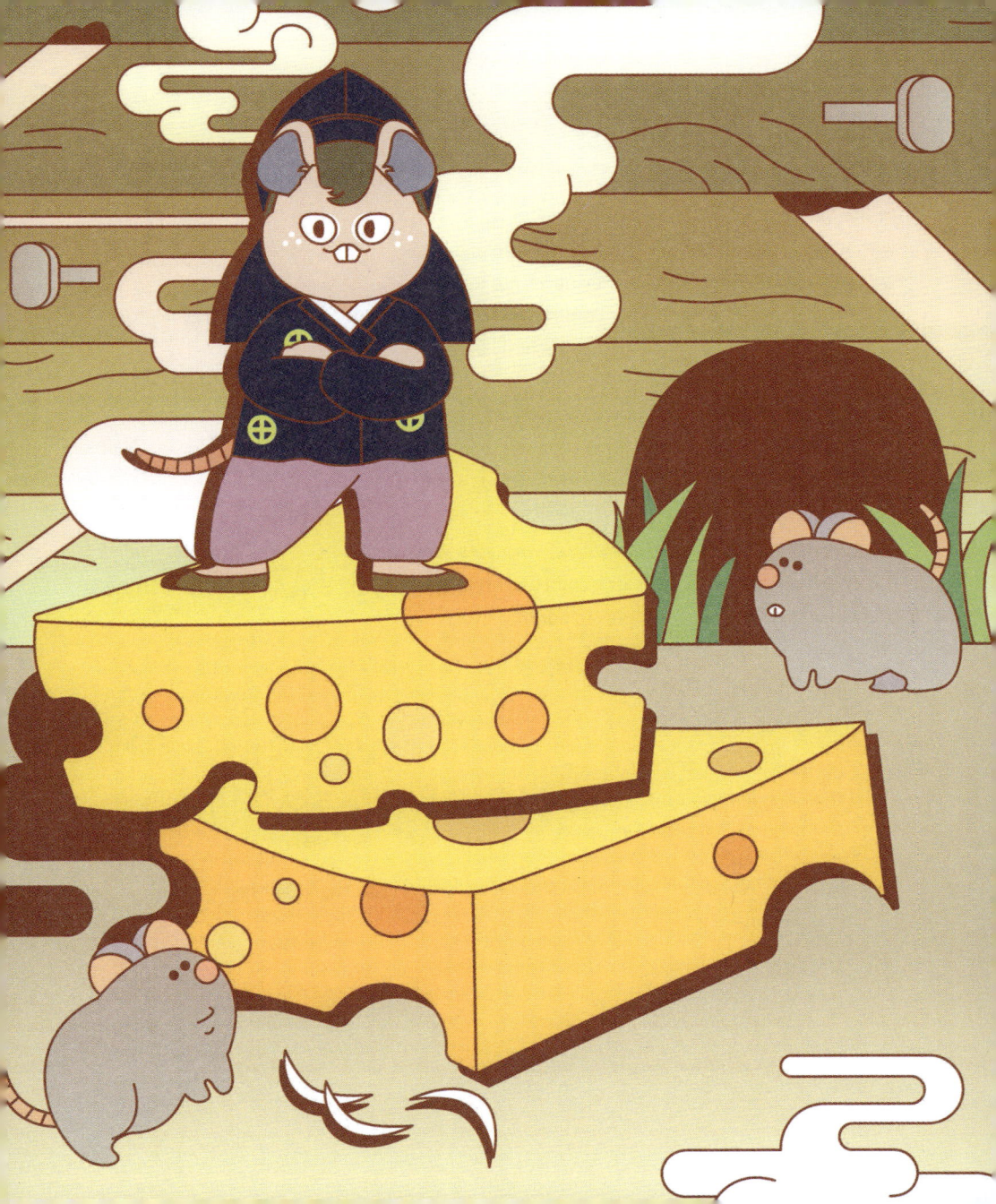

Jigui

지귀

In the Silla dynasty, there was a man who fell in love with Queen Seondeok. To confess his feelings, he waited and waited for her, but they never got to meet. His burning passion eventually combusted his body, turning him into a fire ghost. Jigui is his body of undying flames. He leaves a trail of fire wherever he goes, sometimes setting whole villages ablaze. To calm her people's fears of the crazed fires, Queen Seondeok devised a spell that, when written and posted, would make a place fireproof.

No one wants to come near Jigui, who gets very lonely. He actually loves what little company he can get and means no harm when he tries to approach you.

QUEEN SEONDEOK'S SPELL

Jigui's heart burned up his body, and
now he is a fiend of fire.
I shall cast him out beyond the seas,
never to look after him again.

Reciting Queen Seondeok's spell or posting a paper talisman of it will make a place untouchable by Jigui and his fire.

POWER

Intelligence · Spell-casting · Magic · Ecokinesis · Strength

39

NAME	Jigui
CATEGORY	ghost
TYPE	gwein > typical > spectral
ELEMENT	fire
CHARACTERISTICS	spreads fire
FRIENDLINESS	-2
HABITAT	across the city of Gyeongju
HEIGHT/SIZE	178 cm | 5.8 ft.
WEIGHT	21 g | 0.05 lbs.
AGE	29
ERA	Queen Seondeok of Silla's reign

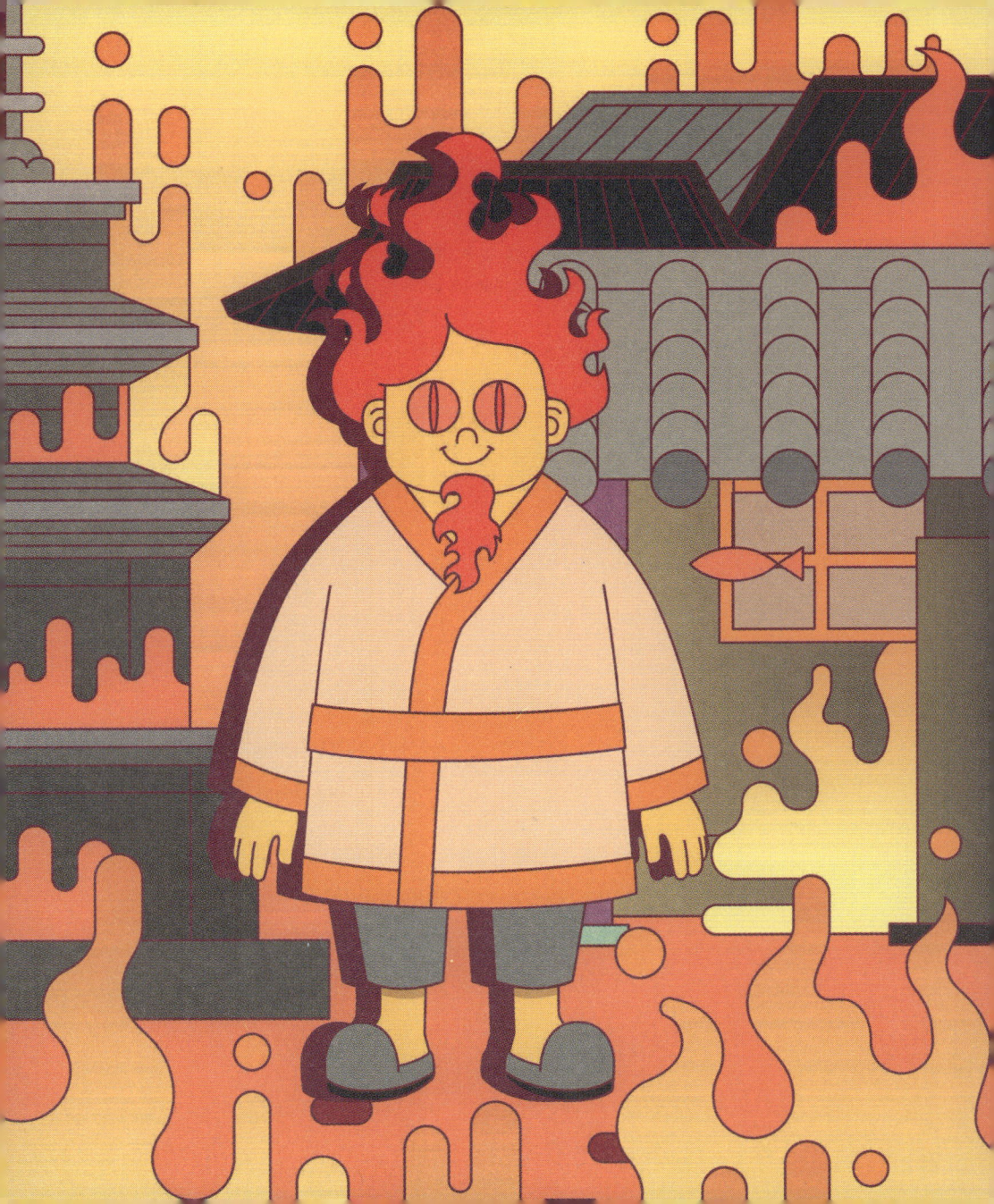

Jiryong

지룡

This peculiar dragon lives only underground, unable to fly but sweeping through the earth with ease. It purifies the energy of the ground and prevents disasters like earthquakes.

The dirt-brown skin of Jiryong is smooth and scaleless, perfect for slipping in and out of soil. It has little bumps for horns and claws ideal for digging. It is not aggressive by nature but may cause an earthquake to punish those who pollute the earth.

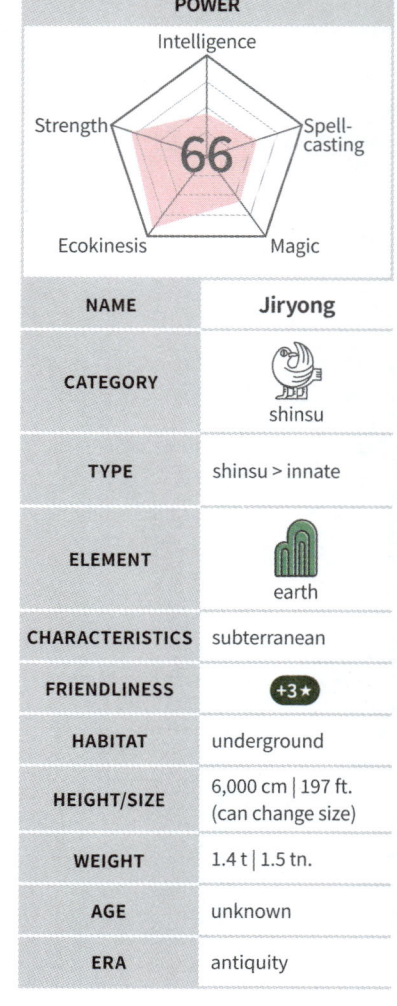

POWER

66

NAME	Jiryong
CATEGORY	shinsu
TYPE	shinsu > innate
ELEMENT	earth
CHARACTERISTICS	subterranean
FRIENDLINESS	+3 ★
HABITAT	underground
HEIGHT/SIZE	6,000 cm | 197 ft. (can change size)
WEIGHT	1.4 t | 1.5 tn.
AGE	unknown
ERA	antiquity

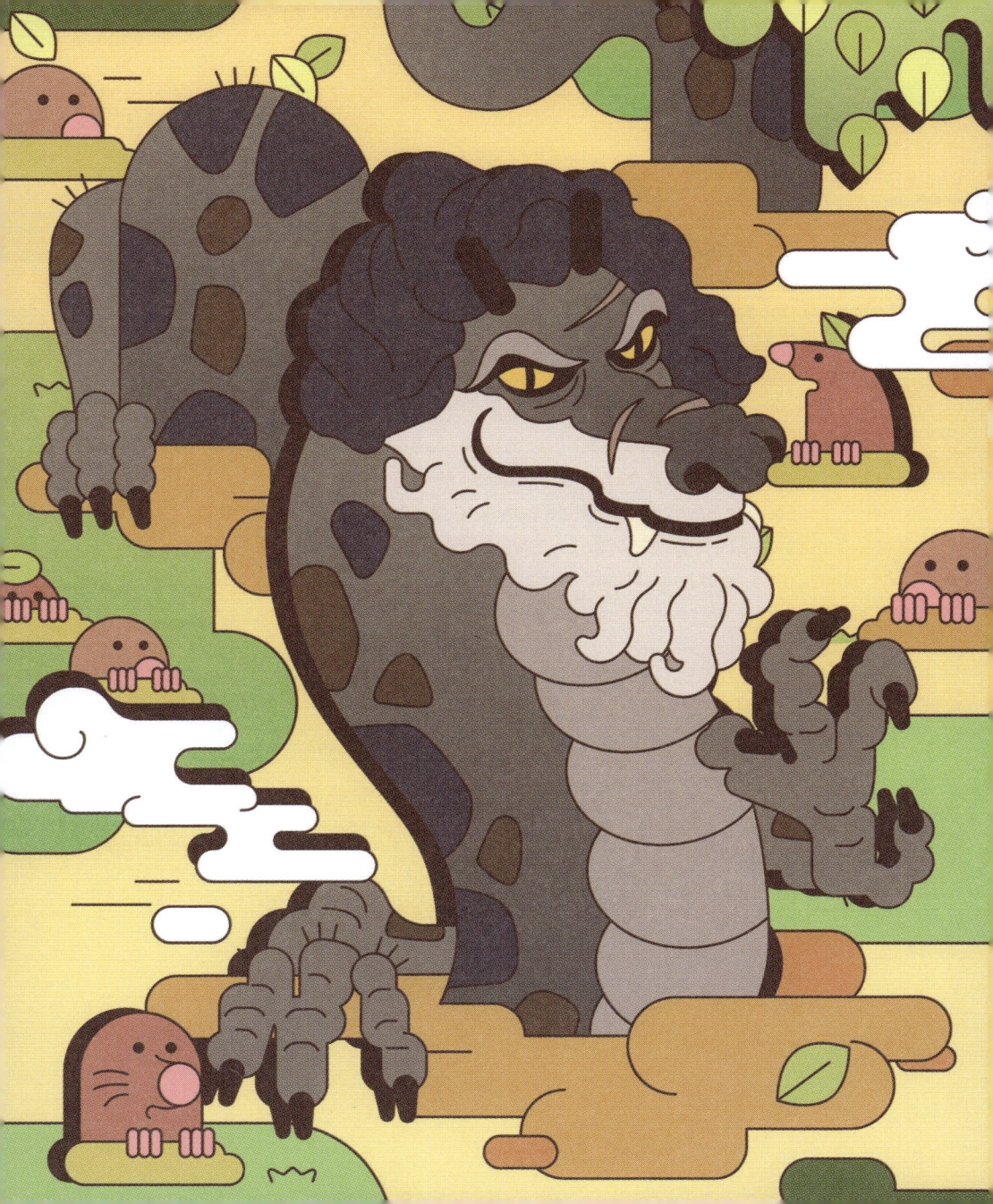

Jeebagryung

Jeebagryung are ghosts tied down to a place by unresolved trauma. They have no fixed form, and their only defining trait is that they stand rooted to a spot like a tree. They stand wearily with vacant eyes. Some may turn into evil spirits depending on the reason of death, their personality when they were alive, and their former relationships.

They are aggrieved ghosts, bound as they are to a place with lingering hurt. A Jeebagryung-turned-fiend harms people who have nothing to do with its death, even innocent passersby. It will do anything to detain its victims, refusing to let go. There is no way to banish a Jeebagryung except to help heal its trauma.

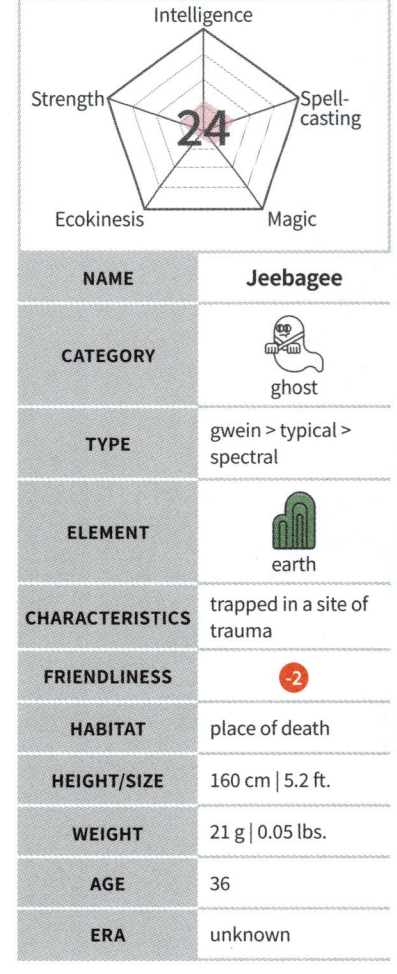

POWER

24

NAME	**Jeebagee**
CATEGORY	ghost
TYPE	gwein > typical > spectral
ELEMENT	earth
CHARACTERISTICS	trapped in a site of trauma
FRIENDLINESS	-2
HABITAT	place of death
HEIGHT/SIZE	160 cm	5.2 ft.
WEIGHT	21 g	0.05 lbs.
AGE	36
ERA	unknown

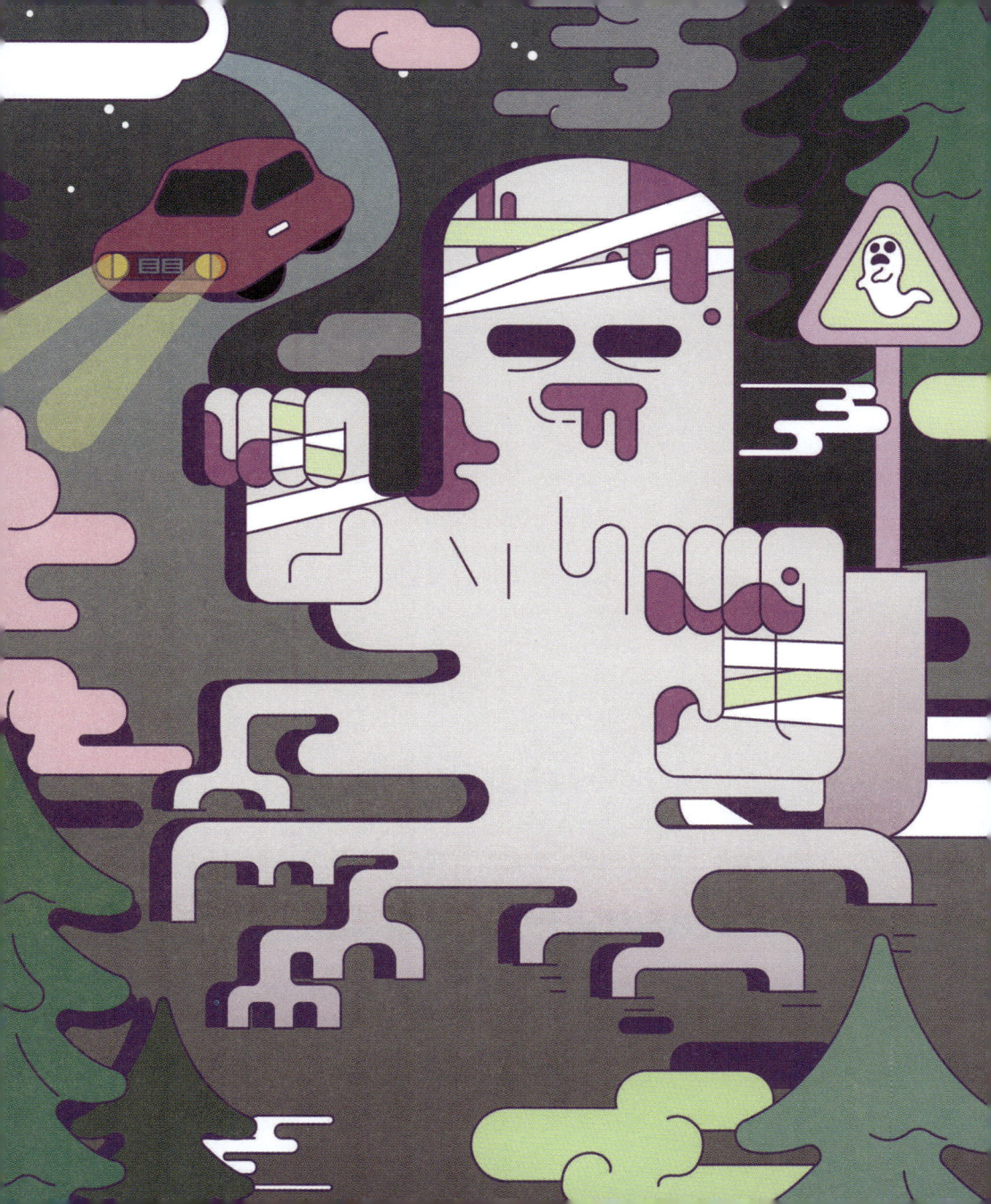

Jihaguk Dejok

Gumori is a monster that dwells in Jihaguk, an underground kingdom home to creatures of mystery and might. Known as Jihaguk Dejok among humans, or the Great Underground Bandit, this ruthless giant can sniff out humans from miles away.

It notoriously has nine heads, each with a unique power that works in parallel instead of assisting one central head. Even when chopped off, the heads grow right back. Jihaguk Dejok carries an equally dangerous weapon called the Treasure Sword of Aagui.[*] Yet, even this seemingly invincible gwein has a weakness: two tiny scales on its armpits. If you pluck them off, all nine of its heads will fall away and shoot up to the sky. Seize that moment to throw ash on its exposed throats. That will stop the heads from reattaching themselves to the necks and kill the gwein.

Every so often, Jihaguk Dejok emerges aboveground to stir up chaos or kidnap humans. Its first appearance in the human world was ages ago when it abducted a princess. Fortunately, a brave warrior used the aforementioned trick to subdue it and save her.

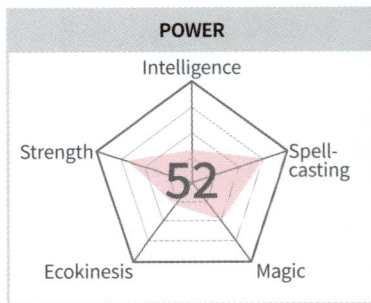

POWER	

NAME	**Gumori**
CATEGORY	yogwe
TYPE	gwein > typical > humanoid
ELEMENT	earth
CHARACTERISTICS	weakness: two armpit scales
FRIENDLINESS	-2
HABITAT	Jihaguk
HEIGHT/SIZE	234 cm	7.8 ft.
WEIGHT	150 kg	331 lbs.
AGE	1,002
ERA	unknown

---

* **Treasure Sword of Aagui:** a deadly sword that can slash an object as easily as if it were a rotting weed

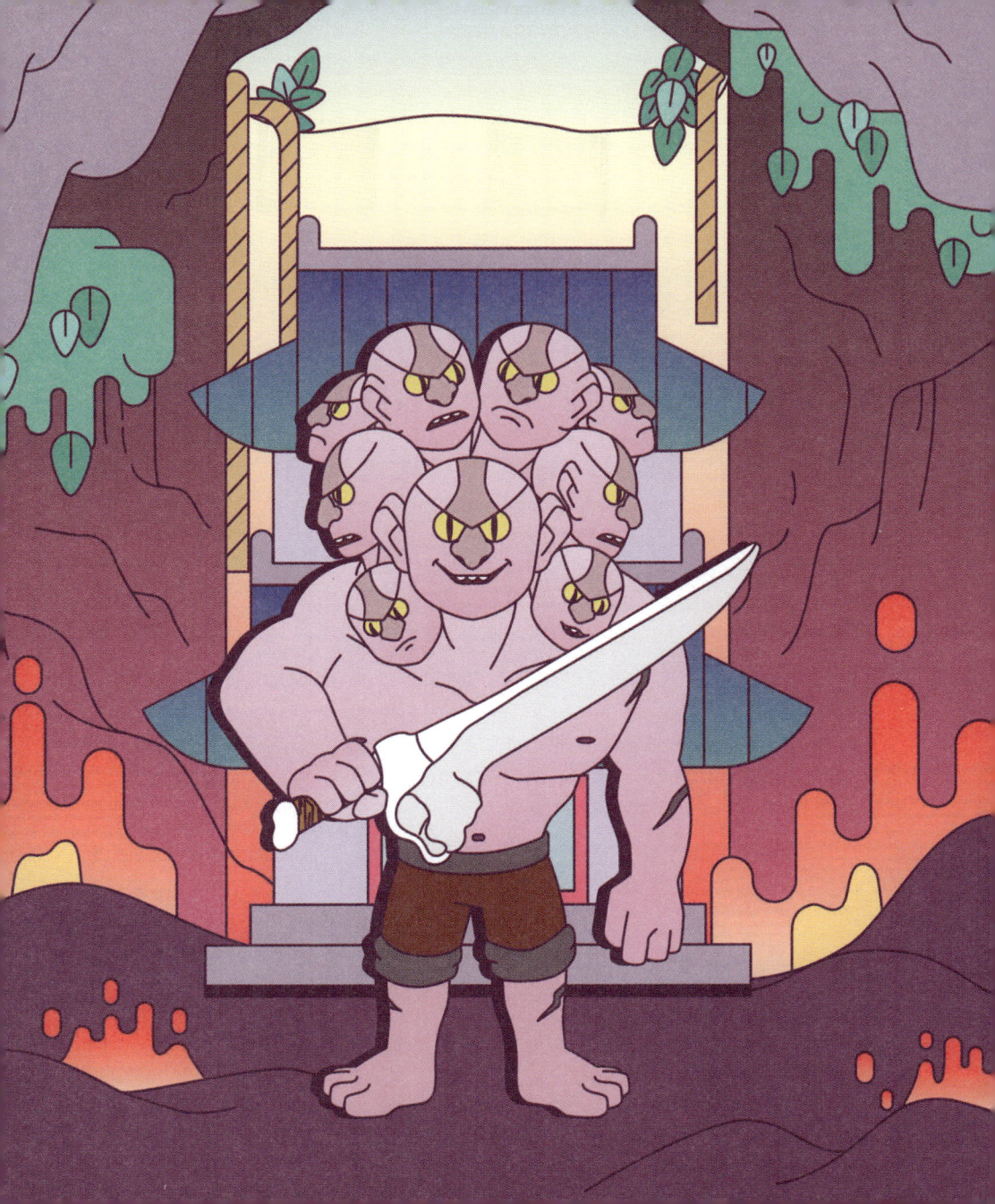

Changgui

Changgui are ghosts of people who were gobbled up by a tiger and have been bound to it ever since. When a tiger scarfs down a human, it leaves the head untouched. It is the ghost of that head that sticks to the tiger, the body long digested.

Humans become enslaved to the tiger that ate them, baiting prey and navigating directions for their master. Their only way to break free is to trick another human into replacing them. They appear as their old selves to fool other humans, not hesitating to sacrifice even friends and family for their own freedom.

Changgui get attached to different parts of a tiger depending on the order they were eaten. The first victim clings to a tiger's armpit and is called "Gulgak"; the second, called "Yiol," clings to its cheekbone; and the third, "Yukhon," to its chin.

Each Changgui plays a different role in capturing prey. They don't particularly get along, however, getting into frequent squabbles about the best dinner menu for their master. As the tiger's injuries or death will impact them, Changgui are quick to detect and sabotage tiger traps set by humans.

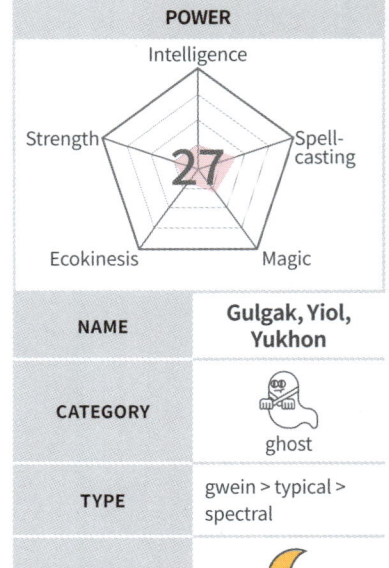

POWER	
	Intelligence
Strength	27 Spell-casting
Ecokinesis	Magic

NAME	Gulgak, Yiol, Yukhon
CATEGORY	ghost
TYPE	gwein > typical > spectral
ELEMENT	moon
CHARACTERISTICS	ghostly head of tiger victim
FRIENDLINESS	-2
HABITAT	mountains
HEIGHT/SIZE	20–30 cm | 0.7–1 ft.
WEIGHT	21 g | 0.05 lbs.
AGE	varies by entity
ERA	mainly Joseon dynasty

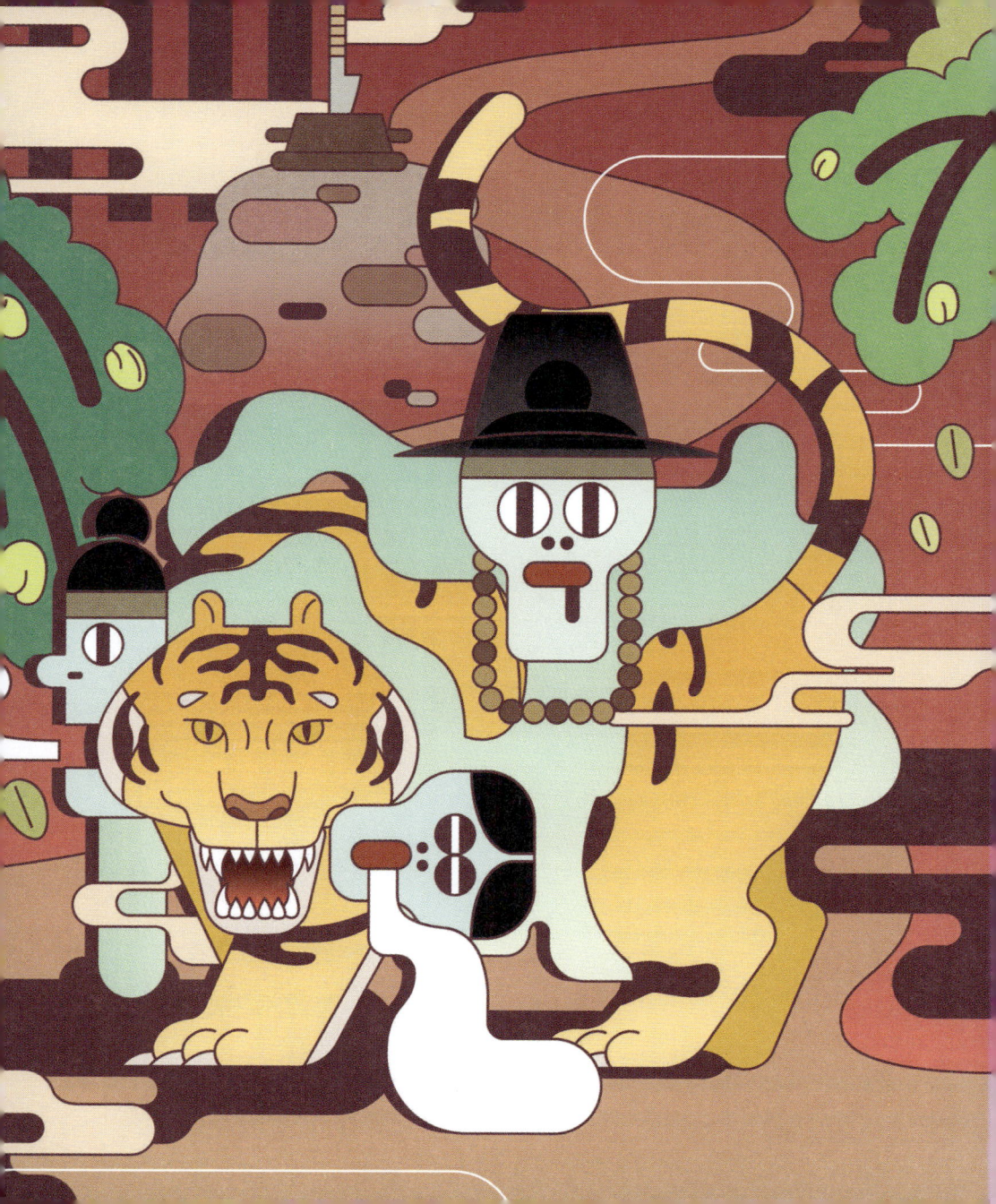

Chungu

Chungu is a sacred puppy living in outer space. Don't let its adorable face fool you, though, because hidden beneath its round, furry brows are eyes brimming with spiritual power. Its tail, nearly three feet long, is made of brilliant rainbow flames and its fur of the same mysterious fire.

If you are lucky, you might catch Chungu twinkling in the sky. It usually swims around the ether high above us, but when it gets injured or dies, it plummets to the ground. There are records of people mistaking it for a shooting star and wishing upon it. Chungu's crash leaves a huge crater that looks like a great fire erupted there. Sometimes, Chungu falls into the sea.

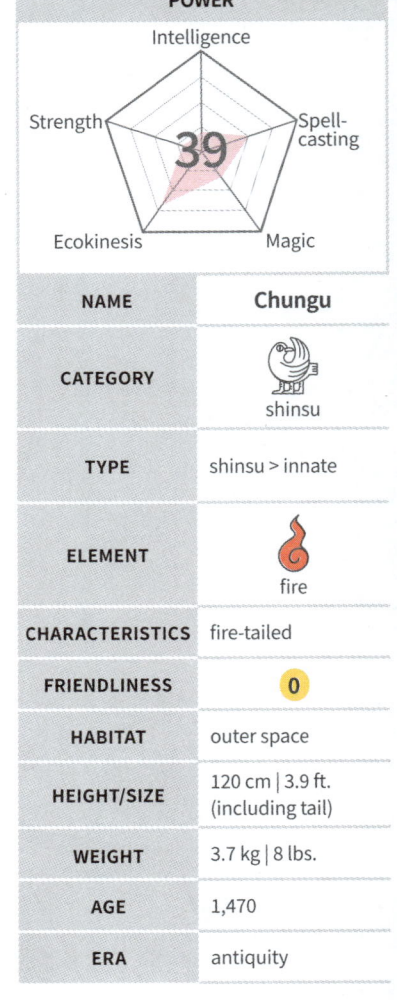

POWER

Intelligence · Spell-casting · Magic · Ecokinesis · Strength

39

NAME	Chungu
CATEGORY	shinsu
TYPE	shinsu > innate
ELEMENT	fire
CHARACTERISTICS	fire-tailed
FRIENDLINESS	0
HABITAT	outer space
HEIGHT/SIZE	120 cm | 3.9 ft. (including tail)
WEIGHT	3.7 kg | 8 lbs.
AGE	1,470
ERA	antiquity

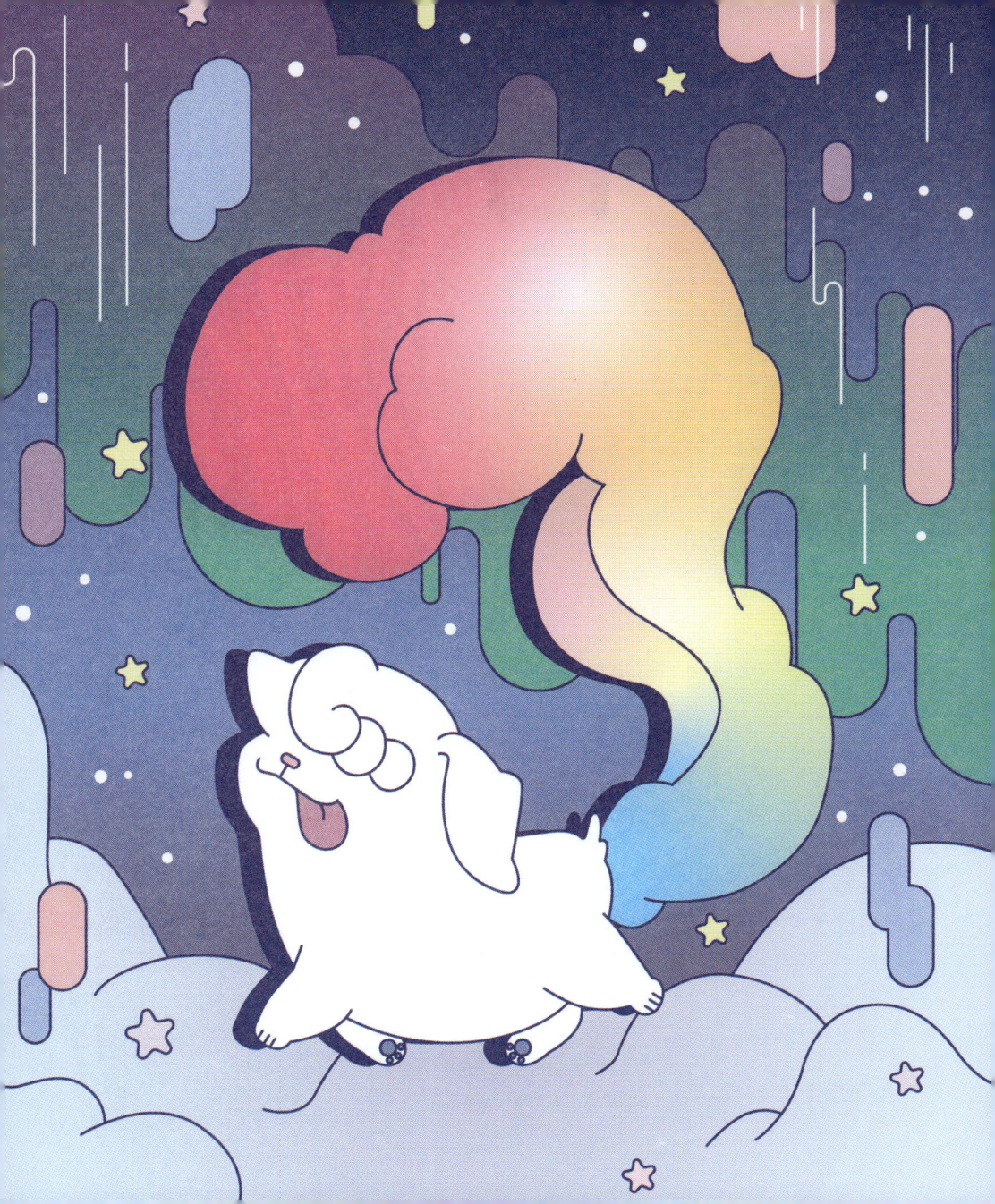

Chunrok Bueksa

Chunrok Bueksa is a pair of majestic shinsu that protects good and vanquishes evil. Chunrok means "heaven's blessing," while Bueksa means "the uprooting of evil." Chunrok has one horn; Bueksa has two. Together, they are "Chunrok Bueksa." They look like tigers with glowing horns in fantastic colors. Bueksa has a snowy mane, and both have imposing talons.

Usually spotted in forests, the pair likes to climb lofty trees. They never leave each other's side. Both are unbeatable runners, galloping four thousand miles in just a day. On encountering a human, Chunrok Bueksa may size up their character and behavior to decide whether to bless them or curse them.

NAME	Chunrok	Bueksa
CATEGORY	shinsu	shinsu
TYPE	shinsu > innate	shinsu > innate
ELEMENT	sun	sun
CHARACTERISTICS	one-horned	two-horned
FRIENDLINESS	+2 ★	+2 ★
HABITAT	forests	forests
HEIGHT/SIZE	106 cm | 3.5 ft.	210 cm | 6.9 ft.
WEIGHT	57 kg | 126 lbs.	170 kg | 375 lbs.
AGE	934	934
ERA	Goryeo dynasty	Goryeo dynasty

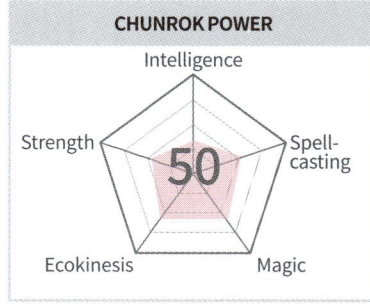

CHUNROK POWER

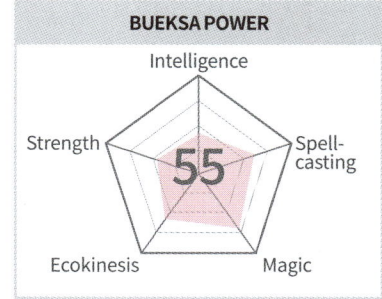

BUEKSA POWER

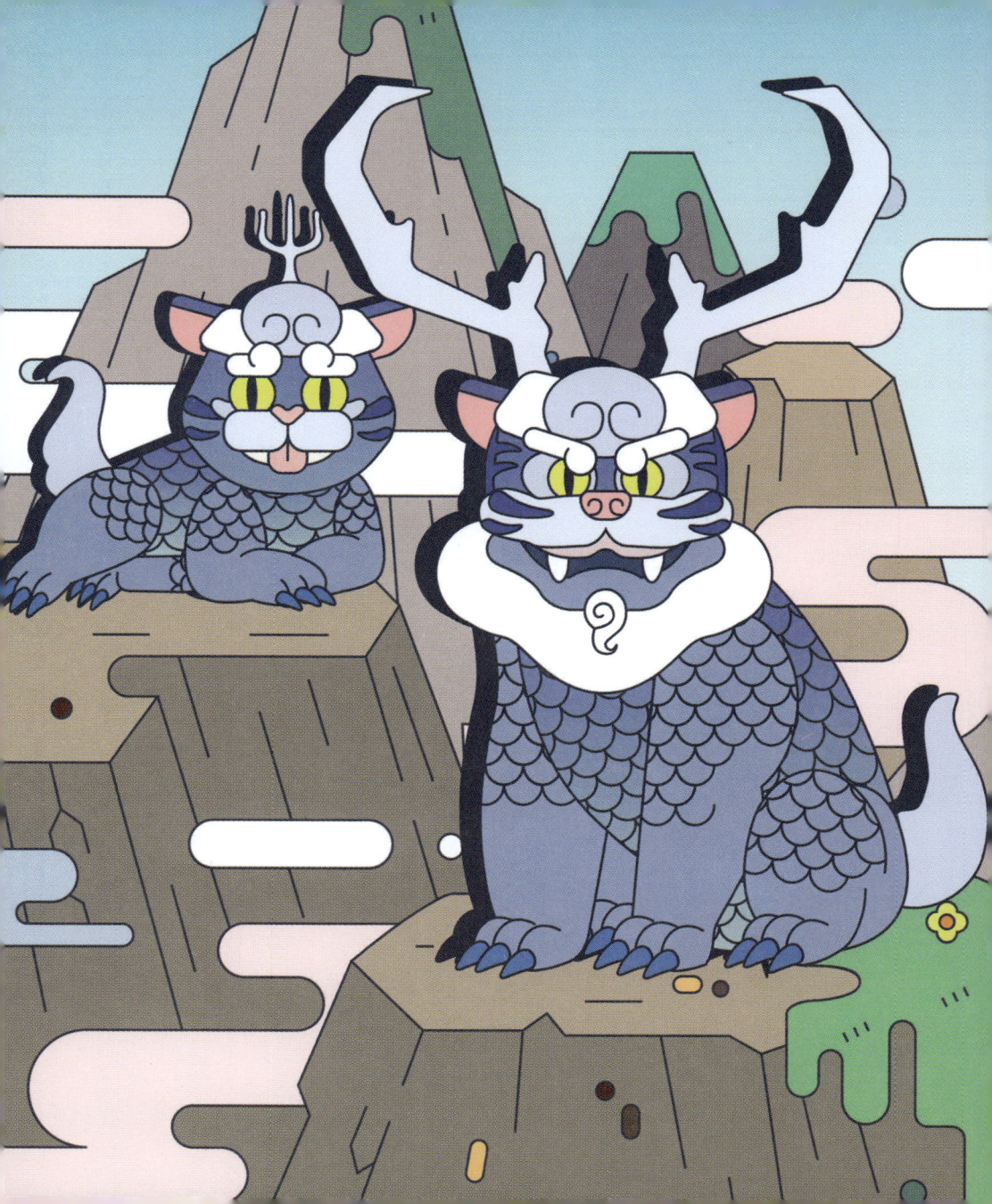

Choonggiyoso

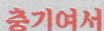

Choonggiyoso, known as Burdlee in MeoShín'Ké, are dust yogwe that look like the fluffy buds of pussy willow. They form suddenly in the air, sometimes in huge numbers, and drift around in a great cloud.

Their cuteness brings people's guard down, but Burdlee are wary little creatures. If you try to touch them when they don't want to be bothered, they can bite you or, worse, dig into your skin and cause skin disease. Burdlee-itis is hard to treat with regular medicine, so best avoid petting them without their permission. If you wait patiently enough, though, they may relax and come to you first.

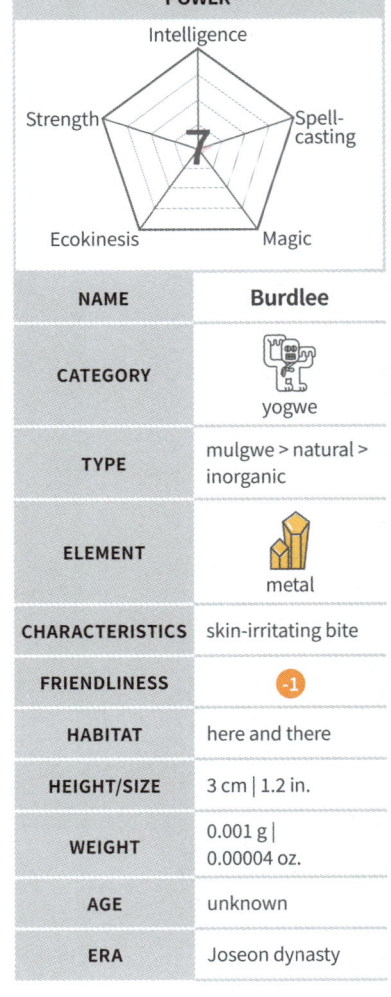

POWER	
	Intelligence / Strength — 7 — Spell-casting / Ecokinesis — Magic
NAME	**Burdlee**
CATEGORY	yogwe
TYPE	mulgwe > natural > inorganic
ELEMENT	metal
CHARACTERISTICS	skin-irritating bite
FRIENDLINESS	-1
HABITAT	here and there
HEIGHT/SIZE	3 cm | 1.2 in.
WEIGHT	0.001 g | 0.00004 oz.
AGE	unknown
ERA	Joseon dynasty

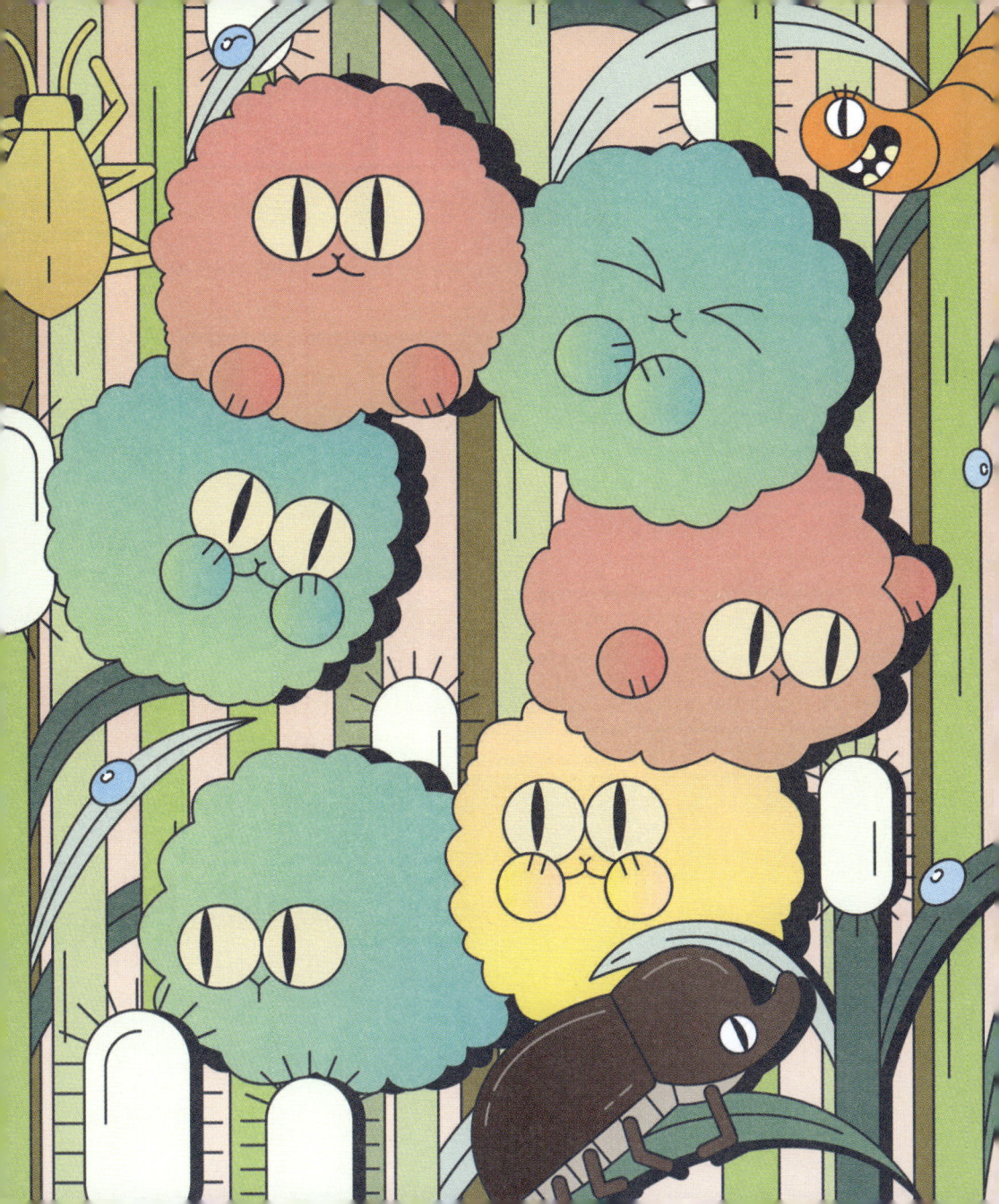

Taktak Guibyung

탁탁귀병

Taktak Guibyung are the ghosts of soldiers who died needlessly in battle. Sightings of them spiked after the Qing invasion of Joseon. Usually active at night and moving in hordes, Taktak Guibyung are always armored and clutching weapons, but the truly frightening sight is their empty eyes.

These ghosts make a *taktak* or *toktok* sound, which is what gave them their name. This sound is so chilling that it scares the sleep away from anyone who hears it. It is said to be the soldiers' last howl of fear and rage before they were killed. To escape them, you must howl louder than they do.

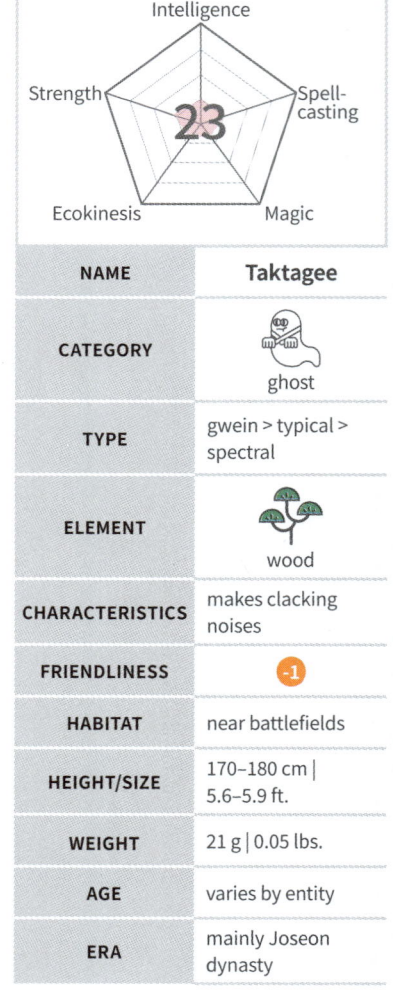

POWER

Intelligence

Strength

Spell-casting

Ecokinesis

Magic

23

NAME	**Taktagee**
CATEGORY	ghost
TYPE	gwein > typical > spectral
ELEMENT	wood
CHARACTERISTICS	makes clacking noises
FRIENDLINESS	-1
HABITAT	near battlefields
HEIGHT/SIZE	170–180 cm | 5.6–5.9 ft.
WEIGHT	21 g | 0.05 lbs.
AGE	varies by entity
ERA	mainly Joseon dynasty

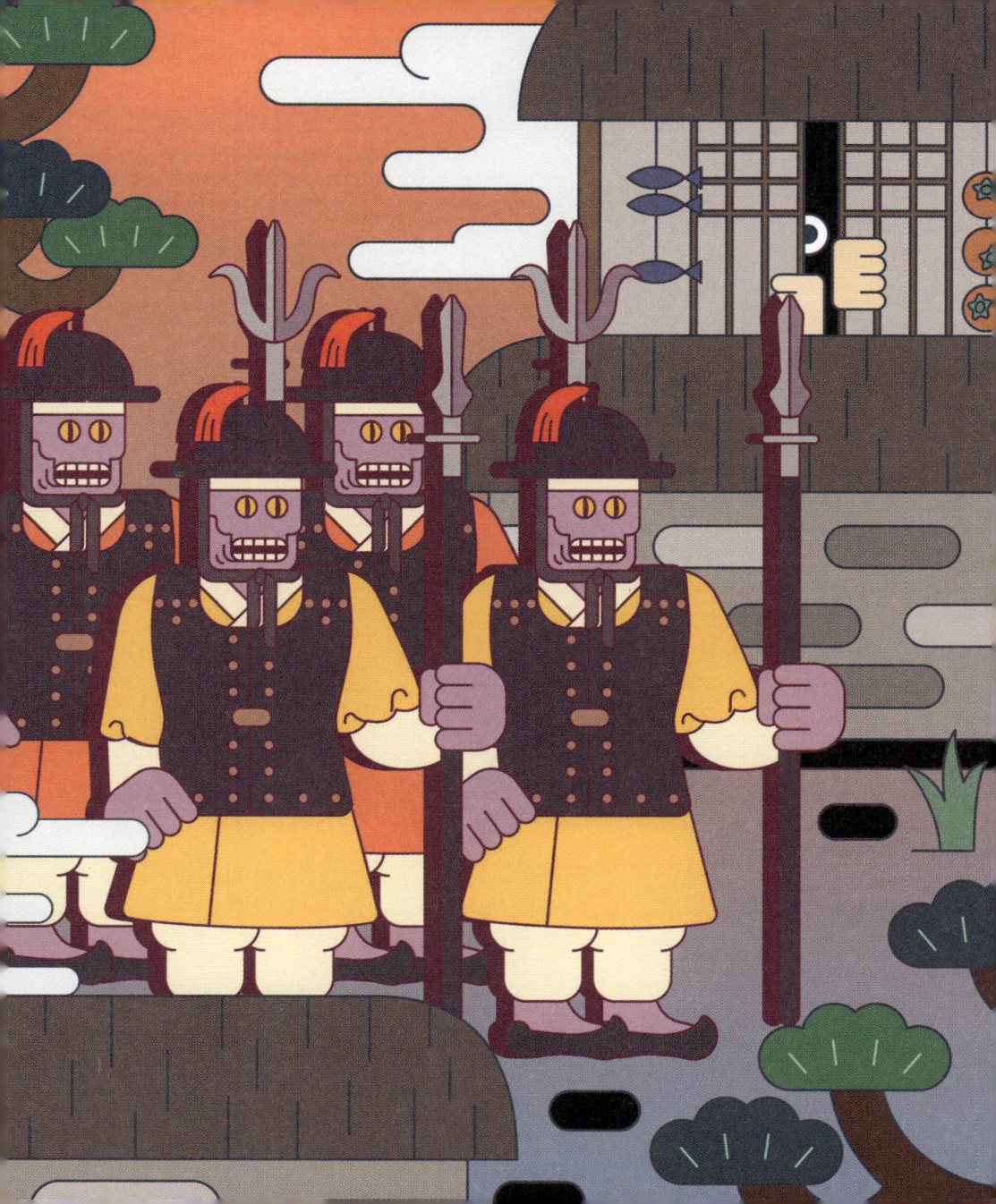

Haetae

해태

Haetae is a noble shinsu that judges right from wrong, good from evil. The name can mean "an official from the heavens" and is used interchangeably with the name "Haechi." The creature resembles an enormous tiger with great, dazzling yellow eyes that discern the nature of things and sharp claws that swipe away evil. Hard, purple scales cover its length, and feathers extend out from its armpits like wings.

As the appraiser of truth and lies, virtue and vice, Haetae takes justice seriously and exacts merciless retribution. And as a water shinsu filled with the energy of holy water, it is resilient against and can prevent fires. In fact, it can predict other types of disasters and stop them from happening. Every bit as mighty as it looks, Haetae is said to outmatch beasts of all kinds.

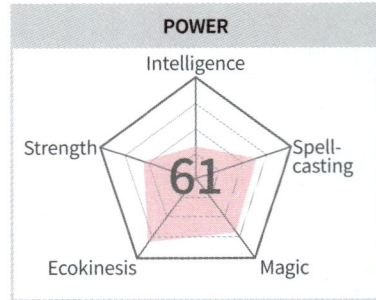

POWER

61

NAME	Haetae
CATEGORY	shinsu
TYPE	shinsu > innate
ELEMENT	water
CHARACTERISTICS	fire-preventing water shinsu; arbiter of morality
FRIENDLINESS	+2★
HABITAT	Jade Emperor's palace
HEIGHT/SIZE	400 cm | 13 ft. (can change in size)
WEIGHT	330 kg | 728 lbs.
AGE	2,278
ERA	antiquity

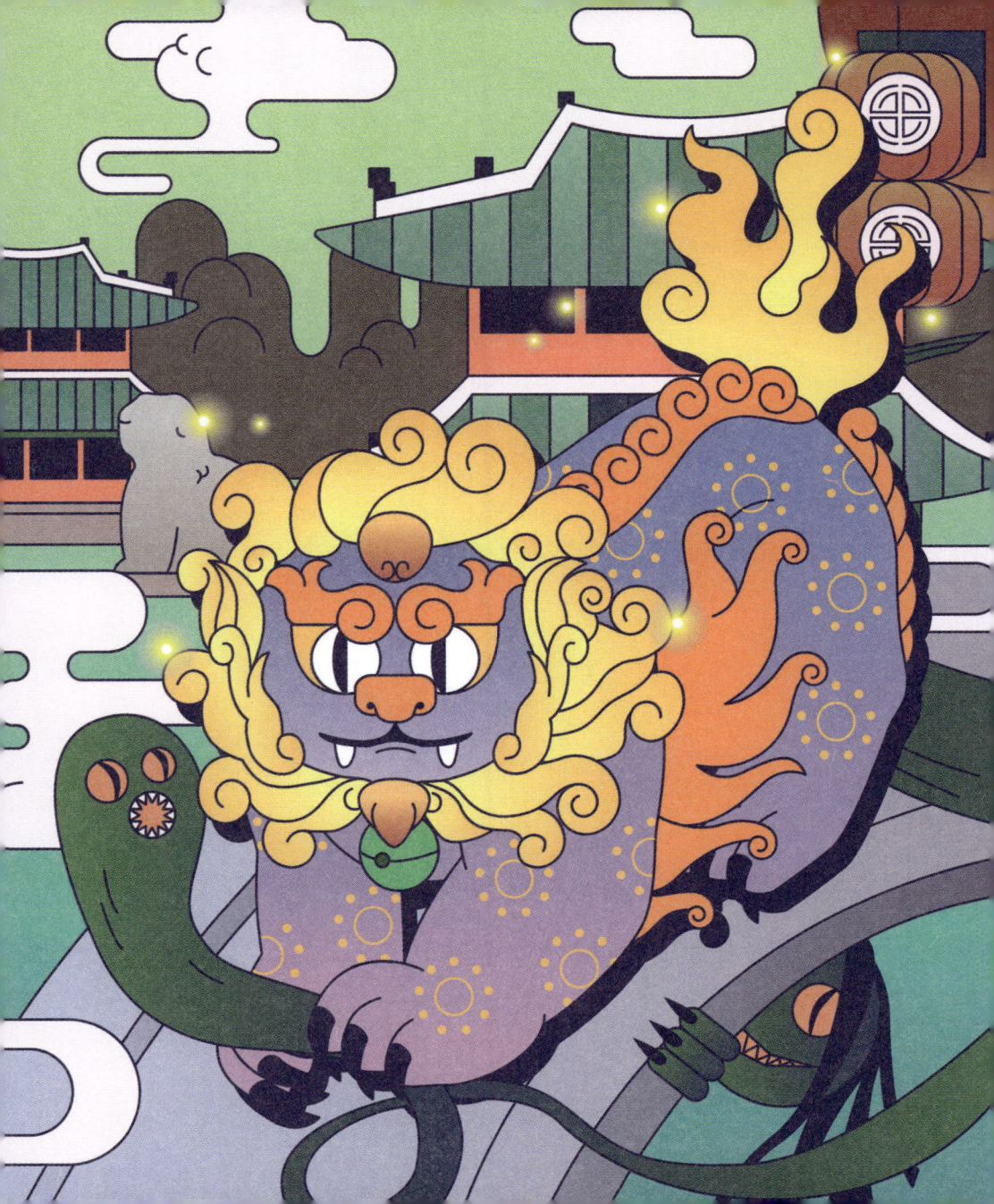

Homoonjo

호문조

Homoonjo is a bird yogwe large enough to swallow a human in one gulp. It has crimson feathers with distinct tiger stripes in an even deeper red. Thanks to its striking plumage, Homoonjo is impossible to miss when it soars over the sea.

The bird nests on small islands and often hunts fishermen. With sharp talons optimized to seize prey, Homoonjo is lightning fast when it hunts but otherwise moves very slowly. It has poor vision and sense of smell, so you can still get away if you hide yourself carefully. If you happen to see Homoonjo in flight, take cover. Fast.

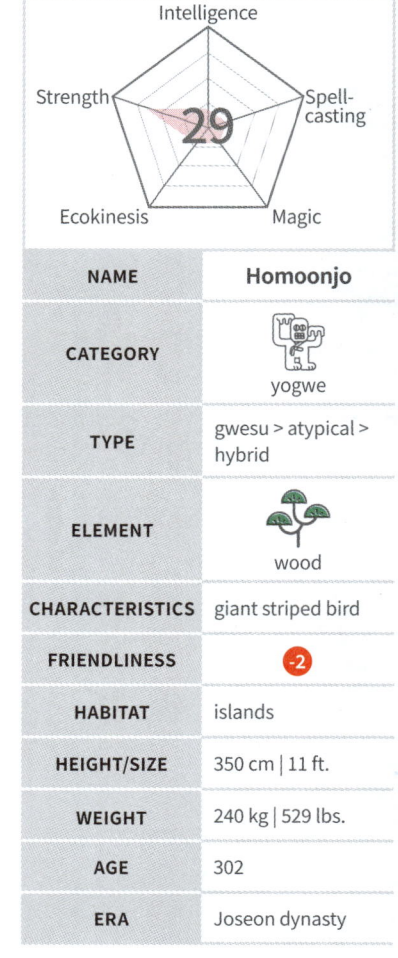

POWER

Intelligence · Strength · Spell-casting · Magic · Ecokinesis

29

NAME	Homoonjo
CATEGORY	yogwe
TYPE	gwesu > atypical > hybrid
ELEMENT	wood
CHARACTERISTICS	giant striped bird
FRIENDLINESS	-2
HABITAT	islands
HEIGHT/SIZE	350 cm | 11 ft.
WEIGHT	240 kg | 529 lbs.
AGE	302
ERA	Joseon dynasty

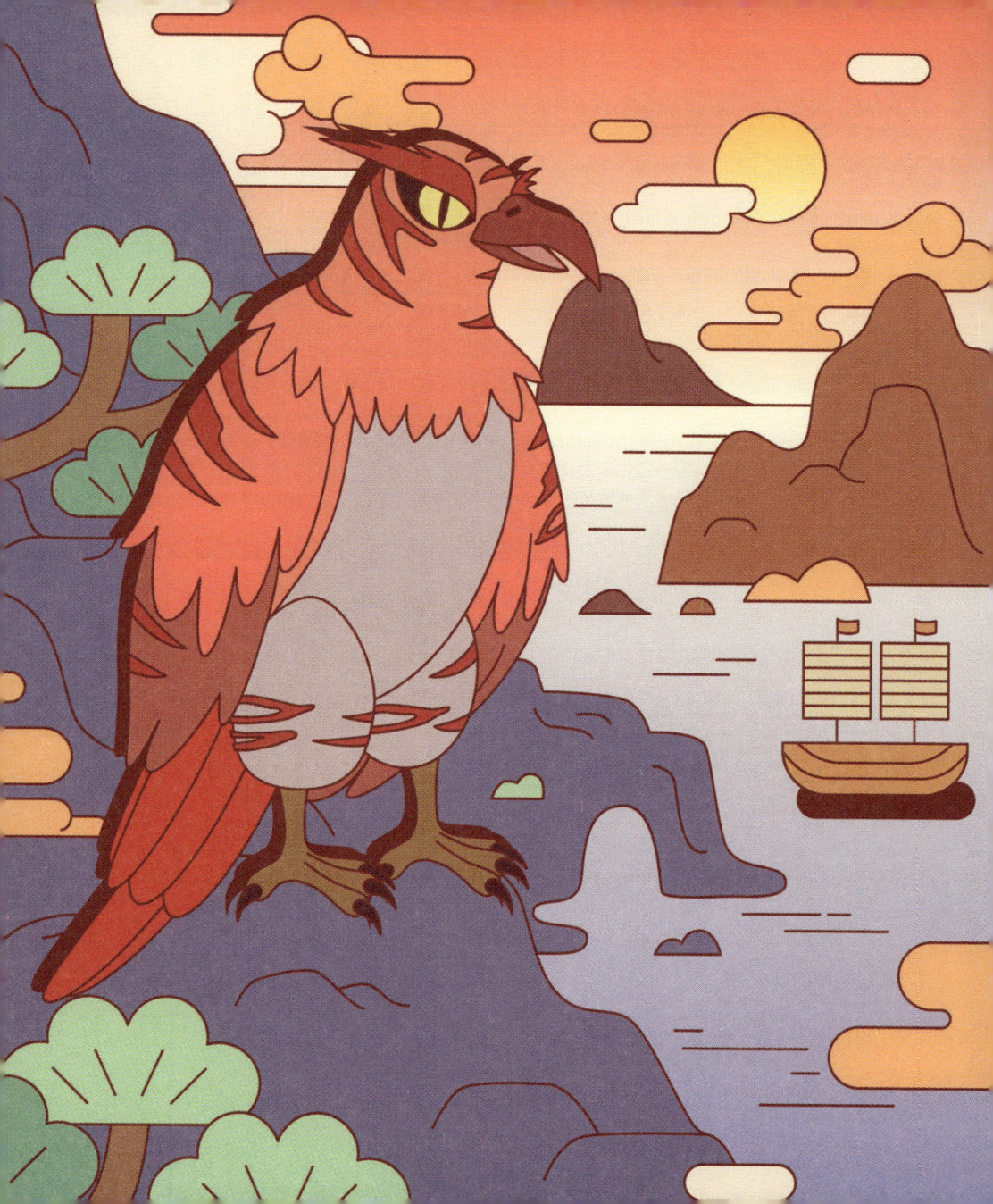

Hwang-Ryong

Hwang-ryong is a sky dragon that symbolizes the center of the cosmos. It guards the heavens and toils to achieve balance in the universe. Shimmering in gold all over, the shinsu is magnificent to behold. Hwang-ryong is the mightiest of all dragons and has all-seeing eyes that most don't dare to meet. As the master of the weather, it appears with a crack of lightning and leaves wisps of clouds in its wake. With many other wondrous powers, Hwang-ryong is a shinsu that is both feared and revered.

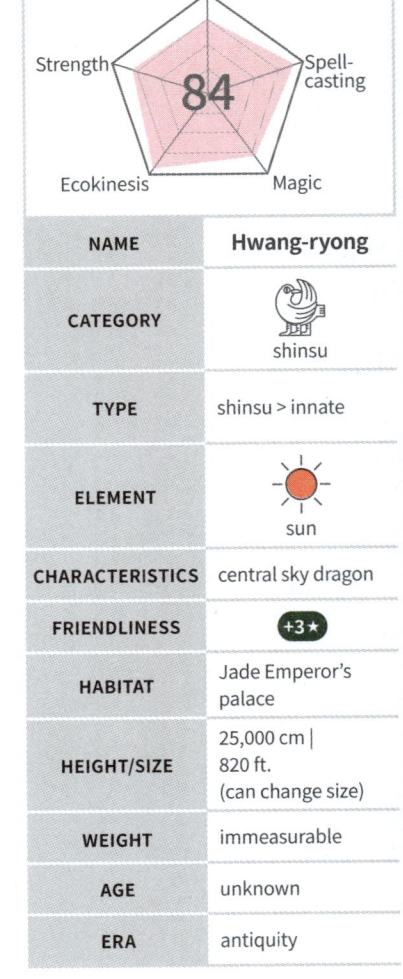

NAME	Hwang-ryong
CATEGORY	shinsu
TYPE	shinsu > innate
ELEMENT	sun
CHARACTERISTICS	central sky dragon
FRIENDLINESS	+3★
HABITAT	Jade Emperor's palace
HEIGHT/SIZE	25,000 cm | 820 ft. (can change size)
WEIGHT	immeasurable
AGE	unknown
ERA	antiquity

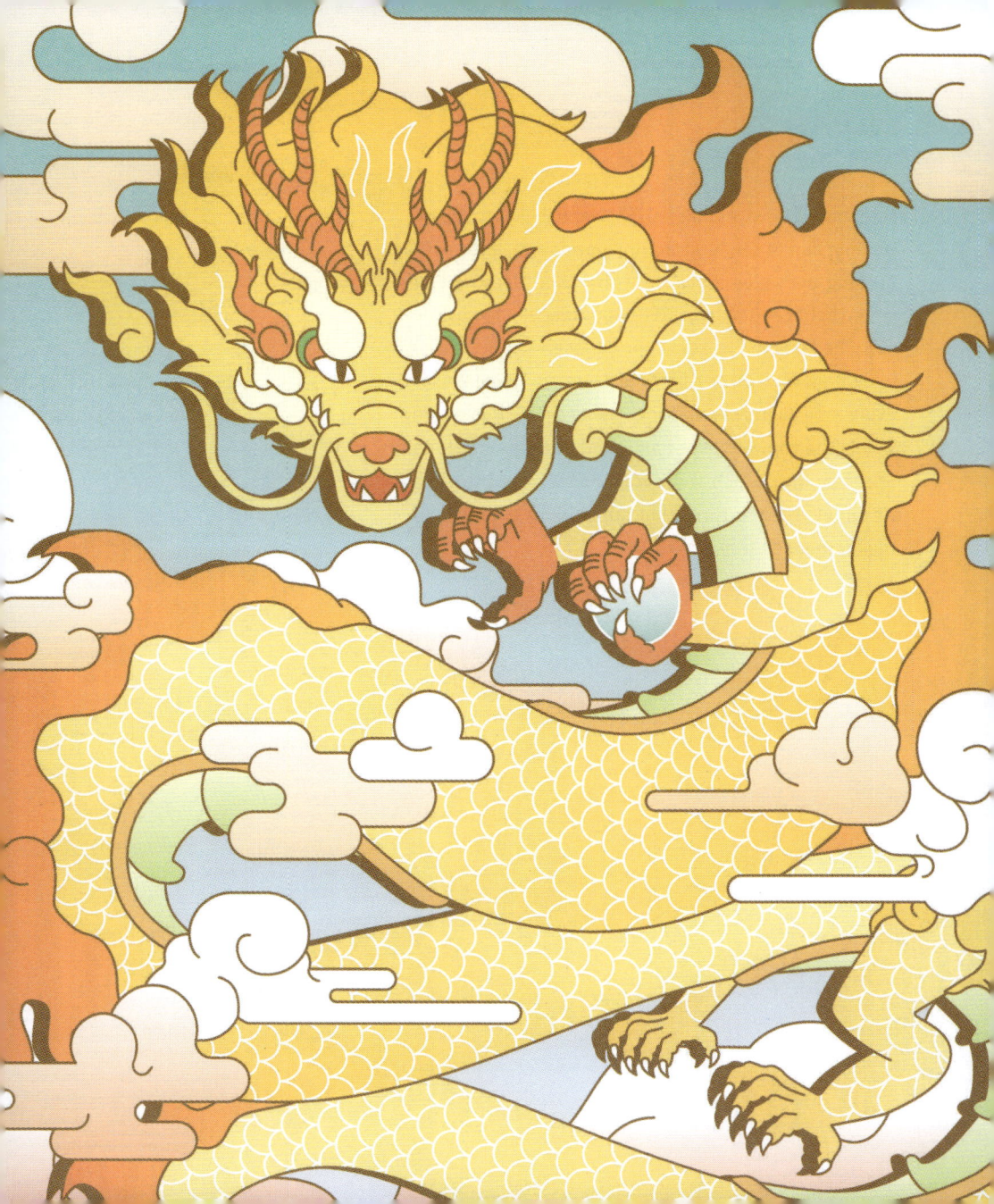

Hoemm

Hoemm is a lewd, monkeyish yogwe that likes to spy on bathing humans. It lurks around ponds and lakes, eyes flashing with glee. Because it dwells in deep waters where light can't reach, it is temporarily blinded by the sun when it emerges above the surface.

Whenever it takes a fancy to a human, Hoemm uses every magical power and trick up its sleeve to capture them. The yogwe is especially good at conjuring cloud and fog, with which it reduces visibility and isolates its target. Then, it turns that human into a ghost and makes them its servant.

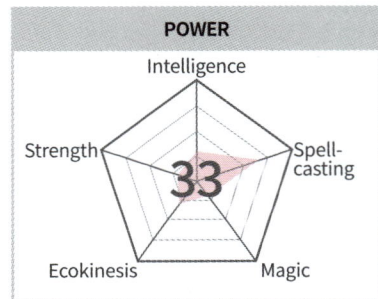

POWER

(radar chart: Intelligence, Spell-casting, Magic, Ecokinesis, Strength — center value **33**)

NAME	Hoemm
CATEGORY	yogwe
TYPE	gwesu > typical > magical
ELEMENT	water
CHARACTERISTICS	turns humans into ghosts
FRIENDLINESS	-2
HABITAT	mountain ponds
HEIGHT/SIZE	132 cm | 4.3 ft.
WEIGHT	50 kg | 110 lbs.
AGE	380
ERA	Joseon dynasty

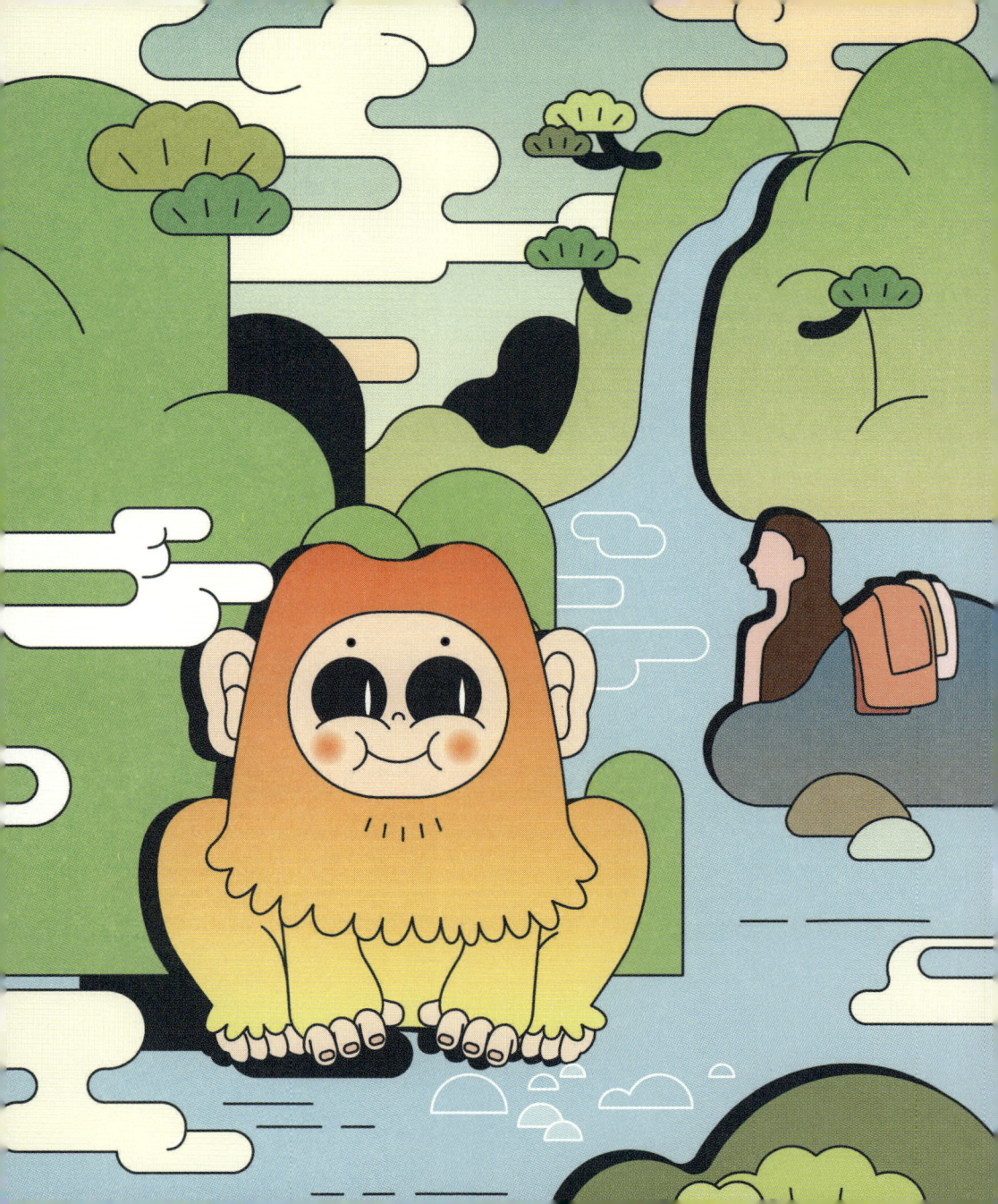

부록

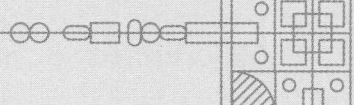

Appendix

Here, you will see the notes left by a human who was personally granted a visit to MeoShín'Ké by MeoShin. You can find surprising snippets about supernatural beings never mentioned in old stories and records. If, however, you divulge these secrets to anyone else in the human world, we cannot predict what will happen next.

cat Head + Snake Body
Meowdusa

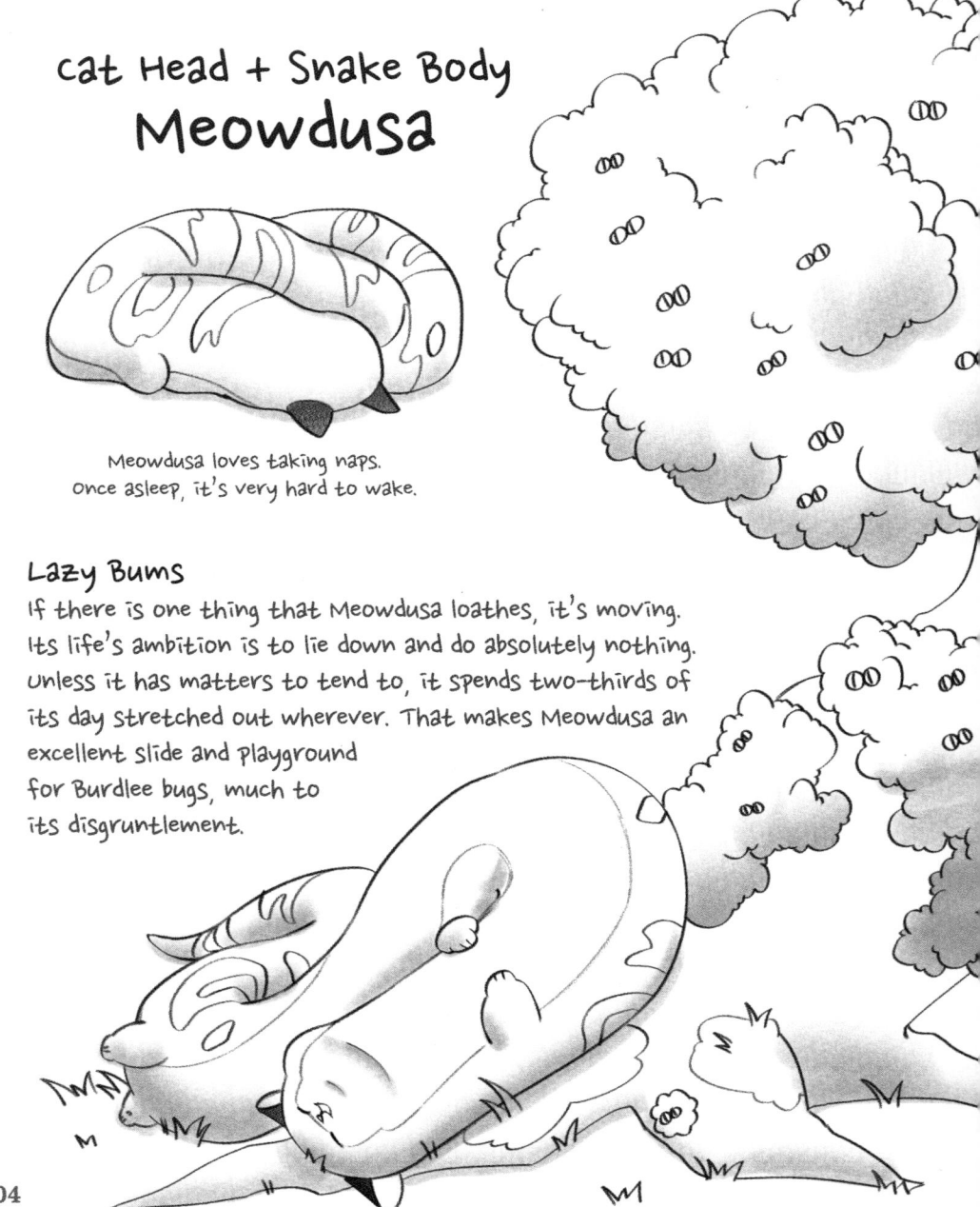

Meowdusa loves taking naps.
Once asleep, it's very hard to wake.

Lazy Bums

If there is one thing that Meowdusa loathes, it's moving.
Its life's ambition is to lie down and do absolutely nothing.
Unless it has matters to tend to, it spends two-thirds of
its day stretched out wherever. That makes Meowdusa an
excellent slide and playground
for Burdlee bugs, much to
its disgruntlement.

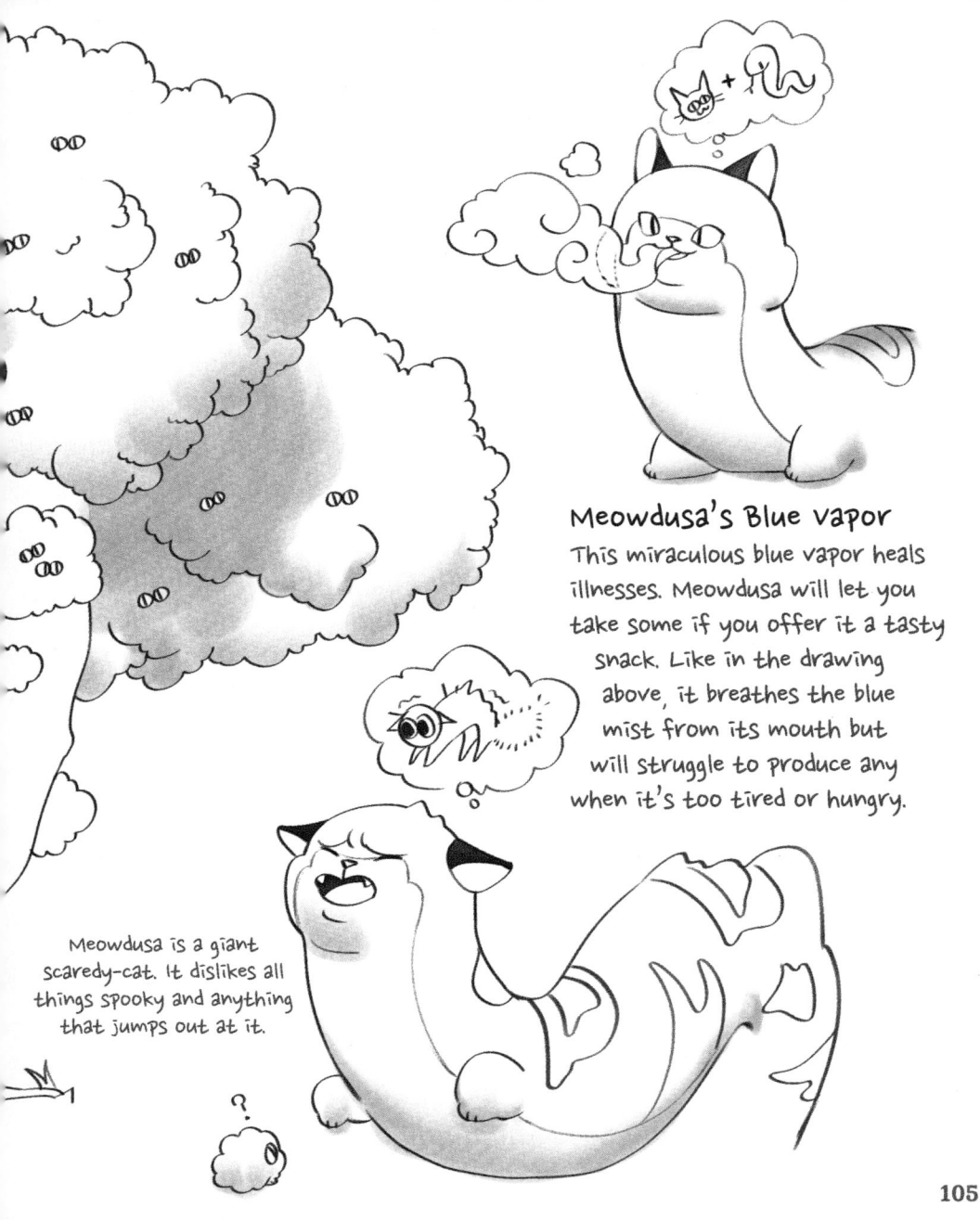

Meowdusa's Blue vapor

This miraculous blue vapor heals illnesses. Meowdusa will let you take some if you offer it a tasty snack. Like in the drawing above, it breathes the blue mist from its mouth but will struggle to produce any when it's too tired or hungry.

Meowdusa is a giant scaredy-cat. It dislikes all things spooky and anything that jumps out at it.

Movement

Meowdusa . . .

1. moves like a snake when
   a. coiling up in one spot
   b. slithering up a tree

2. uses four legs when
   a. walking or running
      (watch its belly
      jiggle when it runs)

3. flies (only rarely, as
   that requires way too
   much energy)

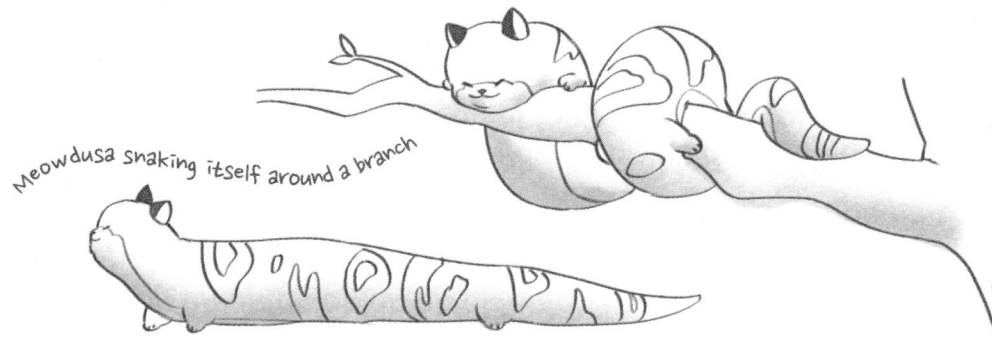

Meowdusa snaking itself around a branch

Flexible Spine

Meowdusa's skeleton consists of the skull and the bones in its body (basically the spine and ribs). Its spine is made up of over 400 vertebrae, which is the secret to Meowdusa's flexibility. Each vertebrae can bend up to about 25 degrees up, down, left, and right, allowing Meowdusa to move as though it were boneless.

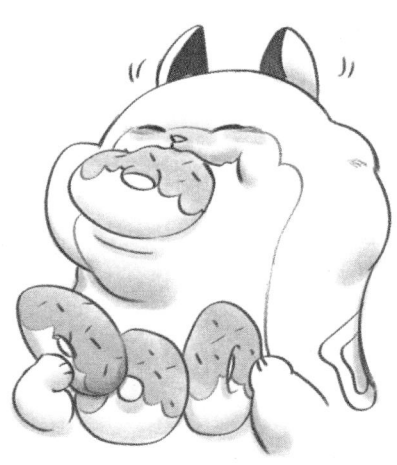

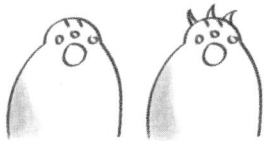

Meowdusa will flex its claws
when you try to steal its food.

Fun fact: Each paw has three toes.

Big Appetite

Meowdusa loves to eat all sorts of things,
but it's especially partial to donuts and
other sweets. More often than not, its
chipmunk cheeks are bulging with food.

Unlike snakes, Meowdusa doesn't
hibernate. But come winter, it
stocks up on heaps of food and
rarely ventures out of its cave.

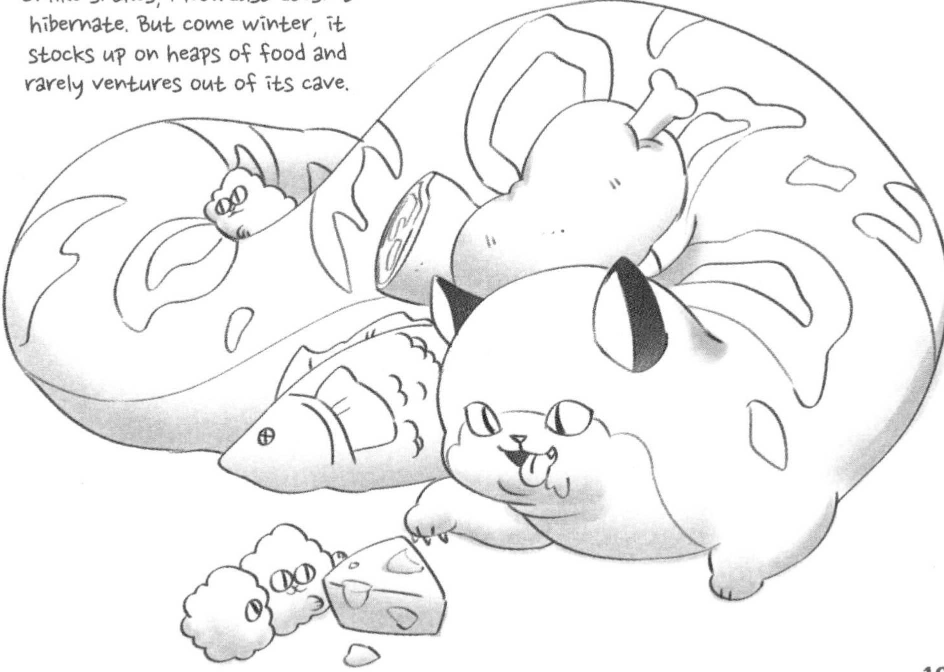

Burdlee Here, Burdlee There

Burdlee bugs are everywhere in Meoshin'Ké, yet they're often invisible as they blend so well into grass, clouds, and other things in nature.

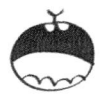 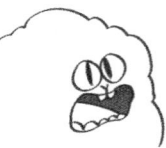

They're tiny, cute, and so fluffy you will be tempted to touch them. But beware, they bite!

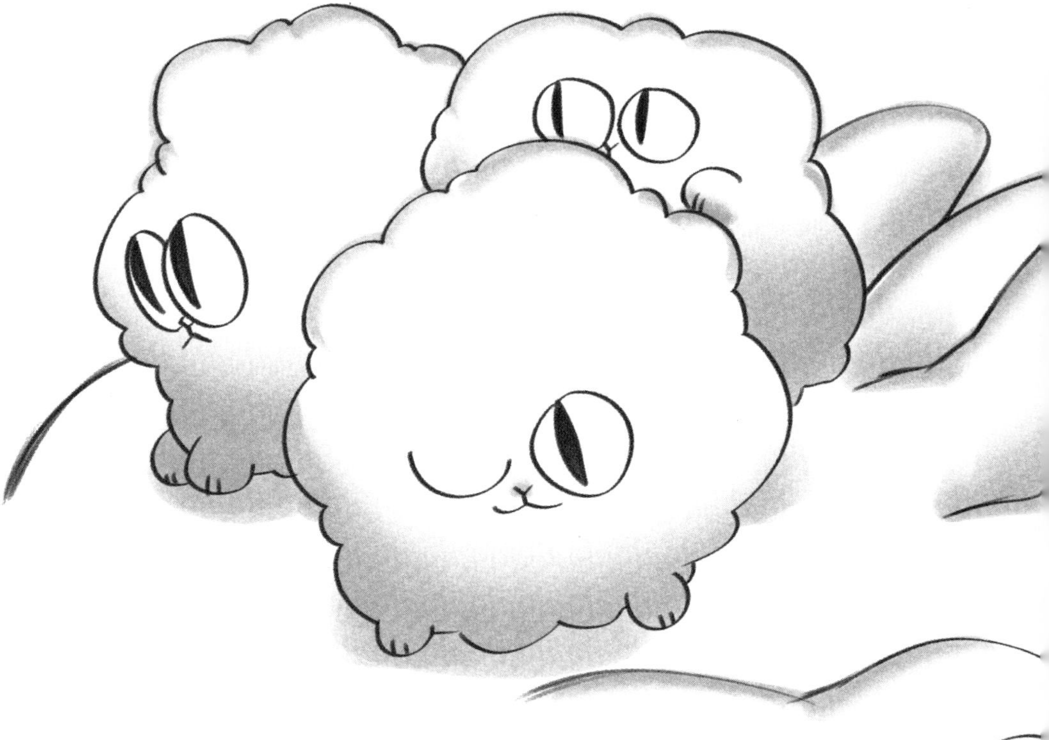

Burdlee are sexless creatures. They shed their coat of fur once it grows impressively poofy. And from these fallen furballs, out pop baby Burdlee bugs!

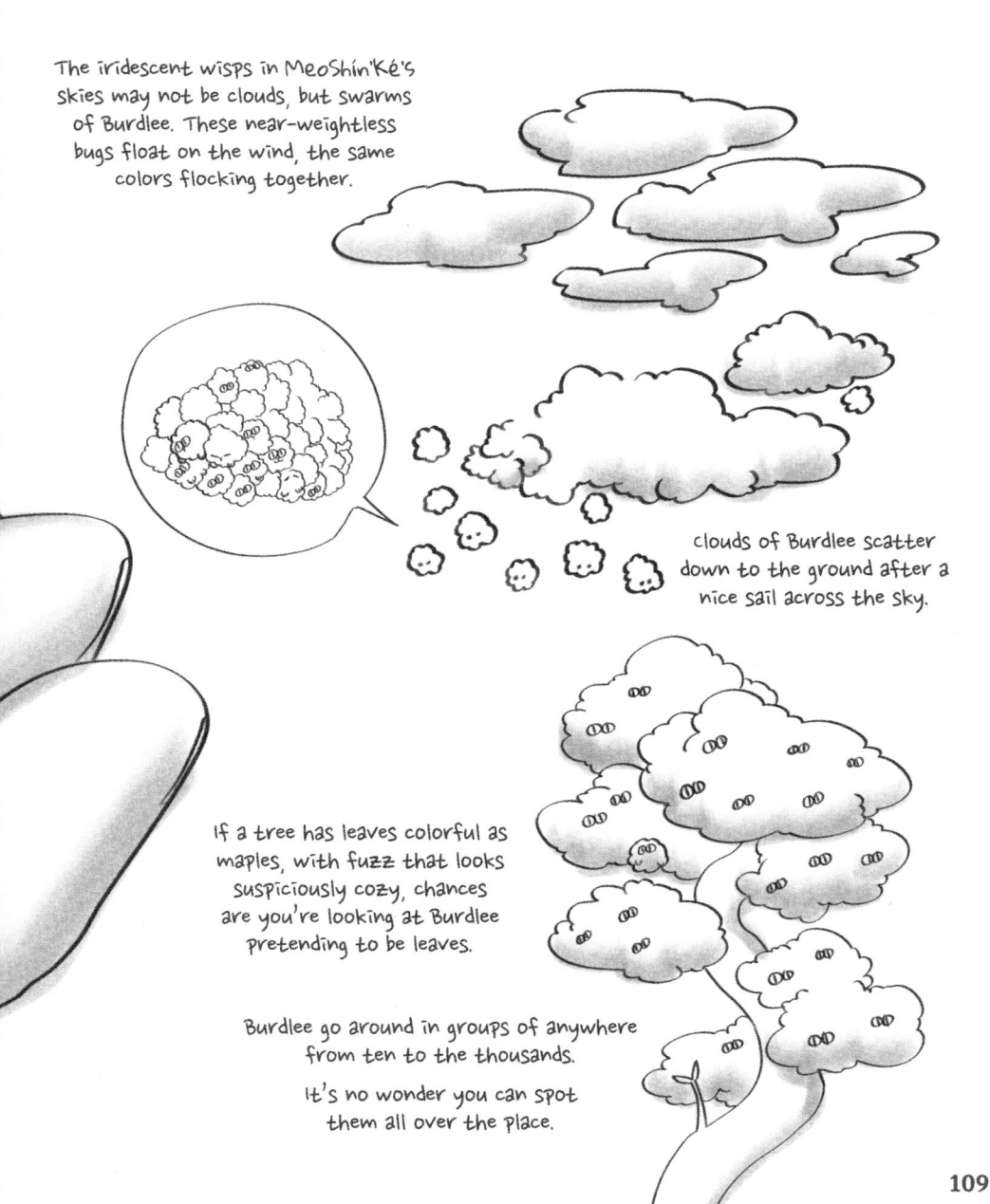

The iridescent wisps in MeoShin'Ké's skies may not be clouds, but swarms of Burdlee. These near-weightless bugs float on the wind, the same colors flocking together.

clouds of Burdlee scatter down to the ground after a nice sail across the sky.

If a tree has leaves colorful as maples, with fuzz that looks suspiciously cozy, chances are you're looking at Burdlee pretending to be leaves.

Burdlee go around in groups of anywhere from ten to the thousands.

It's no wonder you can spot them all over the place.

Types of Goain

1. Goain

Many eons ago, these giants helped create the world. They have moss, starfish, and barnacles stuck on their bodies, as if they've just woken up from a long slumber under the sea.

Some of the starfish are yogwe. Strike up a conversation with them, and they might regale you with the wildest tales.

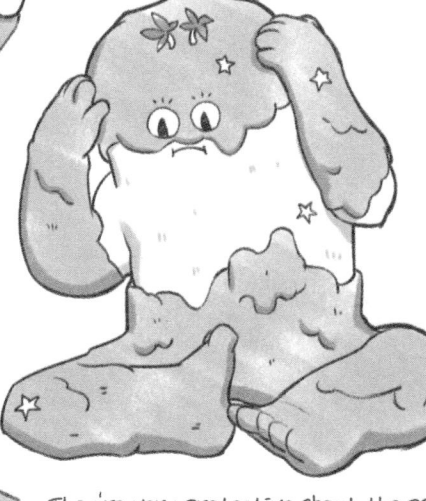

They're very protective about the pair of palm trees growing on their heads.

2. Goain of Tall People Kingdom

The Goain of Tall People Kingdom are a hairy bunch, their entire bodies covered in black fuzz (they can pass for giant gorillas). Maybe all that hair keeps them warm in Tall People Kingdom, which is somewhere up north, though nobody knows exactly where?

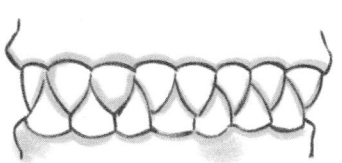

Terrifying saw-like teeth

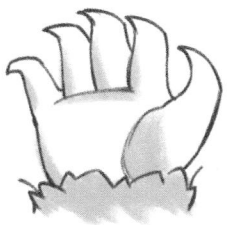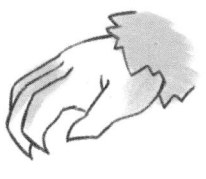

claw-like hands. One swipe and you'd be a goner. If you encounter this Goain, watch out for the hands!

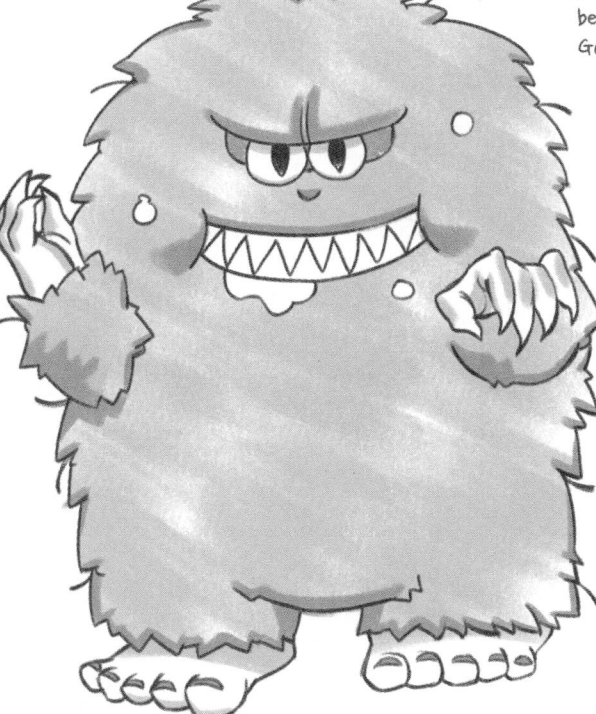

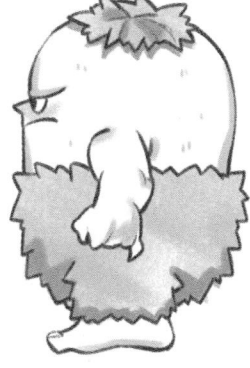

A balding Goain. Tall People Kingdom's Goain are mortally afraid of hair loss. Hair seems to be a symbol of power in these parts.

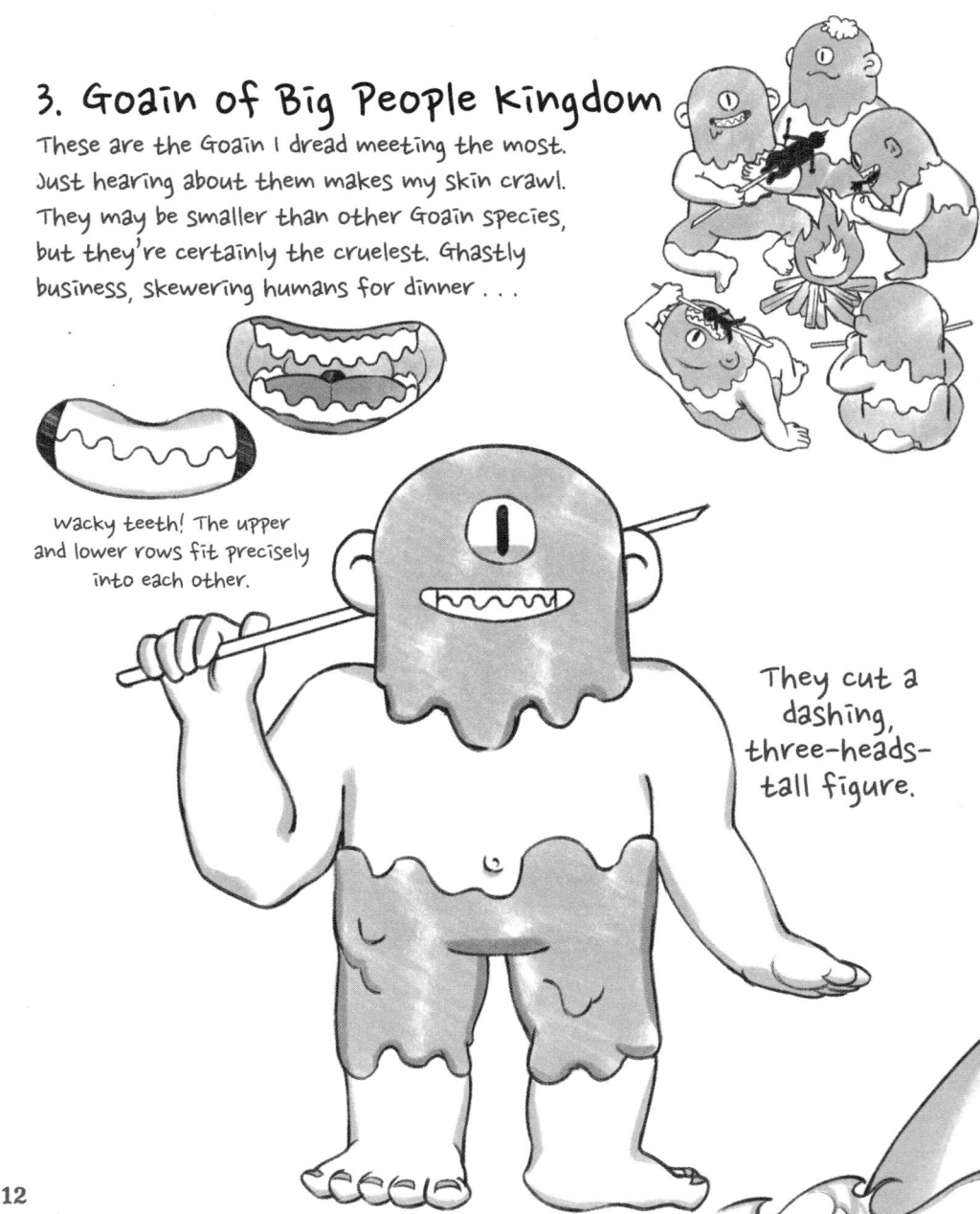

3. Goain of Big People Kingdom

These are the Goain I dread meeting the most.
Just hearing about them makes my skin crawl.
They may be smaller than other Goain species,
but they're certainly the cruelest. Ghastly
business, skewering humans for dinner . . .

Wacky teeth! The upper
and lower rows fit precisely
into each other.

They cut a
dashing,
three-heads-
tall figure.

4. Goain of the Sea

Facing these sea giants—the biggest of the Goain—feels like meeting great cannibal whales. They can talk with humans, but only in simple, childish sentences (forget about persuading them not to eat you; just run).

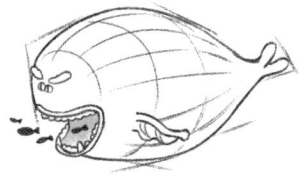

When they find a school of fish, they open their jaws and CHARGE.

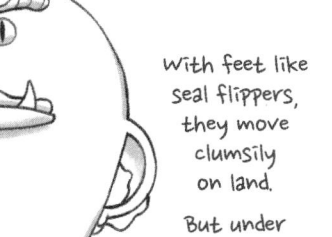

With feet like seal flippers, they move clumsily on land.

But under water, they're unbeatable.

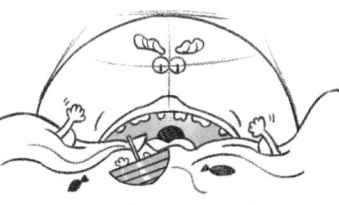

They swallow ships whole.

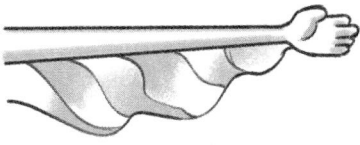

Their arms are similar to human arms but are lined with fins from armpit to wrist.

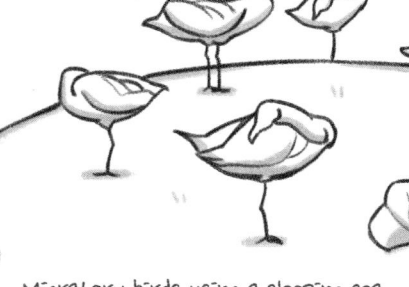

Migratory birds using a sleeping sea Goain's head as a rest stop

Sammoku &
King Sammok the Great

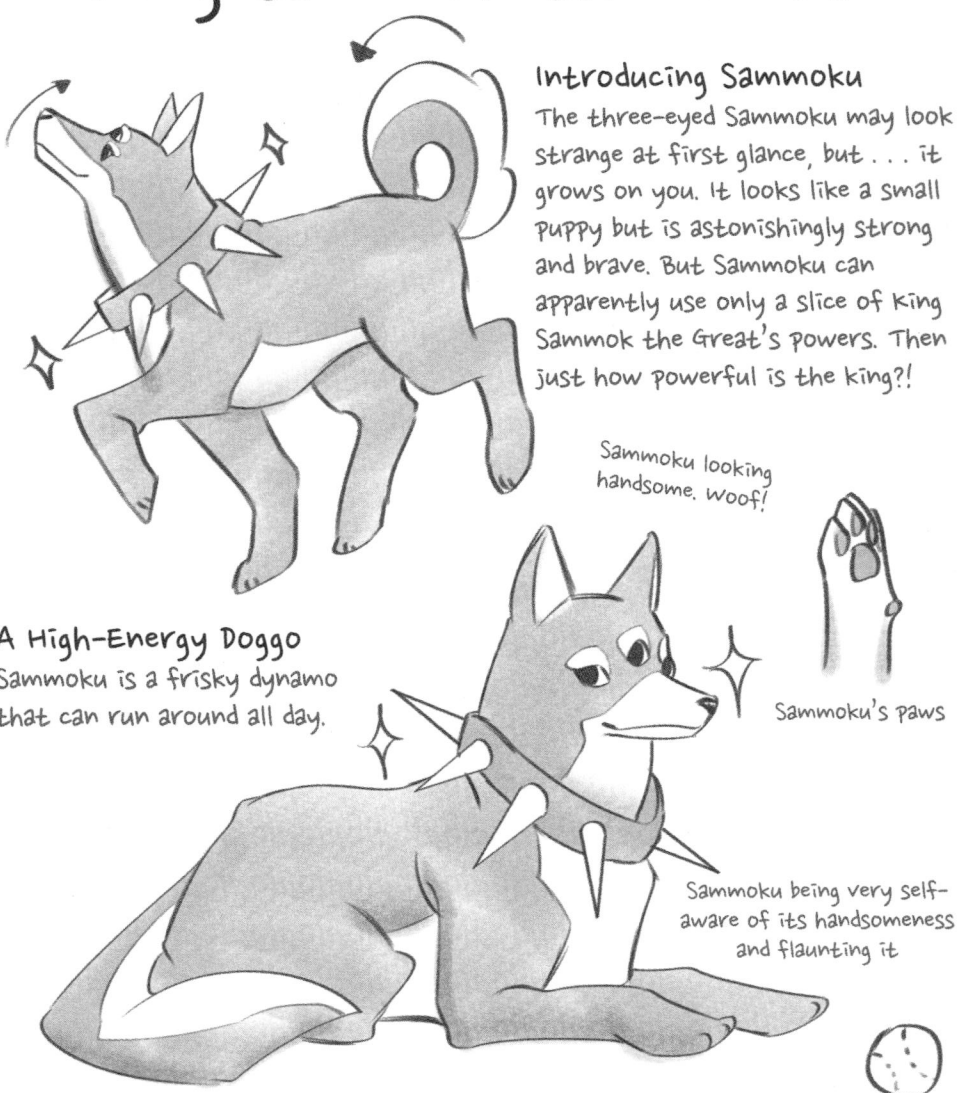

Introducing Sammoku

The three-eyed Sammoku may look strange at first glance, but . . . it grows on you. It looks like a small puppy but is astonishingly strong and brave. But Sammoku can apparently use only a slice of King Sammok the Great's powers. Then just how powerful is the king?!

Sammoku looking handsome. Woof!

A High-Energy Doggo

Sammoku is a frisky dynamo that can run around all day.

Sammoku's paws

Sammoku being very self-aware of its handsomeness and flaunting it

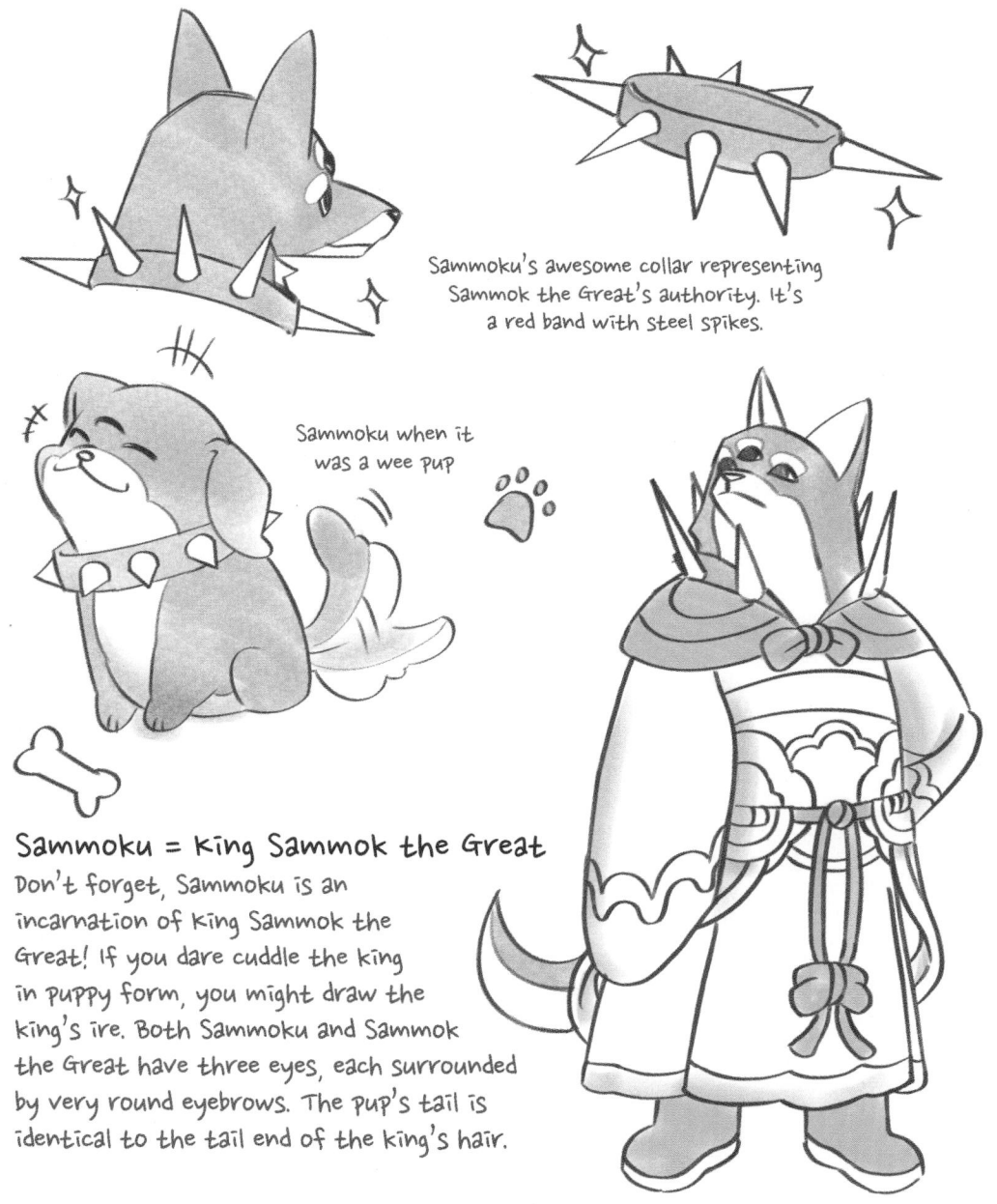

Sammoku's awesome collar representing Sammok the Great's authority. It's a red band with steel spikes.

Sammoku when it was a wee pup

Sammoku = King Sammok the Great

Don't forget, Sammoku is an incarnation of King Sammok the Great! If you dare cuddle the king in puppy form, you might draw the king's ire. Both Sammoku and Sammok the Great have three eyes, each surrounded by very round eyebrows. The pup's tail is identical to the tail end of the king's hair.

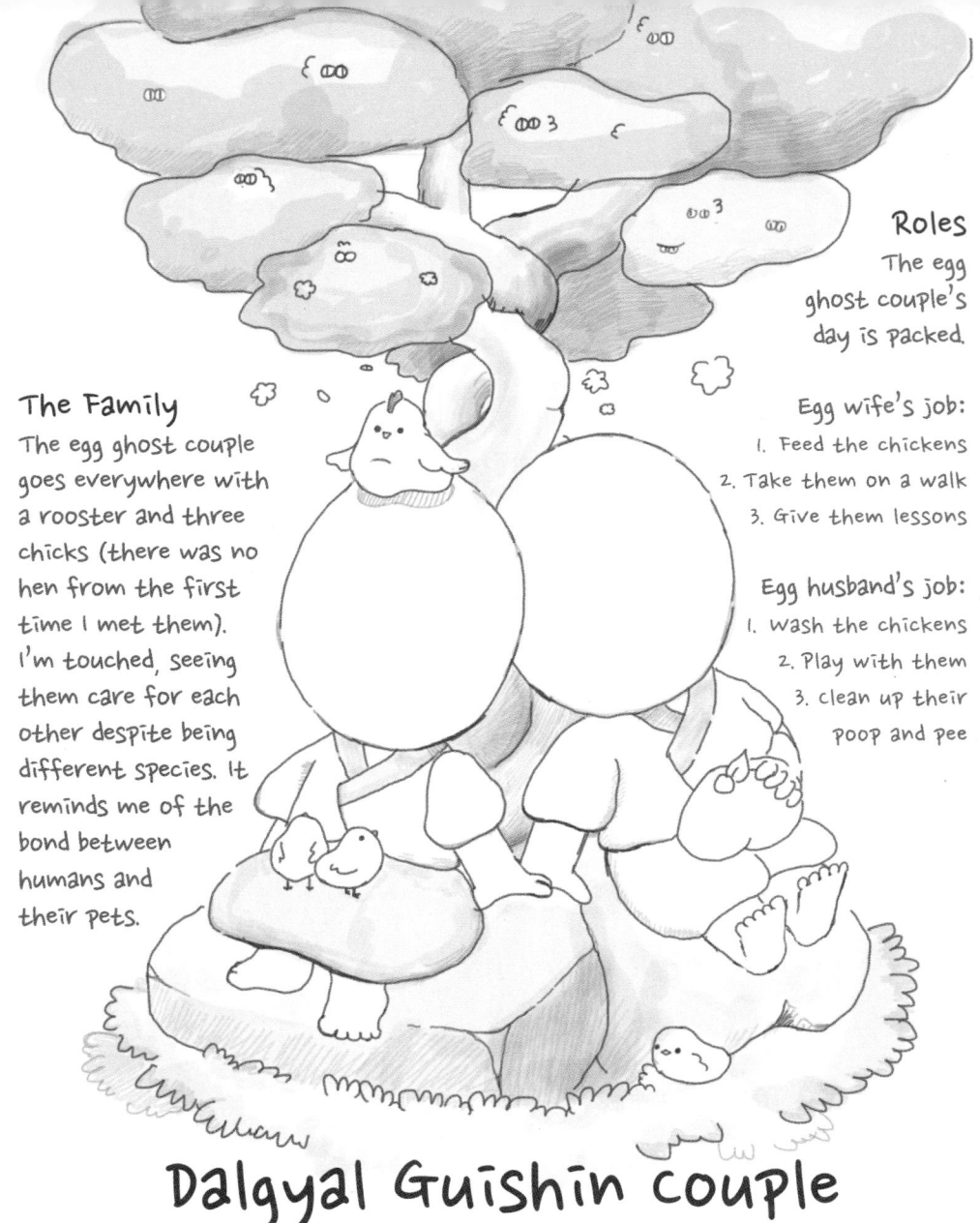

The egg
ghost couple's
day is packed.

Egg wife's job:
1. Feed the chickens
2. Take them on a walk
3. Give them lessons

Egg husband's job:
1. Wash the chickens
2. Play with them
3. Clean up their
poop and pee

The Family
The egg ghost couple
goes everywhere with
a rooster and three
chicks (there was no
hen from the first
time I met them).
I'm touched, seeing
them care for each
other despite being
different species. It
reminds me of the
bond between
humans and
their pets.

Dalgyal Guishin couple

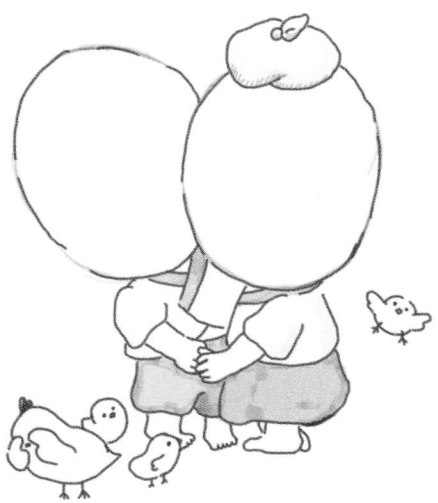

Egg-cellent chemistry

The couple is so lovey-dovey that even the chickens cluck in embarrassment.

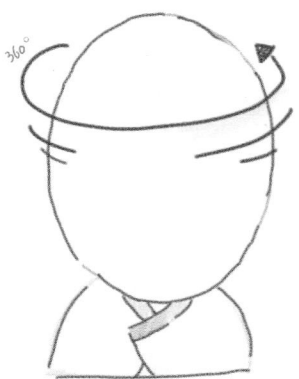

Swiveling Head

Egg ghosts can apparently turn their heads a full 360 degrees—and even spin them very fast!—but you can never tell if you're looking at the back of their heads or the front.

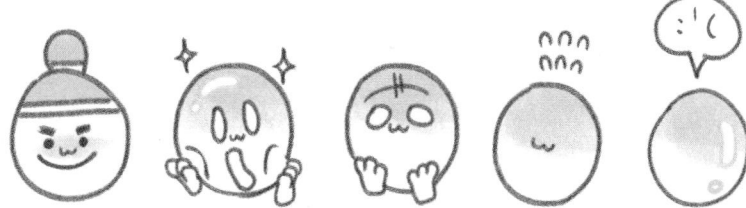

Progression of Egg Face Sickness

DAY 1: You lose all hair on your face and head, including the eyebrows, beard, peach fuzz, everything!

DAY 2: Starting from the corners, your lips start sealing up until you can't open your mouth. Eventually, your lips disappear.

DAY 3: Your eyes slowly seal up until you can no longer see.

DAY 4: Your nose, the last remaining feature, melts away. Your face is smooth as an egg.

Stages of a
Dongjasam's Growth

If an ordinary wild ginseng matures for a very long time, soaking up the earth's energy, it turns into a sentient being called a Dongjasam. Because ginseng is a prized medicinal herb, humans dig it right up as soon as they find one, so precious few grow into Dongjasam.

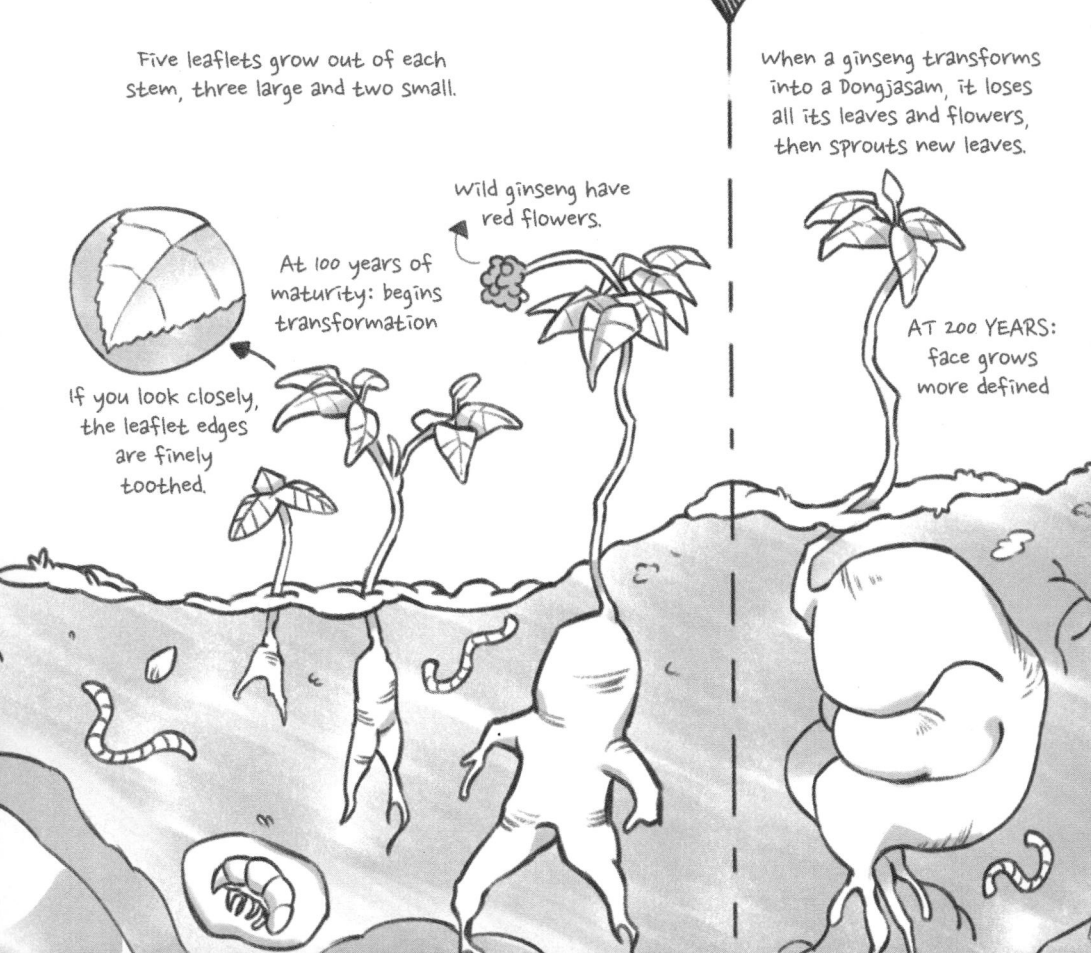

Five leaflets grow out of each stem, three large and two small.

When a ginseng transforms into a Dongjasam, it loses all its leaves and flowers, then sprouts new leaves.

Wild ginseng have red flowers.

At 100 years of maturity: begins transformation

If you look closely, the leaflet edges are finely toothed.

AT 200 YEARS: face grows more defined

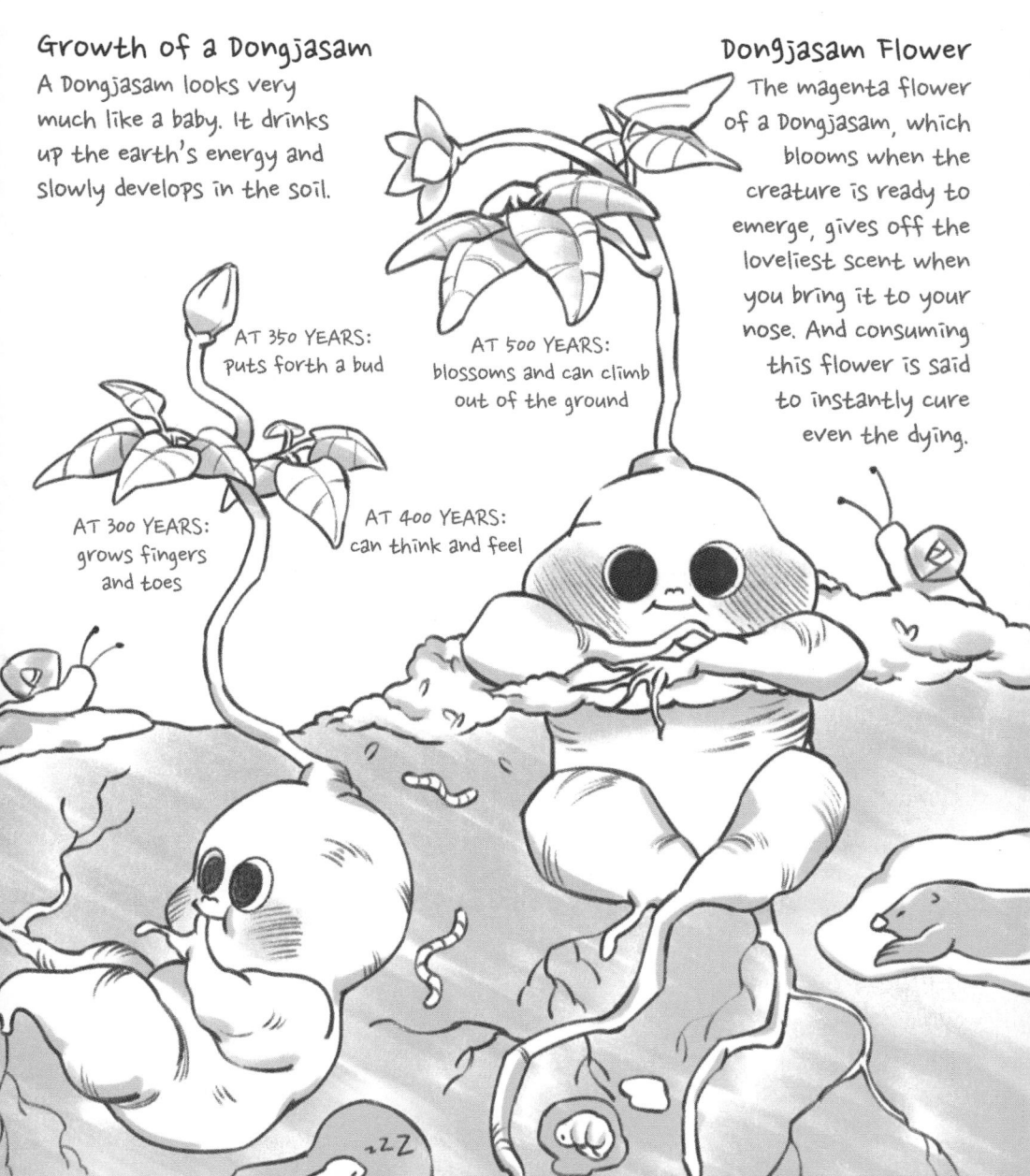

Growth of a Dongjasam

A Dongjasam looks very much like a baby. It drinks up the earth's energy and slowly develops in the soil.

AT 350 YEARS:
Puts forth a bud

AT 500 YEARS:
blossoms and can climb out of the ground

AT 400 YEARS:
can think and feel

AT 300 YEARS:
grows fingers and toes

Dongjasam Flower

The magenta flower of a Dongjasam, which blooms when the creature is ready to emerge, gives off the loveliest scent when you bring it to your nose. And consuming this flower is said to instantly cure even the dying.

Twinkle Twinkle Little Pup:
chungu

Personality
chungu is full of pep! It loves to gambol around and never sits still. It's happy to buddy up with just about anyone. Sometimes it can be too trusting.

chungu used to live in a beautiful bluish-white star, which happens to be blistering hot with an absolute temperature of 15,000 K.

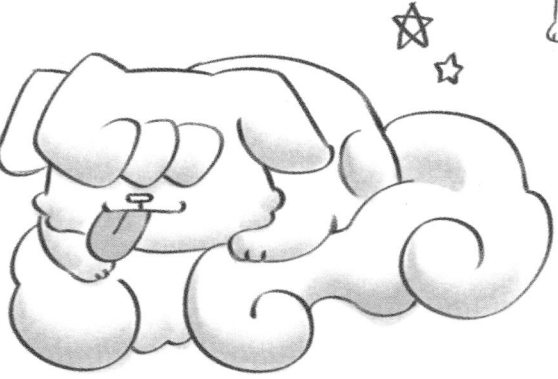

nom nom

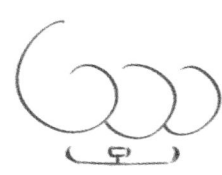

Round Eyebrows
Those heart-shaped eyebrows are everything!!

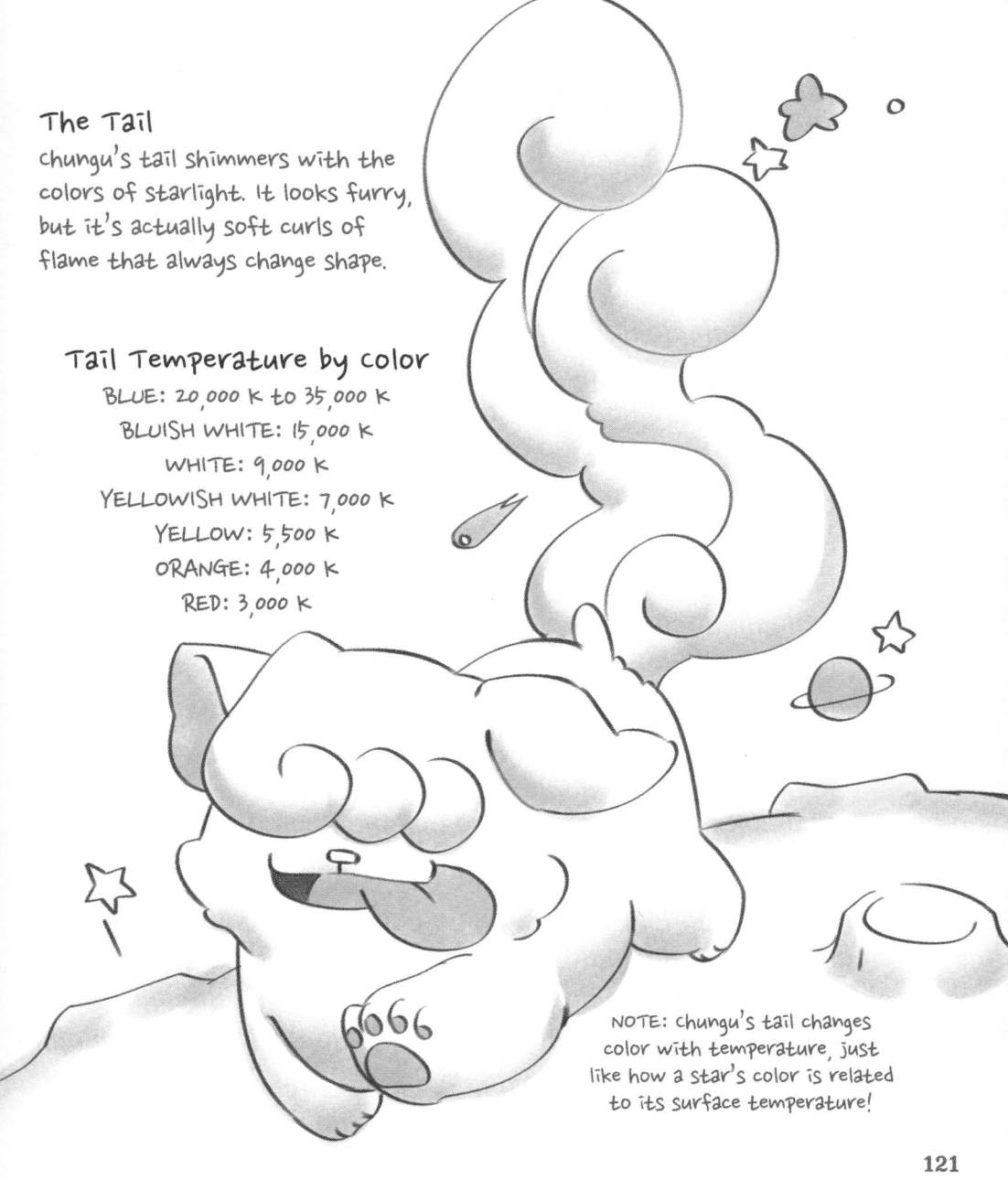

The Tail

chungu's tail shimmers with the colors of starlight. It looks furry, but it's actually soft curls of flame that always change shape.

Tail Temperature by color

BLUE: 20,000 k to 35,000 k

BLUISH WHITE: 15,000 k

WHITE: 9,000 k

YELLOWISH WHITE: 7,000 k

YELLOW: 5,500 k

ORANGE: 4,000 k

RED: 3,000 k

NOTE: chungu's tail changes color with temperature, just like how a star's color is related to its surface temperature!

Olgul Guishin Suffers Pee Problem

The face ghost screams bloody murder at passersby constantly peeing on her wall. Unfortunately, she's forever bound behind the wall.

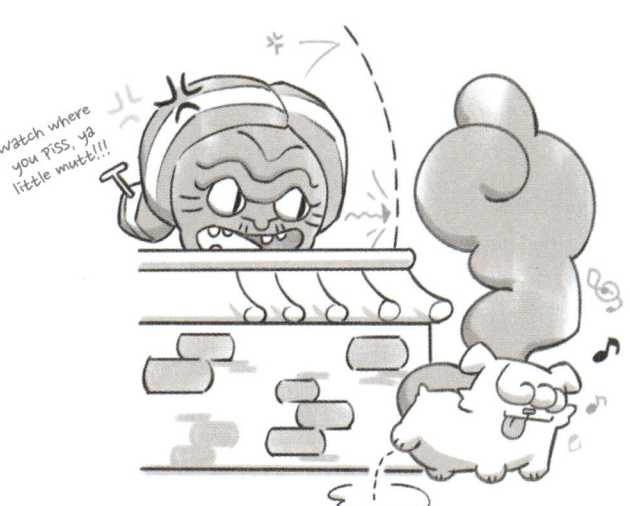

Ginseng Boy Leads Double Life

An innocent-faced Dongjasam has been exposed for his secret nocturnal identity!

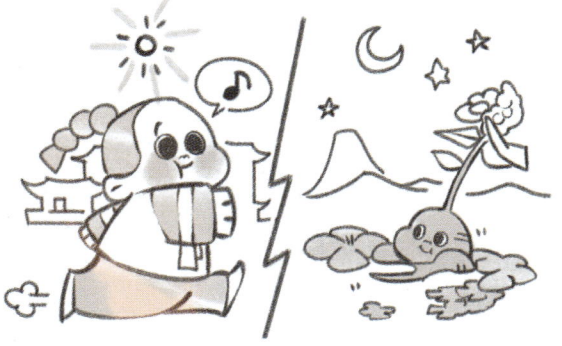

BREAKING NEWS IN MEOSHÍN'KÉ!

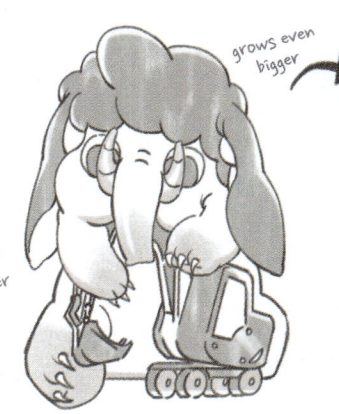

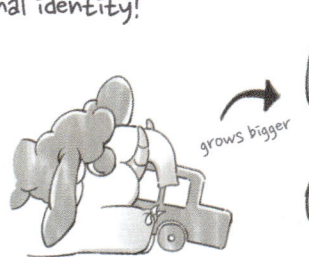

Meowdusa's weather channel

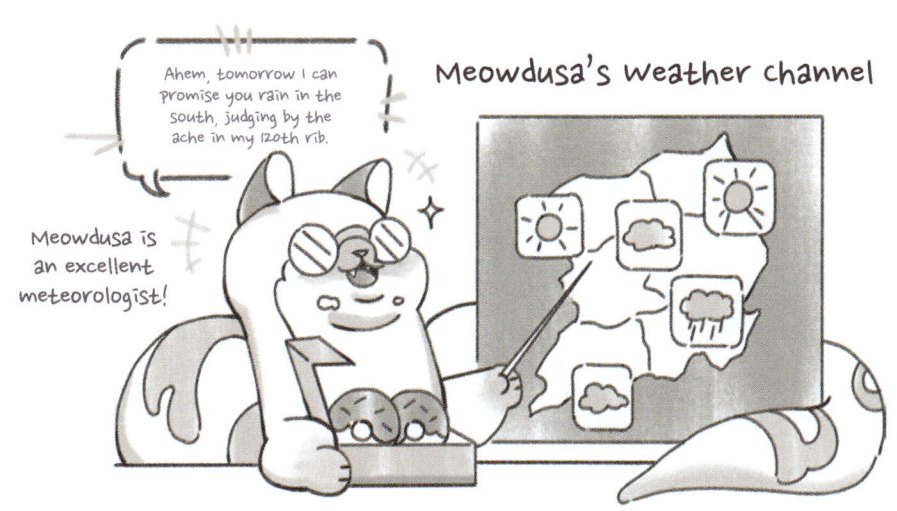

Ahem, tomorrow I can promise you rain in the south, judging by the ache in my 120th rib.

Meowdusa is an excellent meteorologist!

in france

Crisis Hits Steel Industry!

Steel producers worldwide face bankruptcy as Bulgasari goes on a steel-eating rampage. It has just chomped down on the Eiffel Tower!

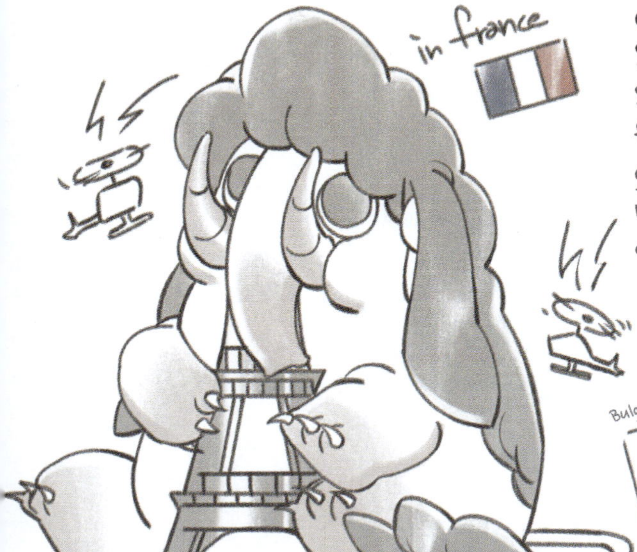

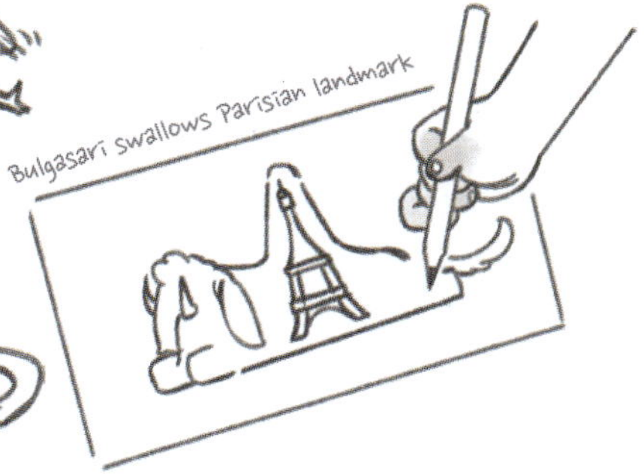

Bulgasari swallows Parisian landmark

Social Survival Tips from Supernatural Beings

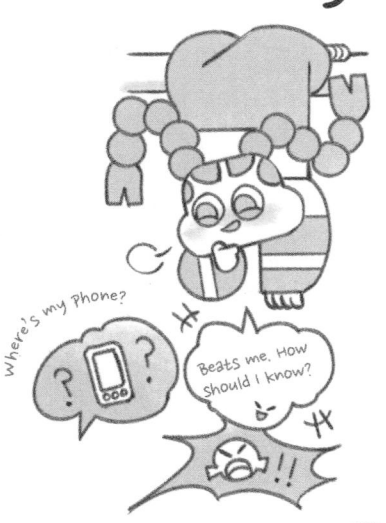

SOKGUL SONSENG: Be kind and patient, even when talking to someone who knows less than you or is hard to communicate with.

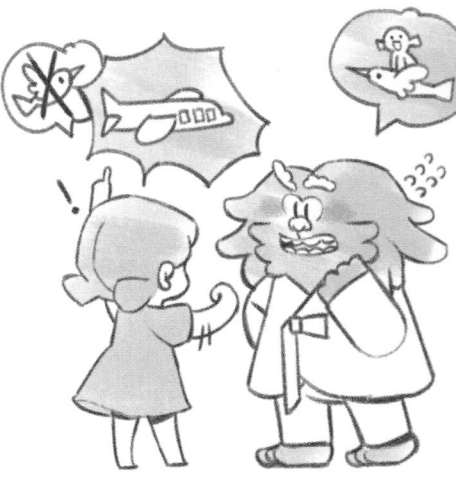

NOENGSOL: Never lose your temper, even when you're frustrated. Angry outbursts and irritability can ruin relationships!

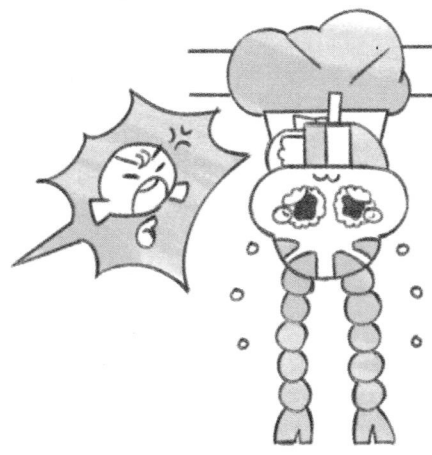

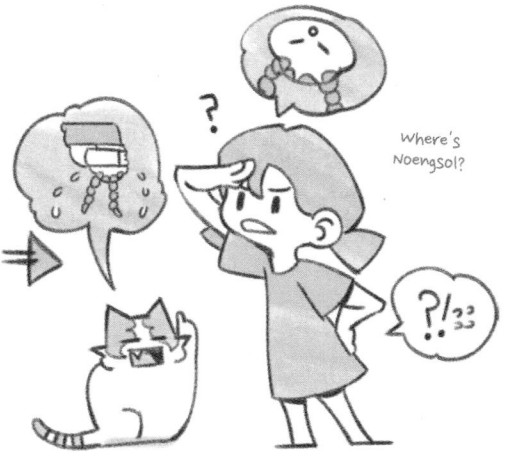

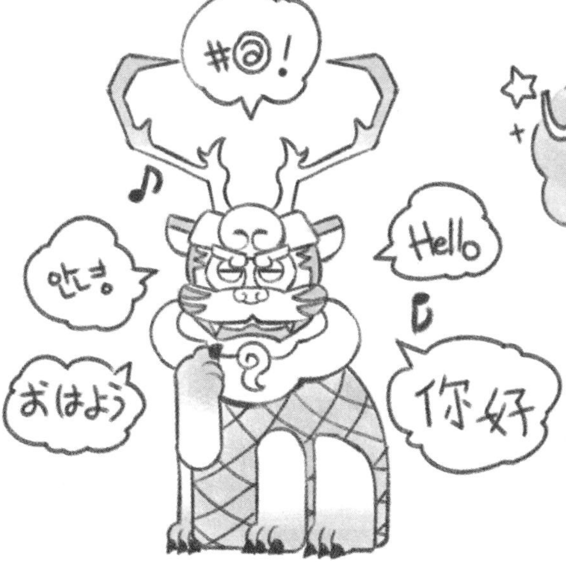

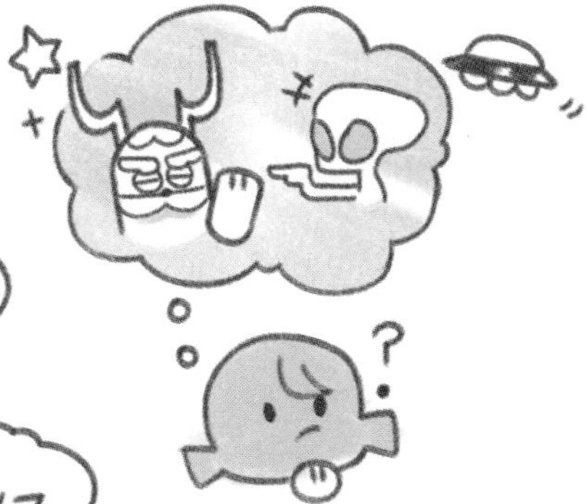

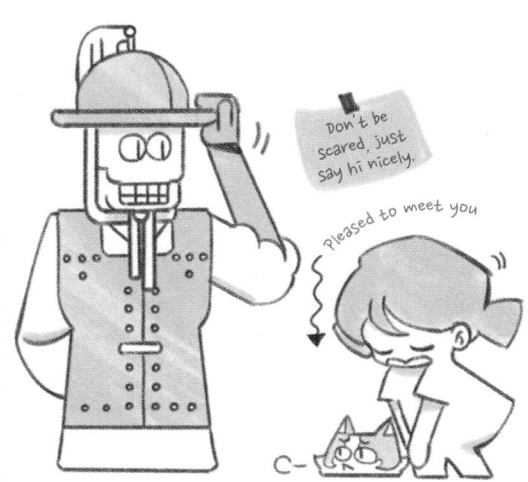

CHUNROK BUEKSA: In this global age, learn different languages like chunrok Bueksa!

(can they even speak Alien?)

TAKTAK GUIBYUNG: Polite greetings can go a long way in building relationships.

MAEHWA NOIN: There's always a fuddy-duddy in the room!

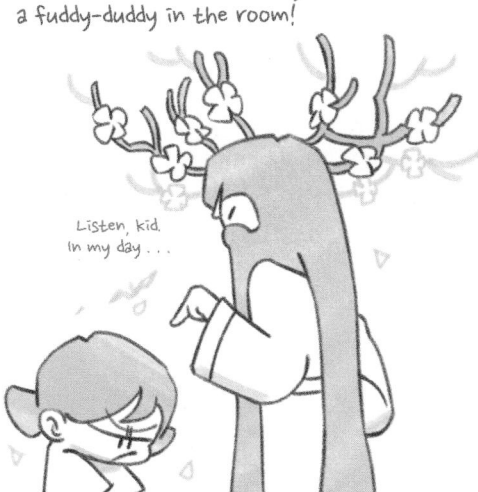

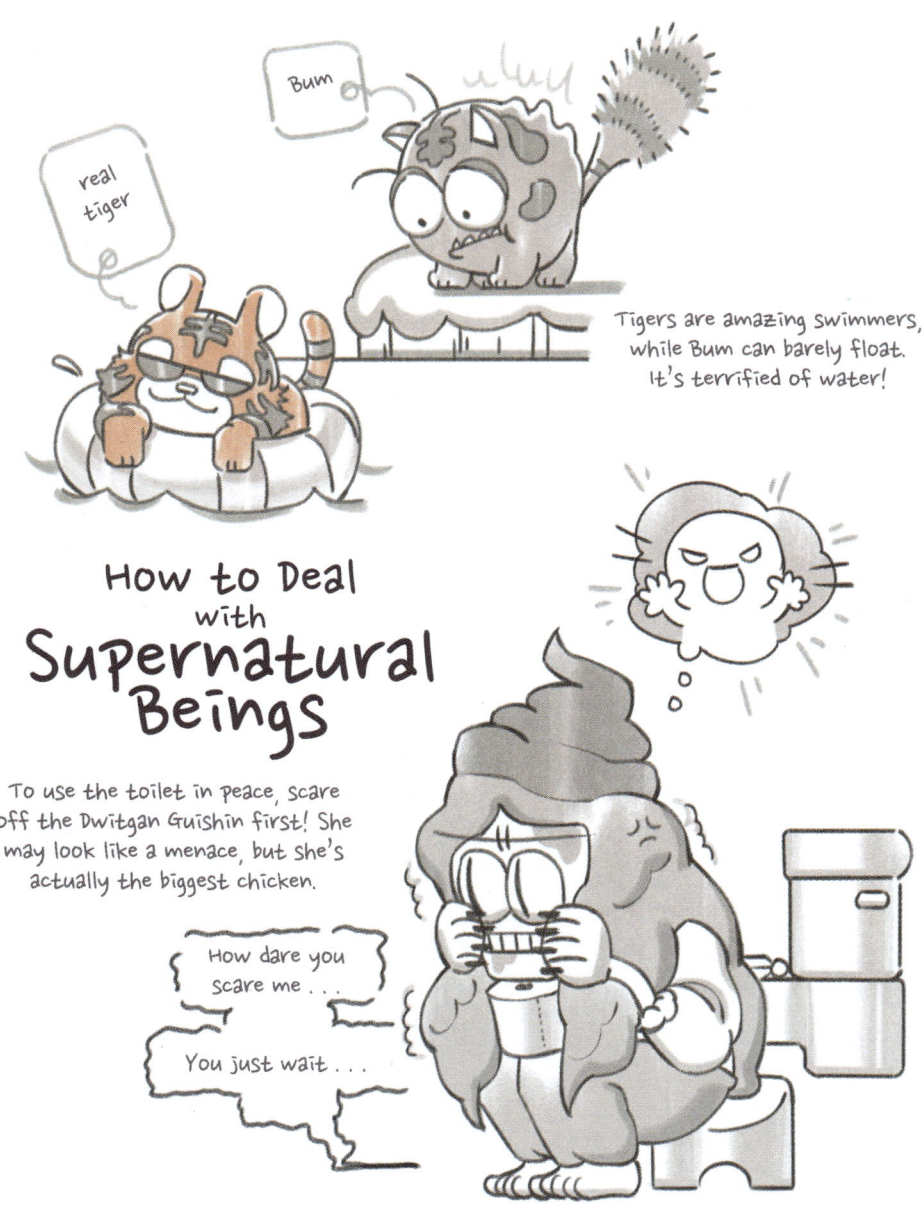

real tiger

Bum

Tigers are amazing swimmers, while Bum can barely float. It's terrified of water!

How to Deal with Supernatural Beings

To use the toilet in peace, scare off the Dwitgan Guishin first! She may look like a menace, but she's actually the biggest chicken.

How dare you scare me . . .

You just wait . . .

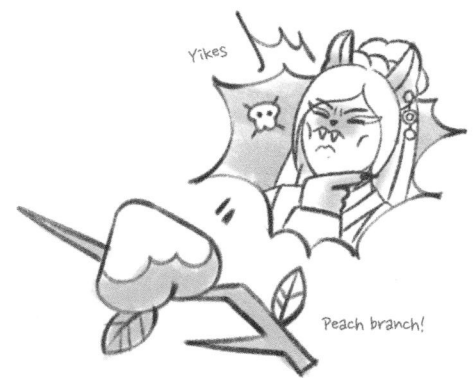

Yikes

Peach branch!

Not a Peach Allergy!
When Gumiho see a peach tree, they turn and run. They're thought to be allergic to peach, but it's actually the branches of peach trees they hate!

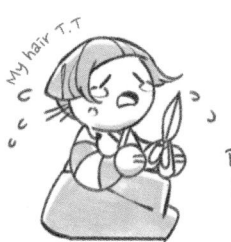

My hair T.T

You can ward off Yagwanggui by burning some of your hair strands at sundown. People are complaining of balding because of these pesky shoe thieves!

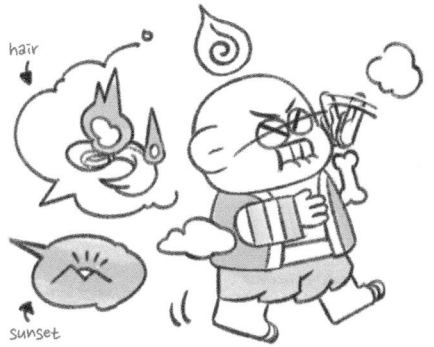

hair

sunset

Not a fan of a pretty bride tidying up your room? If you don't want your house to be magically cleaned up and prefer to be free, just rush Oolung Gaksi in any way.

Oolung Gaksi will leave when she feels pressured.

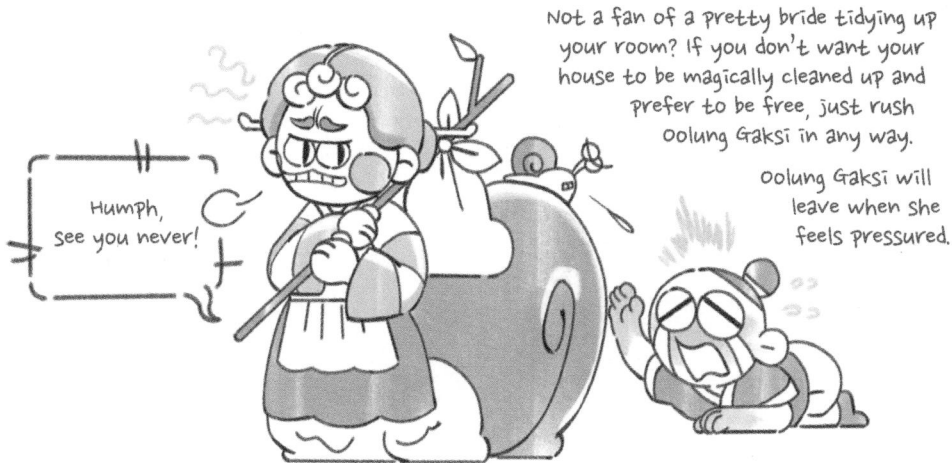

Humph, see you never!

The Question of Food
for
Supernaturals

Aagui's Endless Feast

Once they start eating, Aagui never put their spoons down. No mukbang YouTuber can hold a candle to Aagui.

WARNING: An Aagui's mukbang broadcast only ends when it has squeezed your pantry dry.

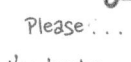

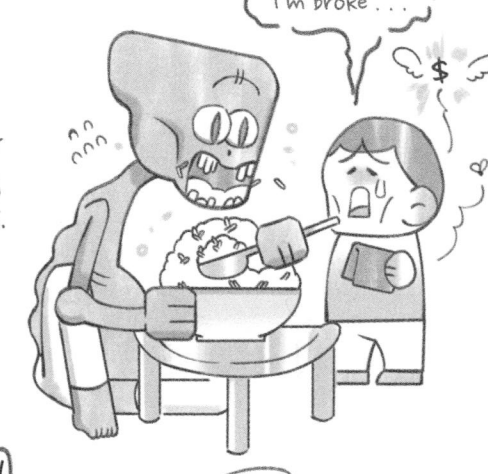

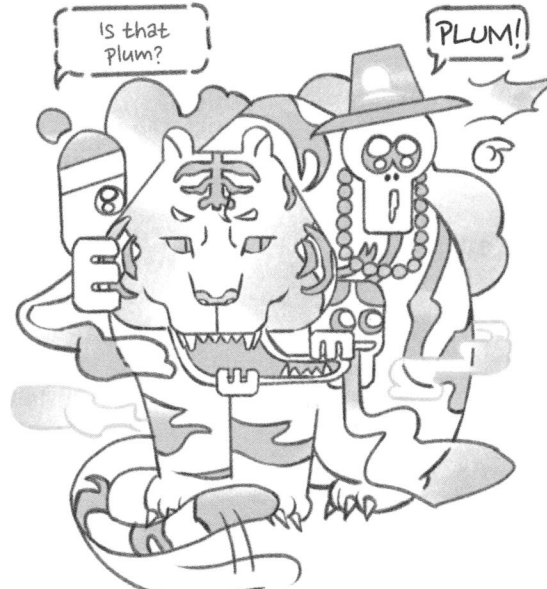

Tigers are carnivores, but changgui adore plums. Their eyes turn dreamy when they spot the fruit.

Here they are coaxing the tiger to steal those plums Burdlee are snacking on!

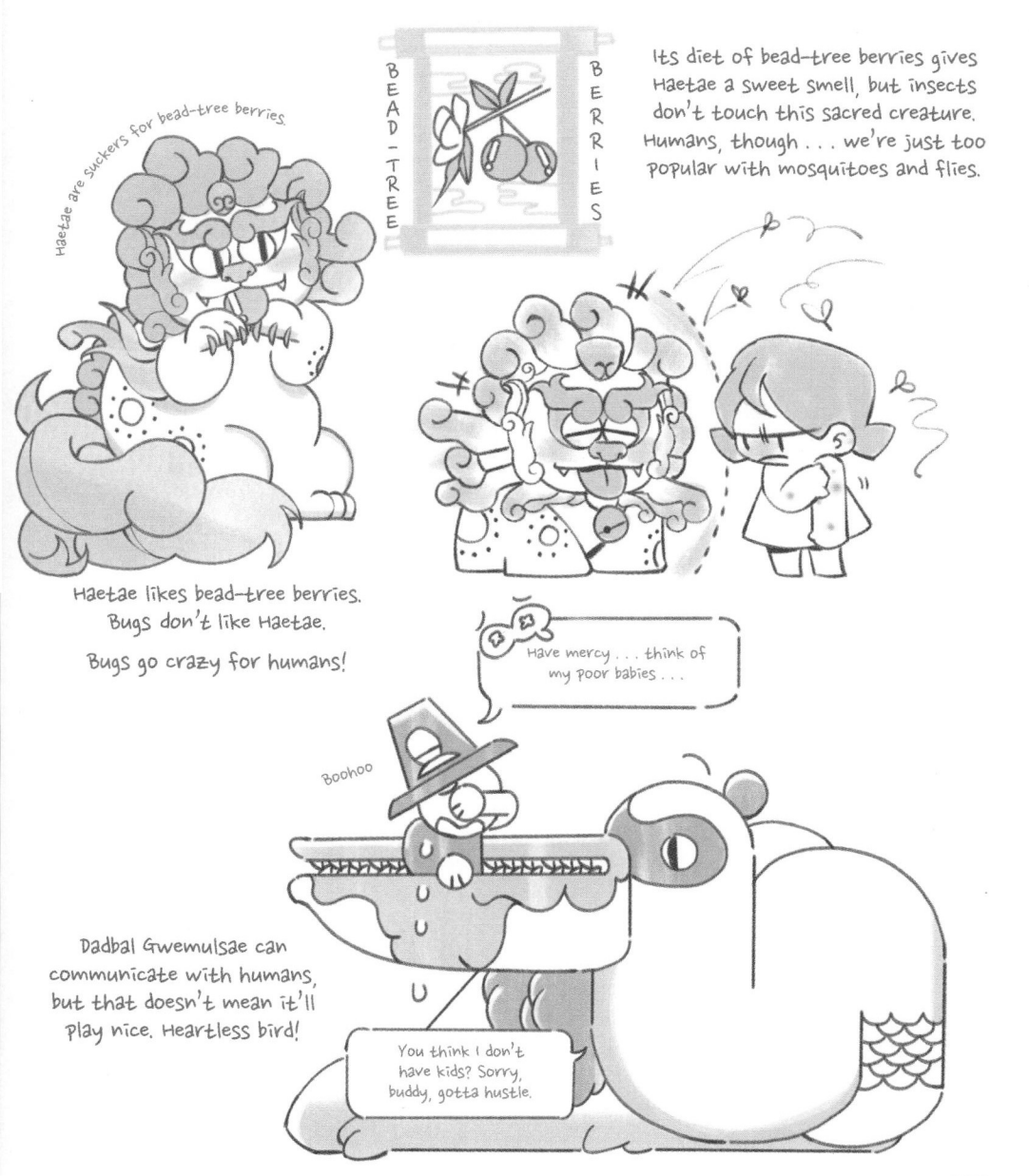

Haetae are suckers for bead-tree berries.

B E A D - T R E E   B E R R I E S

Its diet of bead-tree berries gives Haetae a sweet smell, but insects don't touch this sacred creature. Humans, though . . . we're just too popular with mosquitoes and flies.

Haetae likes bead-tree berries.
Bugs don't like Haetae.

Bugs go crazy for humans!

Have mercy . . . think of my poor babies . . .

Boohoo

Dadbal Gwemulsae can communicate with humans, but that doesn't mean it'll play nice. Heartless bird!

You think I don't have kids? Sorry, buddy, gotta hustle.

129

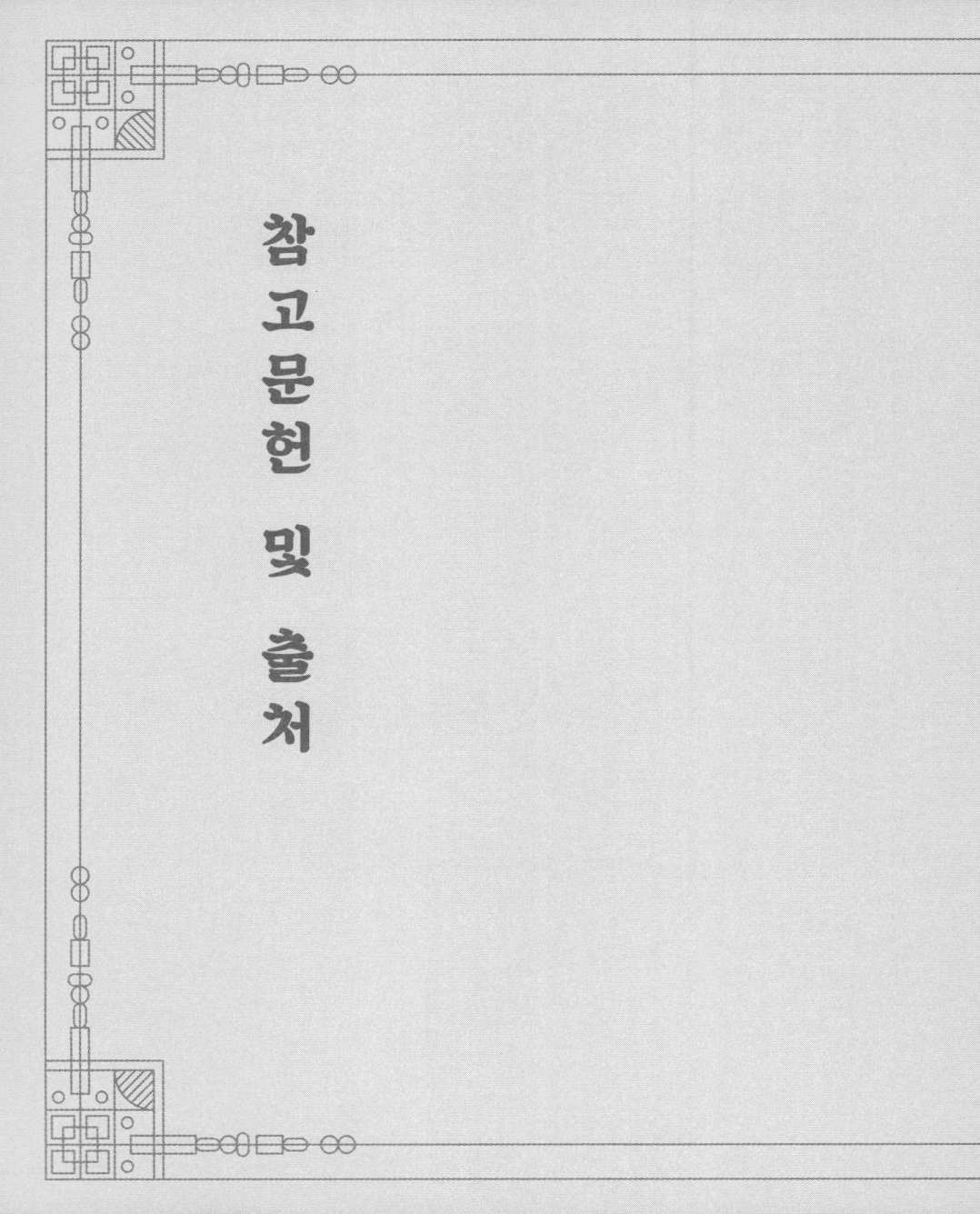

참고문헌 및 출처

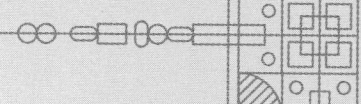

Bibliography

Here are the stories that inspired MeoShín'Ké's fantastical creatures, a compilation of material we've gleaned from Korean classical texts. Exact quotes are shown, including some in regional dialects.

Note from the Publisher: *The following information is from the original source material and includes some graphic details and scenes that can be upsetting to some readers. Please proceed mindfully.*

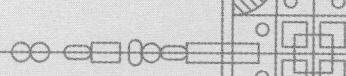

Bibliography

In order of appearance:

CHARACTER	WORK	SOURCE	SNIPPET
GANG-CHOLEE	Damjeongchongseo [담정총서], Seonghosaseol [성호사설], Cheongjangg-wanjeonseo [청장관전서], Hakgojip [학고집]	Shin Donbok. *Haksanhaneon*. Bogosa. Lee Deokmu. *Cheongjanggwanjeonseo*. Minjokmunhwachujinhoe. Yi Ik. *Seonghosaseol*. https://db.itkc.or.kr/.	"A few days ago, a great rainstorm raged and an animal fell out of the sky, landing by the well. It could be a cow, or a horse, or neither. I had never seen the likes of it in my life. Was it a dragon? I wondered. I covered it with leaves in case people saw it."
GOGUGUI	Gimunchonghwa [기문총화], Daedonggimun [대동기문], Eouyadam [어우야담]	Yu Mongin. *Eouyadam*. Dolbegae.	"The monster was blocking the road, its jaws wide open. Its upper lip reached all the way up to the sky while its lower lip rested on the ground. Terrified, his companions backed away and fled down another path, but Shin Sukju strode straight into the gaping jaws."
GOAIN	Dongguktonggam [동국통감], Mago Halmi folktale [마고할미설화], Samguk Sagi [삼국사기]	Yu Mongin. *Eouyadam*. Dolbegae. Sejong Daewang Ginyeom Saeophoe. *Gugyeok Dongguktonggam*. Kim Hyeonryong. *Hanguk Munheonseolhwa*. Konkuk University Press.	"To the southeast of Silla lies Japan, and to its east, Janginguk. Residents of Janginguk are as tall as three jang,* and their fingernails are like claws. They refuse to eat food cooked over fire, hunting animals and sometimes even humans."
GOLCHULGUI	Eouyadam [어우야담]	Yu Mongin. *Eouyadam*. Dolbegae. Im Seokjae. *Hanguk Gujeon Seolhwa Vol. 5 Gyeonggido*, 247.	"The front gate creaked open, and in walked a thing missing a left hand, left leg, and the whole left side of its face. Its right hand was nearly burned off. The left half of its body was wilted—a horrible sight indeed."

---

* **jang:** Unit of length. Three jang are approximately equal to thirty feet.

CHARACTER	WORK	SOURCE	SNIPPET
GUMIHO	Gang Gamchan folktale [강감찬 설화], yeouguseul folktale [여우구슬설화], Uirimchwalyo [의림촬요]	Son Jintae. *Joseon Mindamjip.* Minsokwon. *Hanguk Gubimunhak Daegye.* The Academy of Korean Studies. Vol. 1-2, 167 / Vol. 1-3, 418 / Vol. 2-2, 340 / Vol. 2-6, 639 / Vol. 2-8, 646 / Vol. 4-2, 470 / Vol. 4-2, 649 / Vol. 4-2, 791 / Vol. 5-4, 448 / Vol. 6-5, 687 / Vol. 6-7, 35 / Vol. 6-8, 135 / Vol. 7-16, 578 / Vol. 8-1, 114 / Vol. 8-8, 580 / Vol. 8-9, 621 / Vol. 8-13, 59.	"A boy was on his way to school when a beautiful girl appeared and gave him a kiss, inviting him to play with her. He was smitten and began to see her every day to and from school, stealing kisses. Slowly, the boy's face grew sickly."
GUSUNSE	Eouyadam [어우야담], folklore of Jeju Island	Hyeon Yongjun. Jejudo Mindam. Jejumunhwa, 252–253.	"The Gusunse looks like a straw rain cape that swoops and billows about. When it strikes, it is said to knock the very soul out of a person, leaving them to die."
NOENGSOL	Yongjaechonghwa [용재총화]	Seong Hyeon. *Yongjaechonghwa.* Zmanz Books.	"But she didn't harm the household in any way. Her voice was loud and clear, like an old songbird's. By day she floated in midair; by night she curled up on a collar beam across the ceiling."
DALGYAL GUISHIN	folklore, Paju Tapsakgol legend [파주 탑삭골 전설]	Achimnamu. *Sangsigeuro Ggok Araya Hal Segyeui Jeonseol: Dongyangpyeon.* Samyang Media.	"A young man hiked up the hill, swallowing his fear. But then he came scrambling down and said, 'It was crouching there, a faceless Dalgyal Guishin,' before promptly keeling over to his death. Rumors have since gone around that the forest is haunted."
DADBAL GWEMULSAE	Ggori Dadbal Judungi Dadbal folktale [꼬리 닷발 주둥이 닷발 설화], Hanguk Gubimunhak Daegye [한국 구비문학대계]	*Hanguk Gubimunhak Daegye.* The Academy of Korean Studies. Vol. 1-4, 36 / Vol. 4-6, 188 / Vol. 5-7, 542 / Vol. 6-7, 84 / Vol. 8-2, 322 / Vol. 8-6, 34.	"When the man looked for his mother, someone told him, 'Two birds with a five-bal-long beak and a five-bal-long tail swooped down and ate your mother, leaving only her feet and head in the room, and her skin on the fence.'"

CHARACTER	WORK	SOURCE	SNIPPET
DONGJASAM	supernatural folklore, Korean oral literature, filial-piety-themed folklore	*Hanguk Gubimunhak Daegye*. The Academy of Korean Studies. Vol. 1-4, 241 / Vol. 1-4, 917 / Vol. 2-2, 606 / Vol. 2-3, 92 / Vol. 2-6, 629 / Vol. 2-7, 117 / Vol. 3-4, 284 / Vol. 4-1, 230 / Vol. 4-2, 199 / Vol. 4-4, 452 / Vol. 4-5, 111 / Vol. 4-5, 231 / Vol. 4-5, 416 / Vol. 4-5, 551 / Vol. 4-5, 1065 / Vol. 5-2, 787 / Vol. 5-4, 1012 / Vol. 5-7, 11 / Vol. 5-7, 745 / Vol. 6-3, 96 / Vol. 6-3, 500 / Vol. 6-4, 265 / Vol. 6-9, 237 / Vol. 6-11, 140 / Vol. 6-11, 598 / Vol. 6-12, 630 / Vol. 6-12, 633 / Vol. Vol. 6-12, 900 / Vol. 7-2, 670 / Vol. 7-6, 686 / Vol. 7-6, 689 / Vol. 7-11, 392 / Vol. 7-13, 302 / Vol. 7-18, 573 / Vol. 8-1, 218 / Vol. 8-4, 647 / Vol. 8-9, 355 / Vol. 9-2, 83.	"Turns out, it was one of those things called a Dongjasam. The mountain god had turned it into a person, a doll of sorts. And the good daughter-in-law used it to heal the sick mother. So you see, it wasn't her son she decocted but the Dongjasam."
DUOKSHINI	Dongmunseon [동문선] and other folkore, Songnamjapji [송남잡지], Cheonyerok [천예록]	Jo Jaesam. *Songnamjapji*. Somyung Books. Im Bang. *Gyogamyeokju Cheonyerok*. Sungkyunkwan Publishing Department. *Jeonggamrok: Minjok Jonggyoui Motae*. Translated by Yang Taejin. Yenaru. Sim Jae. *Gyogamyeokju Songcheonpildam*. Translated by Shin Ikcheol et al. Bogosa.	"The next day, a dreadful plague struck the house as well as those of everyone who had been at the banquet. Within a few days, people who had berated and bullied the child, or demanded she be dragged out, or shouted for a good beating—along with all the servants, from the guards to the elderly manservants— were dead. Their heads smashed. Not a single attendee of the banquet survived. The world named that child 'Duokshini,' but why, no one knows."
DWITGAN GUISHIN (CHUKSHIN)	Yongjaechonghwa [용재총화], Munjeon Bonpuri from Jeju shaman songs [제주도 무가 중 문전본풀이]	Seong Hyeon. *Yongjaechonghwa*. Zmanz Books. Shin Dongheun. *Saraitneun Hanguk Sinhwa*. Hankyoreh Publishing.	"Noiljedaeguil's daughter fled from the seven brothers until finally she hooked her hair around the outhouse rafter and hanged herself. Upon her death, she became Chukdo Buin, the goddess of the outhouse. The enraged brothers ripped off the evil woman's legs to make a grain treadmill, her head to make a pot, her hair to toss in all directions, which grew into grassy fields. Her flung fingernails turned into chitons, her scooped out navel into baby beetles, her snipped anus into abalones big and small, and her body, powdered and scattered in the winds, became mosquitos and fleas and bed bugs."

CHARACTER	WORK	SOURCE	SNIPPET
MAEHWA NOIN	Jukchanghanhwa [죽창한화]	Kim Hyeonryong. *Hanguk Munheon Seolhwa*. Konkuk University Press.	"One night, Magistrate Shin dreamed of an ancient, snowy-haired man, who thundered, 'One hundred years I've lived peacefully, but you dare move me to another spot! Now I will perish, and so will you.' Not long after the dream, the plum tree withered up and died, and Magistrate Shin soon followed."
MONGDAL	shamanistic faith, Eouyadam [어우야담], Hwang Jini anecdote [황진이일화]	Yu Mongin. *Eouyadam*. Dolbegae. Kim Seonpung. *Hanguk Minsok Jonghap Josa Bogoseo*. Bureau of Cultural Property.	"Before Hwang Jini became a gisaeng, there was a man who fell madly in love with her, only to die lovesick. His casket was being carried to the burial site when, on reaching Hwang Jini's house, it dropped to the ground—and would not budge. Only when Hwang Jini herself came and placed one of her undershirts on the casket, whispering soothing words, did the casket allow itself to be moved."
MEOWDUSA	Songdogii [송도기이]	*Gugyeok Daedongyaseung*. Minjok Munhwa Mungo Ganhaenghoe.	"Something poked out of the hole: It looked like the head of a kitten, but had brilliant scales. Crows shrieked and birds circled above, so the temple's monks dared not go near it. They had no clue what it was, until they saw the flick of a tongue. It was a snake."
MULGUISHIN	Eouyadam [어우야담]	Yu Mongin. *Eouyadam*. Dolbegae. *Hanguk Gubimunhak Daegye Vol. 8-11*. The Academy of Korean Studies, 477. Murayama Chijun. *Joseonui Guishin*. Translated by Noh Seonghwan. Minsokwon.	"The souls of people who drowned become Mulguishin. These ghosts dislike gold and silver. Hence, you can protect yourself by carrying gold and silver when crossing rivers or seas."

CHARACTER	WORK	SOURCE	SNIPPET
BANGSANGSHI	Goryeosa [고려사]	Goryeosa. Sahoegwahakwon Chulpansa. Encyclopedia of Korean Culture Editorial Team. Hanguk Minjok Munhwa Daebaekgwa Sajeon.	"Bangsangshi drape bearskin over themselves and have four golden eyes. Clad in a black jeogori and a red skirt, spear and shield in hand, they lead a hundred servants and hold seasonal rituals to purge plague-spreading ghosts from homes. For a king's funeral procession, Bangsangshi walk before the casket. When they reach the gravesite, they climb into the pit and stab all four corners to banish graveyard ghosts."
BUM	Jangsanbum [장산범], Haewa Dari Dwen Onui [해와 달이 된 오누이]	Hanguk Gubimunhak Daegye. The Academy of Korean Studies. Vol. 1-2, 422 / Vol. 1-4, 81 / Vol. 1-5, 308 / Vol. 1-7, 272 / Vol. 1-7, 761 / Vol. 1-8, 321 / Vol. 1-9, 209 / Vol. 2-5, 104 / Vol. 2-6, 473 / Vol. 2-6. 560 / Vol. 2-7, 123 / Vol. 2-7, 236 / Vol. 2-7, 513 / Vol. 3-2, 408 / Vol. 3-4, 782 / Vol. 4-5, 178 / Vol. 5-1, 49 / Vol. 4-4, 330 / Vol. 4-5, 751 / Vol. 5-2, 516 / Vol. 5-2, 529 / Vol. 5-2, 629 / Vol. 5-3, 312 / Vol. 6-4, 881 / Vol. 6-5, 388 / Vol. 6-7, 72 / Vol. 6-8, 22 / Vol. 6-8, 728 / Vol. 6-10, 73 / Vol. 6-10, 304 / Vol. 6-11, 613 / Vol. 6-12, 585 / Vol. 6-12, 627 / Vol. 7-1, 427 / Vol. 7-4, 118 / Vol. 7-5, 52 / Vol. 7-8, 342 / Vol. 7-6, 199 / Vol. 7-8, 509 / Vol. 7-10, 330 / Vol. 7-10, 642 / Vol. 7-12, 144 / Vol. 7-15, 481 / Vol. 7-17, 559 / Vol. 8-4, 555 / Vol. 8-12, 350 / Vol. 9-1, 674.	"She left her three children at home and went to help starch cotton yarns. After three, four days of work, she received some buckwheat jelly, which she carried in a wooden bowl as she hurried up the hill towards home. Then a tiger said to her, 'Lady, lady, what have you got there? If you give me that, I won't eat you.' So she handed over a block of jelly, then another block, until she ran out completely, until even her bowl was taken, and now possibly her limbs, the tiger telling her, 'If you give me one of your arms, I won't eat you.' The tiger kept at it as she climbed hill after hill."
BULGASARI	Songnamjapji [송남잡지]	Jo Jaesam. Songnamjapji. Somyung Books. Bulgasarijeon. Hanguk Gubimunhak Daegye. The Academy of Korean Studies. Vol. 2-7, 79 / Vol. 4-4, 345 / Vol. 5-4, 176 / Vol. 7-13, 622 / Vol. 7-15, 517 / Vol. 8-9, 721 / Vol. 8-13, 592 / Vol. 8-14, 189.	"Legend goes that in the last years of Songdo,* a monster devoured any and all metal in sight. Many attempts to destroy the monster failed, so it was named Bulgasal: 'unkillable.' When it was thrown into fire, its entire body turned into a white-hot ball of flames that catapulted itself into human homes, burning everything."

*   **Songdo:** ancient capital of Goryeo

CHARACTER	WORK	SOURCE	SNIPPET
SAMMOKU	Buddhist folklore, Cheongjangg-wanjeonseo [청장관전서]	Lee Deokmu. *Cheongjanggwanjeonseo.* Minjokmunhwachujinhoe. Yun Yeolsu. *Sinhwa Sok Sangsangdongmul Yeoljeon.* Korea Cultural Heritage Protection Foundation.	"One night as he was traveling, he stumbled on a beast atop a hill. Startled, Geo-in stared at the yellow-furred, black-striped creature. It looked like a tiger, but its ears and head resembled a dog's. Stranger still were its eyes: three glinting, blue orbs. Geo-in felt sweat roll down his back."
SAMCHOONG	Danjongshillok [단종실록], Bangyakhappyeon [방약합편], Sallimgyeongje [산림경제]	*Joseon Wangjo Sillok.* https://db.itkc.or.kr/. Hwang Doyeon. *Bangyakhappyeon.* Yeogang Chulpansa. *Sallimgyeongje.* Korean Studies Information.	"When a person's stomach and intestines are empty after a bout of illness, Samchoong begin to feed. They nibble away at the organs, a process called 'hoheuk.' Anyone so affected will die shortly. If Samchoong eat the veins of the upper lungs, the throat will itch; if they eat the lower end of the intestines, the anus will suffer severe irritation. In such cases, burn a mimosa tree branch in the agungi and expose the itchy skin to the smoke for relief."
SOKGUL SONSENG	Dongpaeraksong [동패락송]	Kim Hyeonryong. *Hanguk Munheonseolhwa.* Konkuk University Press.	"The two people alighted from the boat, hiked up the mountain, and entered the rock cave. A vast world opened up before their eyes, and seated on a stone chair was a red-bearded ancient."
SUNGJUSHIN	gasin faith, Dongguksesigi [동국세시기], Joseon Musokgo [조선무속고]	Shin Dongheun. *Saraitneun Hanguk Sinhwa.* Hankyoreh Publishing.	"Every October, believed to be the most glorious of months, villagers welcomed Sungjushin into their homes with the help of shamans, preparing rice cakes and fruit, and praying for a peaceful household."

CHARACTER	WORK	SOURCE	SNIPPET
SONGAKSI (A-LANG SON)	shamanistic faith, Shillip folktale [신립설화]	*Hanguk Gubimunhak Daegye*. The Academy of Korean Studies. Vol. 1-2, 164 / Vol. 1-7, 586 / Vol. 2-2, 416 / Vol. 2-6, 387 / Vol. 2-8, 839 / Vol. 2-9, 814 / Vol. 3-1, 71 / Vol. 3-1, 91 / Vol. 3-1, 182 / Vol. 3-1, 309 / Vol. 3-2, 387 / Vol. 3-2, 703 / Vol. 3-3, 156 / Vol. 3-4, 96 / Vol. 4-1, 294 / Vol. 4-2, 133 / Vol. 5-4, 157 / Vol. 5-4, 674 / Vol. 5-7, 102 / Vol. 6-2, 765 / Vol. 6-4, 523 / Vol. 6-9, 526 / Vol. 6-11, 521 / Vol. 7-5, 278 / Vol. 7-6, 377 / Vol. 7-13, 75 / Vol. 7-13, 308 / Vol. 7-15, 455 / Vol. 7-17, 518 / Vol. 7-18, 343 / Vol. 8-7, 137 / Vol. 8-7, 359 / Vol. 8-8, 66 / Vol. 8-8, 396 / Vol. 8-9, 217.	"He drifted to sleep and in his dream appeared a woman who had a knife through her throat. She told him she was wandering in that state because she had not gotten her revenge, and begged him to help her."
SURYONG	Samguk Sagi [삼국사기], Samguk Yusa [삼국유사], folklore	Kim Busik. *Samguk Sagi*. Hanbulhakyesa. Il Yeon. *Samguk Yusa*. Sinwon Munhwasa.	"Without warning, the sea dragon pulled his wife into the sea. Sir Sunjeong ran about in a panic, screaming at the dragon, but nothing could be done."
SHIGINGUI	folklore		"That was when he heard a *crunch, crunch*. He got up, thinking it was a wounded soldier, but it was a Shigingui biting off the head of a corpse. Horrified, Hwaryong hid himself among his fallen brothers-in-arms. But alas, his turn eventually came."
AAGUI	folklore, Buddhist folklore, Eouyadam [어우야담]	*Daemokgeonryeonmyeonggangu-mobyeonmun*.	"Saved from Hell, Mongnyeon Jonja*'s mother fell into the realm of Aagui. Her neck grew thin as a needle hole and her belly swelled to a great mountain. Mongnyeon Jonja brought food and water for her, but they burst into flames."

---

* **Mongnyeon Jonja:** Korean name for Maudgalyayana, one of the closest disciples of the Buddha

CHARACTER	WORK	SOURCE	SNIPPET
YAGWANGGUI BROTHERS	Gyeongdojapji [경도잡지], Sesigi [세시기], Sesigisok [세시기속], Sesipungyo [세시풍요]	*Hanguk Minsok Daebaekgwa Sajeon.* National Folk Museum of Korea's Folk Research Division. Yu Deukgong. *Gyeongdojapji.* Joseon Goseo Ganhaenghoe. *Hanguk Minsok Jonghap Josa Bogoseo (1971) - Chungbukpyeon Vol. 1.* Bureau of Cultural Property.	"Around the first or fifteenth day of the lunar new year, the ghosts are said to descend on people's homes, try on their shoes, and take what fits. These ghosts are known as 'Yagwanggui' or 'shoe ghosts.' People whose shoes are taken are believed to have bad luck for the year. To prevent this from happening, people hide their shoes in their rooms and hang a sieve on their doors, a custom called 'warding off Yagwanggui.'"
ODUKSHINI	folklore	*Joseon Hyangto Baekgwa.* The Institute for Peace Affairs. "Dokkaebineun Bomyeon Bolsurok Keojinda" (Jeonnam Muan-gun). Hanguk Gubimunhak Daegye DB. https://kdp.aks.ac.kr/inde/gubi. "Dokkaebireul Mannatsseul Ddae Haneureul Bomyeon Andwenda" (Yeosu-si Hwajeong-myeon Jeokgeum-ri). Hanguk Gubimunhak Daegye DB. https://kdp.aks.ac.kr/inde/gubi.	"This is a valley in Chuma-ri, Yangdeok-gun of South Pyongan Province, between Mount Obong and Dol Hill. The valley leads up to Eodwingi Hill, which got that name because a ghost called Odukshini (or Eodwing) showed up there whenever it grew dark."
OLGUL GUISHIN	Haedongjaprok [해동잡록]	*Gugyeok Daedongyaseung.* Minjok Munhwa Mungo Ganhaenghoe.	"When he drew nearer, he saw that the face was so large it filled most of the fence, a true freak of nature. With no other means of escape, he decided to face the ghost head-on and charged. Slowly, the shape faded. When he stood back to get a better look, he glimpsed only the face hanging on the fence."
UPSHIN	gasin faith, Daegam Taryeong from shaman songs [무당굿 중 대감타령], folklore	Encyclopedia of Korean Culture Editorial Team. *Hanguk Minjok Munhwa Daebaekgwa Sajeon.* Hanguk Jeongsin Munhwa Yeonguwon. Seo Daeseok et al. *Anseongmuga.* Jipmundang.	"Upshin is the shinryung presiding over the financial fortune of a family. Unlike Teoju, a household deity worshipped until recently in many homes of the Dobong-gu area, Upshin was worshipped in only a handful of homes there. Once Upshin left a house, the family's fortunes were believed to wane."

CHARACTER	WORK	SOURCE	SNIPPET
WEDARI GUISHIN	Haksanhaneon [학산한언], Cheongguyadam [청구야담]	Shin Donbok. *Haksanhaneon*. Bogosa. *Cheongguyadam*. Translated by Lee Gangok. Munhakdongne.	"The figure's straw hat and cape were not out of place in the rain, but their eyes were like blazing torches, and despite having one leg, they ran like the wind."
OOLUNG GAKSI	folklore	*Hanguk Gubimunhak Daegye*. The Academy of Korean Studies. Vol. 4-5, 775 / Vol. 4-6, 192 / Vol. 4-6, 554 / Vol. 5-1, 265 / Vol. 5-2, 98 / Vol. 5-2, 163 / Vol. 5-2, 224 / Vol. 5-2, 225 / Vol. 5-2, 536 / Vol. 5-2, 751 / Vol. 5-4, 323 / Vol. 5-4, 834 / Vol. 5-4, 1096 / Vol. 5-5, 310 / Vol. 5-5, 702 / Vol. 5-7, 191 / Vol. 5-7, 420 / Vol. 6-3, 666 / Vol. 6-5, 170 / Vol. 6-9, 614 / Vol. 6-11, 106 / Vol. 7-1, 271 / Vol. 7-5, 318 / Vol. 7-12, 169 / Vol. 8-9, 598 / Vol. 8-13, 505 / Vol. 8-14, 774.	"One day, the young man was working the field when he sighed, 'Who will I ever make a home with, when all I've got to plow is this tiny plot of land?' Then a voice replied, 'Why, you can make a home with me. Who else?' The man looked around in surprise, but no one was there. How strange. A moment later, he heard the voice again and this time, he saw who had spoken: It was a large river snail."
YEEMUGI	Seonghosaseol [성호사설], Eouyadam [어우야담], Ojuyeonmunjang-jeonsango [오주연문장전산고], Joseon Mindamjip [조선민담집]	Yi Ik. *Seonghosaseol*. https://db.itkc.or.kr/. Yu Mongin. *Eouyadam*. Dolbegae. *Ojuyeonmunjangjeonsango*. https://db.itkc.or.kr/. Son Jintae. *Joseon Mindamjip*. Minsokwon.	"It is said that Emperor Wu of Han killed the Yeemugi in the Xunyang River with his bow and arrow. This Yeemugi is, in effect, a dragon and is thus one of the Four Holy Beasts. One moment it lies hiding in a deep pond; the next, it soars up to the sky, its every move stirring wind and thunder. What is more, its entire body is an armor of scales. How, then, can a mere arrow kill the beast?"
JANGBALGUI	Eouyadam [어우야담]	Yu Mongin. *Eouyadam*. Dolbegae.	"Suddenly, something came to stand by the corner of the house. It wore a navy robe that reached its heels, and had long, windblown hair that trailed on the ground. Between strands of wild hair shone eyes that were eerily round, like perfect rings."

CHARACTER	WORK	SOURCE	SNIPPET
JOWANGSHIN	gasin faith	Shin Dongheun. *Saraitneun Hanguk Sinhwa*. Hankyoreh Publishing.	"The brothers ran to the spring and wept, at which the water dried up to reveal the body of Lady Yeosan. Just then, a passing cuckoo offered to fly them on its back to Seocheon Flower Garden. So off they went to the garden, where they plucked a Resurrection Flower, and used it to bring their mother back to life. Anxious that their mother might be freezing after spending four seasons in the water, the brothers suggested she become Grandma Jowang of the kitchen, where she could warm herself by the fire thrice a day."
JUIDORYUNG	shapeshifting rat folktales, Eouyadam [어우야담]	Yu Mongin. *Eouyadam*. Dolbegae. *Hanguk Gubimunhak Daegye*. The Academy of Korean Studies. Vol. 1-4, 154 / Vol. 1-7, 782 / Vol. 2-6, 405 / Vol. 2-7, 395 / Vol. 2-9, 125 / Vol. 3-1, 338 / Vol. 3-2, 221 / Vol. 3-2, 485 / Vol. 3-4, 892 / Vol. 4-3, 414 / Vol. 4-5, 631 / Vol. 4-6, 501 / Vol. 5-1, 497 / Vol. 5-4, 603 / Vol. 5-4, 967 / Vol. 5-5, 431 / Vol. 6-3, 682 / Vol. 6-5, 27 / Vol. 6-5, 30 / Vol. 6-11, 519 / Vol. 7-6, 93 / Vol. 7-8, 162 / Vol. 7-13, 111 / Vol. 7-18, 528 / Vol. 8-6, 835 / Vol. 8-14, 180 / Vol. 8-14, 653 / Vol. 9-3, 713 / Vol. 9-3, 726. Im Seokjae. *Hanguk Gujeon Seolhwa Vol. 7*, 62.	"When the son went back home, hiding a cat in his sleeve, his family called him an imposter and tried to throw him out. But he pleaded to have a word with their supposed son. The fake son was lazing about in his room when the real son knocked. As soon as the former opened the door, the latter released the cat in his sleeve. The cat bit the fake son, who, still lying down, turned back into a rat and died."
JIGUI	Daedongunbu-gunok [대동운부군옥], Samguk Yusa [삼국유사]	Gwon Munhae. *Daedongunbugunok*. Translated by Nammyeonghak Yeonguso Gyeongsang Hanmunhak Yeonguhoe. Somyong Books. Il Yeon. *Samguk Yusa*. Sinwon Munhwasa.	"When Jigui awoke, he realized that the Queen had come and gone. Stricken by grief, he fainted and the fire in his heart surged, swallowing the pagoda. He had turned into a fire-raising fiend."
JIRYONG	pungsu jiri principles		

CHARACTER	WORK	SOURCE	SNIPPET
JEEBAGRYUNG	folklore	The term "Jeebagryung" was coined only in modern times, but many records exist on similar creatures.	"Since the farmer's death, guests who stayed at the inn would hear the dawn call of the rooster and set out for somewhere in a frenzy, only to be found dead at the same spot the farmer was found."
JIHAGUK DEJOK	battling bandit king folktales	Im Seokjae. *Hanguk Gujeon Seolhwa.* Vol. 1, 144 / Vol. 2, 80 / Vol. 2, 90 / Vol. 2, 592 / Vol. 3, 173 / Vol. 5, 248 / Vol. 12, 73 / Vol. 12, 75. *Joseon Jeollae Donghwajip*, 200 / 372. *Joseon Seolhwajip*, 267 / 270 / 274 / 279 / 283. *Gangwon Gubimunhak Jeonjip*, 179 / 188. *Hanguk Gubimunhak Daegye.* The Academy of Korean Studies. Vol. 1-1, 505 / Vol. 1-3, 302 / Vol. 1-7, 564 / Vol. 1-7, 625 / Vol. 5-2, 579 / Vol. 5-4, 788 / Vol. 5-7, 210 / Vol. 6-1, 362 / Vol. 6-7, 712 / Vol. 7-5, 276 / Vol. 7-14, 646 / Vol. 7-16, 39 / Vol. 8-5, 1097 / Vol. 8-6, 88 / Vol. 8-8, 388 / Vol. 1-3, 353 / Vol. 1-4, 67 / Vol. 1-7, 292 / Vol. 2-5, 143 / Vol. 4-3, 491 / Vol. 6-3, 677 / Vol. 7-16, 420 / Vol. 8-9, 957. Choi Inhak. *Hanguk Mindamui Yu-hyeong Yeongu*, 422. Park Yeongjun. *Hangugui Jeonseol Vol. 5*, 153. Choi Yunsik. *Chungcheongnamdo Mindam*, 128. Hong Taehwan. *Hangugui Mindam*, 91. Im Donggwon. *Hangugui Mindam*, 221. Choi Unsik. *Hangugui Mindam*, 45 / 53. Kim Gyuntae. *Buyeoui Gubiseolhwa Vol. 2*, 121.	"Once upon a time, there lived a nine-headed monster in Jihaguk. It turned up in human society from time to time, wreaking havoc and kidnapping beautiful girls. One day, it snatched all three princesses of a kingdom. The king ordered his court to make a rescue plan at once, but no one came forward."

CHARACTER	WORK	SOURCE	SNIPPET
JIHAGUK DEJOK (continued)		Choi Raeok. *Jeonbuk Mindam*, 106.	
		Kim Gwangsun. *Gyeongbuk Mindam*, 116 / 233.	
		Jin Seonggi. *Namgugui Jeonseol*, 106.	
		Haeundae Minsok, 163.	
		Banpilseokjeon.	
		Kimwonjeon.	
		Leesumunjeon.	
		Choigounjeon.	
		Geumbanguljeon.	
		Honggildongjeon.	
		Chwichwijeon.	
		Unsujeon.	
		Seohaemureunggi.	
		Ihwaseoljeon.	
		Imjinrok.	
CHANGGUI	Seonghosaseol [성호사설], Eouyadam [어우야담], Yeolha Ilgi [열하일기], Cheongjangg-wanjeonseo [청장관전서]	Yu Mongin. *Eouyadam*. Dolbegae. Lee Deokmu. *Cheongjanggwanjeonseo*. Minjokmunhwachujinhoe. Yi Ik. *Seonghosaseol*. https://db.itkc.or.kr/. Park Jiwon. *Hojil*.	"A person eaten by a tiger will turn into a Changgui called 'Gulgak,' which will attach itself to the tiger's armpit and live there. When a tiger sneaks into the kitchen of a home and licks the rice pot, the owner will feel a sudden pang of hunger and ask his wife to make him a late-night snack. The moment she walks into the kitchen, the tiger will seize her and carry her away."
CHUNGU	Gieon [기연], Dongsagangmok [동사강목], Samguk Yusa [삼국유사]	Heo Mok. *Gugyeok Gieon*. Institute for the Translation of Korean Classics. Minjokmunhwachujinhoe. *Dongsagangmok*. Minjok Munhwa Mungo Ganhaenghoe. Il Yeon. *Samguk Yusa*. Sinwon Munhwasa.	"Its head is as big as a clay pot, and its tail, about half the size of a human, dazzles like bonfire. It is a creature of the sky but will at times plummet to the ground. Because Chungu falls so quickly from so high up, its crash leaves a wide crater and can even cause a small earthquake."

CHARACTER	WORK	SOURCE	SNIPPET
CHUNROK BUEKSA	Imokgusimseo [이목구심서]	*Gugyeok Cheongjanggwanjeonseo Vol. 8: Imokgusimseo (Gojeon Gugyeok Chongseo Vol. 191).* Minmungo.	"The animal was the size of a young deer, with a fierce, feline face like a tiger's. One horn protruded out of its forehead, and scales enveloped its length. Its toes looked formidable. And yet, the creature didn't look particularly terrifying, being so small."
CHOONGGI-YOSO	Eouyadam [어우야담]	Yu Mongin. *Eouyadam*. Dolbegae.	"Flying in droves, they are tiny balls of fluff that resemble pussy willows. They pester people in swarms massive enough to fill entire rooms. Their bites cause skin disease."
TAKTAK GUIBYUNG	Yeollyeosilgisul [연려실기술]	Lee Geungik. *Yeollyeosilgisul*. Kumsung Publishing.	"One night, rumors flew across the castle that the guibyung were coming—the ghost soldiers that went *taktak*. The second watch of the night saw a flurry of preparations to chase them away, cannons blasting, drums beating. Everyone stared fearfully up at the strange glow suffusing the sky. The startled king appointed someone to fend off the freakish phenomenon."
HAETAE	Dongguksegi [동국세기], folk superstition, folk art	Yun Yeolsu. *Sinhwa Sok Sangsangdongmul Yeoljeon*. Korea Cultural Heritage Protection Foundation.	"It only eats fruits yet is stronger than a hundred kinds of beasts. It can also rule right from wrong and virtue from vice; if it senses the presence of evil, it will pounce and bite."
HOMOONJO	Cheongjangg-wanjeonseo [청장관전서]	Lee Deokmu. *Cheongjanggwanjeonseo*. Minjokmunhwachujinhoe.	"The vicious seabird is several times the size of humans. Its head is especially big, like a hefty clay pot, and its tiger-striped wings are massive enough to support its bulk. Most of its plumes are crimson. Its movements are slow and laborious due to its size, but up in the sky, it is remarkably agile."

CHARACTER	WORK	SOURCE	SNIPPET
HWANG-RYONG	Goryeosa [고려사], Samguk Sagi [삼국사기], Eouyadam [어우야담], Hanguk Minsok Munhak Sajeon [한국민속문학사전]	*Goryeosa*. Sahoegwahakwon Chulpansa. Kim Busik. *Samguk Sagi*. Hanbulhakyesa. Yu Mongin. *Eouyadam*. Dolbegae. *Hanguk Minsok Munhak Sajeon*. National Folk Museum of Korea. Yun Yeolsu. *Sinhwa Sok Sangsangdongmul Yeoljeon*. Korea Cultural Heritage Protection Foundation.	"In ancient China, Hwang-ryong was a symbol of the emperor. It is the noblest of dragons, a dragon god and king that reigns supreme. It is also an auspicious omen, appearing on the earth for great joyous occasions."
HOEMM	Seonghosaseol [성호사설]	Yi Ik. *Seonghosaseol*. https://db.itkc.or.kr/.	"Long ago, a pretty woman took a trip to Bagyeon pond, where she bathed, baring her bosom. But a black mist rose around her and from the water surfaced a monster. She couldn't make out its face or head, just its eyes, which flashed like lightning. Storm and thunder quaked the air but not beyond the mountain. Within moments, the woman was lost."

The authorised representative in the EEA is Simon and Schuster Netherlands BV, Herculesplein 96 3584 AA Utrecht, Netherlands. (info@simonandschuster.nl)

Andrews McMeel Publishing
a division of Andrews McMeel Universal
1130 Walnut Street, Kansas City, Missouri 64106

www.andrewsmcmeel.com

25 26 27 28 29 IGK 10 9 8 7 6 5 4 3 2 1

ISBN: 979-8-8816-0292-5

Library of Congress Control Number: 2025933769

Editor: Hannah Kimber
Art Director: Diane Marsh
Production Editor: Kayla Overbey
Production Manager: Jeff Preuss

ATTENTION: SCHOOLS AND BUSINESSES
Andrews McMeel books are available at quantity discounts with bulk purchase for educational, business, or sales promotional use. For information, please email the Andrews McMeel Publishing Special Sales Department: sales@andrewsmcmeel.com.